BLACK AGE

Black Age

Oceanic Lifespans and the Time of Black Life

Habiba Ibrahim

NEW YORK UNIVERSITY PRESS
New York

NEW YORK UNIVERSITY PRESS
New York
www.nyupress.org

© 2021 by New York University
All rights reserved

References to Internet websites (URLs) were accurate at the time of writing. Neither the author nor New York University Press is responsible for URLs that may have expired or changed since the manuscript was prepared.

Library of Congress Cataloging-in-Publication Data
Names: Ibrahim, Habiba, author.
Title: Black age : Oceanic lifespans and the time of Black life / Habiba Ibrahim.
Description: New York : New York University Press, [2021] |
Includes bibliographical references and index.
Identifiers: LCCN 2021003079 | ISBN 9781479810888 (hardback ; alk. paper) | ISBN 9781479810895 (paperback ; alk. paper) | ISBN 9781479810925 (ebook) | ISBN 9781479810932 (ebook other)
Subjects: LCSH: African Americans. | Blacks. | Age—Social aspects. | Human body—Social aspects. | Racism.
Classification: LCC E185.86 .I27 2021 | DDC 305.896/073—dc23
LC record available at https://lccn.loc.gov/2021003079

New York University Press books are printed on acid-free paper, and their binding materials are chosen for strength and durability. We strive to use environmentally responsible suppliers and materials to the greatest extent possible in publishing our books.

Manufactured in the United States of America

10 9 8 7 6 5 4 3 2 1

Also available as an ebook

As the original locus of the human race, Africa is ancient, yet, being under colonial control, it is also infantile. A kind of old fetus always waiting to be born but confounding all midwives.
—Toni Morrison, "The Foreigner's Home"

CONTENTS

Introduction: Emmett's Face, Emmett's Flesh   1

1. Shape-Shifters and Body Snatchers   43

2. Vampires and Relics   81

3. The Mass and Men   123

4. Ghosts   165

Epilogue: And with Black Children   203

Acknowledgments   209

Notes   211

Index   247

About the Author   261

Introduction

Emmett's Face, Emmett's Flesh

Oh, certainly, I will be told, now and then when we are worn out by our lives in big buildings, we will turn to you as we do to our children—to the innocent, the ingenuous, the spontaneous. We will turn to you as to the childhood of the world. You are so real in your life—so funny, that is. Let us run away for a little while from our ritualized, polite civilization and let us relax, bend to those heads, those adorably expressive faces. In a way, you reconcile us with ourselves.
—Frantz Fanon, *White Skin, Black Masks*

On rainy days my sister and I used to tie the short end of a scarf around our scrawny braids and let the rest of its silken mass trail to our waists. [. . .] There was a time when I would have called that wanting to be white, yet the real point of the game was being feminine. Being feminine *meant* being white to us.
—Michele Wallace, "A Black Feminist's Search for Sisterhood"

Morrison savors the irony that black writers are descending deeper into historical concerns at the same time that the white literati are abolishing it in the name of something they call "postmodern." "History has become impossible for them. They're so busy being innocents and skipping from adolescence into old age."
—Paul Gilroy, "Living Memory: A Meeting with Toni Morrison"

In a photograph of Emmett Till, the 14-year-old boy whose lynching near Money, Mississippi, awakened the nation in 1955, a child's face is missing. Emmett's mother, Mamie Till-Mobley, insisted on an open casket so that the destroyed, faceless—seemingly ageless—body could be seen, photographed, circulated in the black press, and entered in the annals of US history. Through the now-famous photograph of her son that first appeared in *Jet* magazine, Till-Mobley invited "all the world" to be a part of Emmett's flesh, to witness the precariousness that comes from not quite owning one's own body, from not quite achieving the liberal individualism that makes innocence make sense. Till-Mobley waged a reclamation of Emmett's childhood through the horrific exposure of how his childhood had been violently denied and, consequently, how the appearance of childhood had been stolen from his faceless flesh.

Emmett's facelessness testified to an alternative childhood. As Rebekah Sheldon suggests, the ideal child is "all face": The affective attachment to a child's innocence relies on the presumptive capacity of the face to signify a lack of guilt within.[1] In the photograph of Emmett in his coffin, we see a destroyed body that interrupts thinking of Emmett in classical psychoanalytic terms of human consciousness and in the Foucauldian terms of a child's biopolitical management of sexuality, which takes the child's empty interiority as the precondition for adulthood yet to come. Simply put, the child who is innocent and imperiled, who must be managed, protected, and saved, has a face. Photography has played an essential role in defining childhood through the preservation of this face after death, as Karen Sánchez-Eppler argues of the mid-nineteenth century.[2] During that era, the photo of the dead child's face functioned as a repository for the values and memories of the middle-class family. The tangible photo, integrated with the dead child, transforms the family's unmanageable grief into an experience of bounded mourning, dignified loss. Yet, the photo of Emmett's faceless body expressed an alternative mode of relating to childhood. From Emmett's flesh arose an alternatively affective attachment to a face that was not there. Till-Mobley's redemption of her child occurred through claiming a form of embodiment that could not signify childhood—Emmett's missing face—while simultaneously exposing the social, historical problem that the absence marked.[3]

When Till-Mobley chose to display her child's unchildlike corpse, she was also putting in full view what black communities in the United States already knew—that no age or life stage protects black people. From the vantage point of what modern blackness signifies, which is exclusion from western humanity, the fallacy of innocence is laid bare. Till-Mobley reclaimed her son's childhood after his death and in so doing, she reset the terms of protection. She situates the unchildlike child as the figure of non-differentiation that leads us toward a critique of racial capitalism, defined as a political-economic rationality that casts divisions between people and communities, prevents recognition of shared interests, and works against collective action and collectivist means of retrieving history.[4] In a word, it prevents relationality, a principle borne out of Indigenous epistemologies that names our relations with and responsibility to each other and the world.[5] The child who is viciously dispossessed of childhood is figurative of social protection that comes from radical connection in the flesh. As Ruth Wilson Gilmore suggests, skin is connective tissue in more ways than one: Emmett's flesh, like the stolen appearance of age, eschews the separation between innocents and everyone else, since such a separation prevents all people, across social categories, from getting free.[6] From this vantage point, black age is an analytical category, and as such, a vector into an alternative humanism—if we dare to imagine it. Such imagining is precisely what this book attempts to do.

Black Age: Oceanic Lifespans and the Time of Black Life begins with the destruction of Emmett Till's face and reclamation of his flesh, laid bare without the appearance of age, to illustrate a major premise of this book: Black age is the prism through which the abuses of liberal humanist dispossession, as well as black cultural, political, and historical reclamation, are visible. This dialectic between abuse and reclamation resonates in *black don't crack*, an old, familiar adage, which places emphasis on the flesh. The colloquial phrase suggests that there is asynchrony between *actual age*, as a matter of chronological, biological time, and *apparent age*, which simultaneously conceals the number of years lived and reveals an alternative temporality—the apparent temporality of untimely youth. Melanin, the iconic sign of blackness as a social category, leads to the untimely appearance of youth. And yet, neither the actual nor apparent youthfulness of black embodiment has historically aligned with dominant conditions of being young. Taken as a metaphor for what I call "untimeliness," the phrase alludes to an alternative humanism that exists between subjective experience and appearance, the sociogenic result of black exclusion from hegemonic measures of time. I understand black age as a figure of a counter-historical temporality of modernity with which the black body is endowed. Age names the locus from whence alternatively modern temporalities arise, and how such temporalities are inhabited, embodied, and expressed. *Black Age* focuses on the fault line between western humanism and its vibrant alternatives. In short, having a body that has been constituted through counter-normative meanings of age creates the potential for experiencing an alternatively historical time. This book focuses on how the abusively fluid formation of black age has a profound, and yet under-considered, impact on the black literary imagination of the twentieth and early twenty-first centuries. In the black literary imagination—and in the black cultural imagination overall—black age is explored as a site of contested meanings over the epistemic conditions of humanity itself. The age of black embodiment expresses both the conditions of racializing abuse and the ongoing reclamation of time and humanity.

Over various phases of the transatlantic slave trade, the black body had been separated from its hegemonic relation to time. I describe how black age became contingent, malleable, and suited for the needs of enslavement. Black embodiment could be figured not only as childlike, but as any age at all. Black age is construable as anything because black subjects have been alienated from the time of their own bodies. As historian Walter Johnson notes with regard to how temporal alienation worked over the course of plantation slavery, "Slaveholders thought they owned their slaves' biological time: they recorded their slaves' birthdays in account books that only they could see; they determined at what age their slaves would be started into the fields or set to a trade, when their slaves would be cajoled into reproduction, how many years they would be allowed to nurse the children they had, and how old they would have to be before retiring."[7] I argue that such a historical process of alienating black subjects from their own age continues to be felt throughout the twentieth century and into the present.

This introduction traces relations between the meanings attributed to black age and a formative process that separated blackness from humanity and history. To think of black age in these terms is to run squarely into a problem of method. What are the current indications of a condition I refer to as "black age," and are they too spurious to count as evidence of historical developments? When one encounters and touches the jagged edge of an evidentiary shard, a piece of something that happened historically and continues to happen—*black children are routinely mistaken for adults*—how might one use it to go about proving that black age substantively and qualitatively differs from hegemonic versions of age?[8] This book does not take on a task as ambitious as proving such a distinction.

Rather, *Black Age* treats age as a tool for analyzing how historical transformation happens. More specifically, black age tracks historical transformation through the struggle between the abuses of black exclusion from western humanism and the reclamation of non-normative black life. This dialectical view emerges from African Americanist, Americanist, and feminist critiques of liberalism, which have all revealed the contradictions of liberalism's logic as it pertains to universal freedom. What we think of as "age," the life stages of lifespans, changes over historical time, is socially mutable, and contains its own set of categorical differences along the lines of class, gender, sexuality. Preeminent scholars of childhood studies, aging studies, and queer studies such as Sánchez-Eppler, Kathleen Woodward, Jack Halberstam, and Elizabeth Freeman, respectively, have meticulously theorized embodied temporalities of young, old, transgender, queer subjects in relation to various registers of normative time, and thus these works reveal how social, cultural, and subjective meanings of age in the United States are the effect of specific historical and political-economic transformations.[9] In its own theorization of age, this book benefits from the insights of these scholars, the field-based debates to which they contribute, and a large body of work that constitutes the burgeoning area of scholarship known as black girlhood studies. Yet, this book also dwells on the methodological problem of saying a true word about a social condition that is as simultaneously specific and broad as black age—black lifespans across incremental life stages. Rather than establish a fixed ontological basis for the ages and aging of black people, this book ultimately turns to black age as a method, an analytical framework for discerning how the past relates to the present. Something happened; there were historical abuses and reclamations—*black children are adult-like, black adults are infantile, black don't crack*—and yet it is difficult to know with certainty what that something was and is.

As an analytic, age works like a hinge insofar as it enables flexible movement between the past and the present, the individual and the collective, the scope of a single lifespan and the scope of an entire epoch. My treatment of black age swings between broad historical scales on which modern black racial formation occurred through colonialism and enslavement and a smaller, national scale spanning from the mid-twentieth century to the present. The purpose of making age swing is to discern how the historical constitution of black subjectivity within the purview of liberal humanism opens epistemic and discursive space for being human otherwise. What interests me are the possibilities that black age opens in relation to the possessive individual, the free-willed subject, a normative gender binary, a presumptive separation between public and private life.

In this respect, *Black Age* treads on grounds well-traveled by scholars who work in a historical materialist tradition, whose work explains how liberalism's political-economic rationalities are reproduced through its institutions, ideologies, and cultural forms, and how they are constitutive of proper subjectivity. Across this work, literary culture is revealed to be the territory of ideological contestation, the site where liberalism's contradictions arise. When Grace Hong argues that coming-of-age narratives of women of color feminists reveal previously repressed alternatives to the possessive subject, I see an implicit use of age as an analytic that uncovers an overlooked moment of crisis in an American nationalist phase of capital's development.[10] Indeed, age—such as Pecola's girlhood in Toni Morrison's *The Bluest Eye* (1970)—is a constitutive aspect of an alternative subjectivity that the dominant ideology of possessive individualism suppresses and disavows. As an analytical tool, age reveals such suppression and disavowal. In contrast to Hong's interest in women of color feminists' narratives of development, Lisa Lowe argues that the genres of liberalism—and specifically, the autobiography—affirm some subjective and historical possibilities while casting others beyond the realm of the thinkable. The autobiography constitutes a subject whose lifespan is a microcosmic proxy for liberalism's dominant historiography. Thus, Lowe disentangles autobiography from its ideological function in order to read it for another history, which is that of property relations across four continents.[11] In both Hong's and Lowe's work, I see the potential to think of aesthetic work as a site where counter-hegemonic representations of black age track repressed or unthought-of schemas of, and narratives about, the past, present, future. Strange or conspicuously unusual images of black age—the children who refuse to grow, the adults who live forever—are routes that lead us away from normative modes of time, such as the liberal time of the individual's linear development into free-willed, possessive adulthood, or the straight time of reproductive futurity. Through the aesthetic and literary, it is possible to imagine the time of another humanity, beyond the time of Man. I imagine black age as one route to take us there.

Similar potentials for thinking of age in relation to historical time arise when Roderick Ferguson argues that black revolutionary nationalism of the 1960s and 1970s appropriated the historiographic tools of western liberalism, enabling young black activists to occupy a position of authority in relation to older members of the black community.[12] Having sidelined the elders as symbolic guarantors of history from below, a history needed for revolutionary action, the young purported to speak for the elderly. This book addresses a key implication of Ferguson's argument: The regulatory norms of black radical nationalism relied on western humanist ideologies about proper *adulthood*, a measure of humanity that supported modern European dominance over brutes, savages, and natives unfit for self-governance.[13] By dint of this exclusionary humanist rationality, young black radicals who saw themselves as fit to lead became the only adults. Since political adulthood is the outcome of social relations, one can see how this "adulthood" is operative in relations between young black revolutionaries and elderly black folk *as well as* in relations between black men and black women of the movement. In other words, an analysis of how "adulthood" operates in this case allows us to think in precise terms about how hierarchies are reproduced at any given moment. At the same time, it renews the potential for liberating modes of relationality. Age is an ideological category that is revealed to be such when we focus on both social and property relations. With our vision trained there, we notice cracks between the embodiments of black subjects and the sometimes conspicuously incongruous social meanings of age attributed to them. We have already trained our vision to see race and gender in this way, rather than as biological or ontological facts, and age is no different. To be sure, our concerns will be set on the intersection of blackness, gender, and age throughout this book. As the effect of historical developments, social and property relations, age tracks both hegemonic and counter-hegemonic historiographical practices and possibilities. In another capacity, age serves as a heuristic tool for exploring and then dismantling anti-relational forces in social life. How do we recognize what "age" speaks in the name of, and when it functions as a means of preventing us from establishing "patterns for relating across our human differences as equals," to borrow the words of Audre Lorde?[14] At stake in *Black Age* is the offering of a new image with which to imagine patterns for relationality.

In what follows, I provide a winding road map through the themes that shape this book, beginning with a historiographic and diasporic turn that focuses on the Atlantic Ocean as a key site for conceptualizing modern blackness. As *Black Age* argues, Hortense Spiller's under-thought retooling of Sigmund Freud's concept of the "oceanic feeling" offers a theory for the coeval unmaking of black gender and age. With what I refer to as an "Oceanic" unmaking at the forefront of our concerns about historiography, we turn to the murders of Emmett Till in 1955 and Trayvon Martin in 2012 as bookends to an era in which the Oceanic and sociogenic aspects of black age are discernable. Frantz Fanon's meaning of sociogeny functions as a philosophy of history that reveals how liberal nationalist categories upon which rights, inclusion, and protection depend—gender and age—confront us with the historical unmaking of these categories and the thingification of blackness. As I reveal, black feminist scholars during the 1980s—a key flashpoint for the historiographic and diasporic turn in black studies, to which Spillers contributes—consistently thought at the intersection of race, gender, and age in their own critiques of liberal nationalist logic. Panning out to the broader scale of western modernity, we briefly consider how such nationalist logic relied on liberal humanism's discursive production of age to conflate human time with historical time. As a signifier of non-humanity, blackness signifies the lack of both age and history. This introduction closes by turning to black feminist cultural production of the 1970s and '80s outside of the university. The Combahee River Collective and Alice Walker developed critiques of liberal humanism with references to the fluidity of black age, as it emerged through the lived experience of black girlhood. As I claim, black girlhood was not simply the temporal and subjective locus of a key feminist and intersectional analytic, "the personal is political." Rather, black girlhood is a whole world, capacious enough for adultish, masculine, lady-like, mimetic, and inventive play. To a large degree, *Black Age* is indebted to this richly dynamic dimension of age that I suggest underwrites contemporary black feminist thought.

This book's engagement with broad and narrow scales of time depends upon one premise: Black racialization is constituted through an emptying process in that "blackness" is drained of both humanity and history. That emptying out of humanity and history is the condition of possibility for the radical alterity of black age. Although this book does not explicitly delve into black sexuality, black age shares a queer and conceptual affinity with black trans analysis and historiography.[15] For instance, *Black Age* moves along with the fluid analytic, Trans*, which, as Kai M. Green notes, raises "a question of how, when, and where one sees and knows" while also making "different scales of movement or change legible."[16] If there is anything that distinguishes black studies from other knowledge projects, it could very well be the necessity to think between different scales of time in order to explore the conditions for seeing and knowing. Further still, it could be the necessity to identify epistemic, barely perceptible cracks that break off one mode of rationality from an unthinkable other, in order to think the unthought-of.

Age is a temporality that crosses multiple epistemological barriers and exists on numerous scales, and the remaining challenge is to devise a precise account of how black age—the whole of black lifespans—has been formed over time. In recognition of this challenge, I turn to age to explore an aspect of black life and embodiment that has a history, and yet is difficult to historicize. Black age—the life stages and lifespans of black people in the diaspora—is the key to producing what Saidiya Hartman has called a "subterranean history."[17] It is history that is unthought-of as officially historical, submerged in the oceanic where, as Christina Sharpe asserts, the diasporic dead continue to live long lives as part of the ocean, and where the progressive linearity of chronological time gives way to fluid, multidirectional movement. It is a history of temporal disruption and suspension, of subjective unmaking and reinvention. Black age is unthought-of history turned into flesh, time that is inadequately translated into the biological, legal, and social discourses about human development. The evidence that supports a counter-history of modernity can be found in what we say, think, and imagine about black age. Ultimately, this book's goal is to work toward approaches to historicizing seemingly non-evidentiary experiences of time that shape our social world.

The Oceanic

The Atlantic Ocean has inspired a multitude of approaches to theorizing the history of modernity. Paul Gilroy influentially thought of the "black Atlantic" as a geopolitical site from whence black diasporic philosophers and cultural producers leaned into modernity's racial contradictions and transnational affiliations. Gilroy's theory of transatlantic cultural and intellectual exchange is one key example of scholarship in black diaspora studies that draws conceptual inspiration from the ocean. More recent examples of such work come from Dionne Brand, Christina Sharpe, and Omise'eke Tinsley.[18] Although *Black Age* turns to various historical and spatial frameworks in order to think of black modernity, such as the plantation of the American South and the "First Passage" through continental Africa, it begins by engaging a dominant schema of black studies, which situates modern blackness in relation to the ocean. From this starting point, "Oceanic lifespans," which I describe below, is the theoretical condition of possibility for reimagining black age as a route to an alternative humanity.

From the trade along West African coasts to the journey across the Atlantic, the temporality of black age shifted into something alienating and artificial as a matter of necessity for the political economy of slavery. The Portuguese slave trade transformed human age into a sliding scale of export taxes based on the size of bodies packed into ships. According to Paul Lovejoy, prior to 1850, "Age was estimated by the height of children, and hence was arbitrary."[19] If age became an integral component of racial capitalism during the Portuguese trade, it also bore out in the British trade. Stephanie Smallwood describes the conditions of the slave trade toward the end of the seventeenth century, in which "it was with approval that officials in London noted the use of children as filler to top off the cargoes put aboard the company's ships."[20] Childhood—or adulthood, for that matter, since either refers to the size, and not the temporality, of embodiment—signified an economic calculus, from lower taxes to packing Portuguese and British slave ships to the brim. Sowande' M. Mustakeem explains that the negotiations between slave traders contributed to the "imagined bodies" of a captive labor force. The gender and age of black bodies were reimagined, so that "descriptors interchangeably used throughout slave trade documents make contemporary understandings of the inclusion of different captives somewhat difficult to discern."[21] What is known is that "Opinions on captives' ages differed among investors, traders, and slaveholders, projecting their own needs and desires through an economic lens."[22] When discussing the antebellum slave market in *Soul by Soul*, Walter Johnson reveals what I refer to as "Oceanic lifespans" as an enduring calculus such as existed after the Middle Passage. No longer seeking to pack people into ships, "traders packed people into price categories according to gender, age, height, weight, and skin color."[23] Fixed into a system of comparative embodiment all its own, the enslaved "were fully fungible." Johnson claims, "The distant and different translated into money value and resolved into a single scale of relative prices, prices that could be used to make even the most counterintuitive comparisons—between the body of an old man and a little girl, for example."[24] As these historians of slavery suggest, bodies become the screen upon which to project anything at all. The conditions of possibility for such projection are the transformation of people into commodities which, in part, occurred on the Atlantic Ocean.

My use of the term "Oceanic" in "Ocean lifespans" is indebted to an under-considered aspect of Spillers's 1987 essay, "Mama's Baby, Papa's Maybe."[25] Spillers's assertion that black bodies have been "ungendered" during transatlantic transport implies a critique of how western modernity racialized temporality. In the opening of Freud's 1930 book, *Civilization and Its Discontents*, he puzzles over a feeling of religious capaciousness—a boundless connection one feels to a larger, external, mystical presence that exceeds the ego of rational adults.[26] He attributes the oceanic feeling to a pre-ego stage of human development, when infants cannot discern where they end and the external world—figured as the mother's breast—begins. Freud concludes that such a feeling is a regressive desire for protection that can exist in later stages of development. Spillers applies that pre-ego lack of differentiated identity to the formation of New World blackness. Psychic distinctions such as "self" and "other," like social distinctions such as "male" and "female," are profoundly disrupted in the "nowhere" of oceanic space:

> Those African persons in "Middle Passage" were literally suspended in the "oceanic," if we think of the latter in its Freudian orientation as an analogy for undifferentiated identity: removed from the indigenous land

and culture, and not yet "American" either, these captive persons [. . .] were in movement across the Atlantic, but they were also *nowhere* at all.[27]

Through her reworking of the Freudian schema of human development, in which the "oceanic" is attributed to a residual, infantile feeling of being non-differentiated from other subjects, Spillers evokes the racialist logic of uneven human development that Freud's nod to recapitulation theory supports.

By opening with Freud, Spillers transforms the nonlinear temporality of the Freudian *oceanic* by mapping it onto the Atlantic *Ocean*, an alternative cradle of modernity. In the afterlife of the Oceanic, the black subject bears a complicated relationship to temporality. On the one hand, the individual supposedly never advances beyond the "primitive core" of humanity in relation to "the healthy adult" that is Western Man.[28] On the other hand, in a moment when bodies were severed from their humanity, the cargo they became could have signified any version of temporal relations. What was human development, with its metaphorical life stages, when the social meaning of age no longer applied to cargo in transit? The Oceanic makes clear that part of what is inscribed within what Spillers calls the "hieroglyphics of the flesh" is fluid time; it is a temporality comprised not of "natural" development, but of being made and remade. By evoking the Atlantic, the Oceanic reorients Freud's key spatial analogy, which maps psychic development onto ancient and present-day Rome. Spillers represents human geography by emphasizing a condition of non-differentiation that is not embedded within a European locus of civilization, nor is it the linear logic of normative human development. Bodies, once "*nowhere* at all," can be completely untimely, since the "nowhere" would then apply to what Freud calls a "psychical entity" that is undecipherable within the codes of a modern social order. The Oceanic marks an alternatively human temporality.

Although my use of psychoanalytic models in this book is sparing, I see a valuable opportunity to situate Spillers's retooling of Freudian thought to theorize the conditions of modern black subjective formation along with Kathleen Woodward's groundbreaking work on aging, which also turns to Freudian and other psychoanalytic models. In *Aging and Its Discontents*, Woodward argues that the Freudian tradition has played a key role in societal repression of old age, and this repression is evidenced in the persistently negative ways that old age and aging are represented in culture. Woodward meticulously details just how thorough the erasure of old age is: We cannot see it, comprehend it, or identify with it from outside of the psychic registers of trauma, aggression, mourning, and anxiety. One outcome of this phenomenon is that the interior life of old age is largely unthinkable, other than as "empty."[29] As we will see later on, this insight is applicable to reading an under-remarked-upon moment in *Black Skin, White Masks*, when Frantz Fanon encounters an elderly farm woman while in clinical practice. Woodward's work remains a unique example of how to think of age—old age, in this case—as the primary prism through which to analyze social subjectivities tout court. More profoundly, her work demonstrates how old age works as a diagnostic tool, which reveals that we knowingly and unknowingly eliminate a common mode of human existence—being old—from the realm of what is thinkable as human.

Although Woodward focuses on white-authored modernist texts, "old age" and "black age" share analytical ground: They converge around the task of denaturalizing the norms of developmental discourse. As I have drawn from Spillers's essay, modern blackness is metaphorical of suspended development on the scale of both the individual and the species. Subjective non-differentiation, which applies to both gender and age, is a route toward an alternative humanism that the supposedly constitutive non-development of blackness engenders. In turn, Woodward asserts that Freudian developmental models focus on infancy and childhood but offer nothing for the analysis of old age except the suggestion that getting old is disintegration. As a result, "We may have the uncanny impression that processes have reversed themselves, are *undoing* themselves, are coming undone."[30] As I see it, this "undoing" bears theoretical likeness to "ungendering"—which is also an unmaking of social age—even as the uncanny "undoing" that Woodward describes pertains to a radically different context than Spillers's concept does. One takes place in the genteel settings of white bourgeois life, according to Woodward's archive, while the other occurs in the dehumanizing conditions of the slave ship. Still, this presumptive "undoing" is a social technology that casts old people outside of the realm of the human, which is to say that undoing, like ungendering—and the untimeliness of un-aging—is an artificial process. And what arises from the undoing that *is* old age is an *artificial childhood*. As Woodward points out, "The equation between childhood and old age has passed into everyday speech (he is in his second childhood, we will say), and it makes people patently anxious (we will avoid it for ourselves but attribute it to others)."[31] If this "second childhood" is a matter not just of the objectively apparent signs of physical and mental decline, but also of social subjection in the modern epoch, then I suggest that the uncanniness of old age arises from unknowing recognition of racial infantilism. Both the second childhood of disintegration and the racial infantilism of non-development reveal how age works as a technology of dehumanization in ways that are socially and historically contingent, and yet, I suggest that one process haunts the other. Conceivably, the anxiety that a second childhood evokes is due to a tacit recognition that to enter such a condition is to be marked by an imperceptible, yet deeply historical, mode of racialization—to become something other than fully human. While Woodward's prime objective is to unbury old age from the layers that conceal it, I want to hold onto the potential of relation I see in her work: Old age is made to speak in a language that sounds, on the lower frequencies, like something related to the Ocean.

Oceanic lifespans illustrate how a historical process of transforming black gendered age into the categories of inhuman time and embodiment is extended into the contemporary cultural imagination. It signifies both a reckoning with historic dehumanization and emancipatory re-figuring. Consider Spillers's concept of the flesh as the chunk of bleeding matter torn out of captive bodies, evidence that human beings have been violently unmade in slave ships. Consider Emmett Till's flesh as evidence of age dispossession and Till-Mobley's radical reclamation. Oceanic lifespans entail demeaning projections with long afterlives as well as the outcome of our own self-fashioning: It is the black that doesn't crack, the elders and ancestors, black girl magic, black boy joy, the past and the redemptive, invented future.[32] It suggests that the evidence of the flesh is concealed in plain sight as skin color. If the untimeliness of black age is the evidence of things not seen, then at the very least, gender is a framework with which to inquire about the imperceptible.

As the theoretical condition for the contemporary reimagining of black age, Ocean lifespans illustrate the methodological fluidity that characterizes treatments of modern history in black studies. In the post–civil rights era, various historical, theoretical, and imaginative connotations of the Atlantic Ocean were related to how black writers troubled the status of evidence, contributing to the project of social history that arose during the 1970s. As I discuss below, shifting methodological ground of black literary studies was precisely the condition of possibility for age to emerge as what is still an under-considered framework for the study of black life. But prior to these developments, the politics of black liberalism was entangled with a problem: how to mend the fracture between black untimeliness and the time of the nation. In the postwar era, the political centrality of black male adulthood was part of the entanglement.

From Emmett to Trayvon

Events of the 1950s and the 2010s respectively announced and returned to the conceptual significance of black age for thinking the limits of liberal humanism in relation to black liberation. In 1952, just a few years prior to Emmett Till's lynching, the Martiniquais psychiatrist-philosopher, Frantz Fanon, published his landmark exploration of colonialism's psychological effects, *Black Skin, White Masks*. Fanon theorizes black dehumanization as being constituted through white fears and fantasies that trap black subjects in alienating personas within the social world. Thus, it must be accepted that "beside phylogeny and ontogeny stands sociogeny."[33] I think of sociogeny as a theory of historical consciousness, and a feeling of temporality that emerges in the afterlife of modern racialization. Sociogeny marks the historicity of colonialism and transatlantic slavery that permeates the seemingly neutral domain of ontogeny, with which classical psychoanalysis is concerned. In the properly bourgeois realm of ontogeny, the white subject develops from childhood into adulthood in a patriarchal family, which shares the same patriarchal logic as the nation. Thus, the subject of classical psychoanalysis is also the liberal subject of nationhood. That subject achieves psychic maturity by the political, economic, and civic standards of liberal society.

Sociogeny, as the psychic life and embodiment of history, reveals a temporal rift between the normatively developmental subject and the black subject who is constituted differently within history. For the black Antillean, there was no route to adulthood, stuck as he was in what Fanon refers to as the "zone of nonbeing." Fixed in time and space without achieving full recognition of the other, the zone of nonbeing is one of untimeliness and non-protection. To think of sociogeny this way does not mean rigidly adhering to a binary schema comprised of white adults and black Antillean children who, having "adorably expressive faces" imagined onto them, were considered more childlike than Emmett was in 1955. Rather, the historicity of colonialism more profoundly seals off the black Antillean from hegemonic, developmental time. Sociogeny names the way history, which constitutes the social order, splits humans from non-humans across the axis of developmental time. Ontogeny, which applies to humans, determines how hegemonic, developmental age appears in social life. Sociogeny reveals that when the (white) viewer sees "blackness" projected onto the other, what is *not seen* is normative, human age. What the white viewer sees is black children with adorable faces and fully grown bodies, a historical heaviness that prevents black people from coming "lithe and young into a world" made for humans.[34] Or the white viewer sees a monstrosity that could be of any age: "Look, a Negro!" Fanon wants to crack the layer of fantasy that seals the person in his untimely blackness, in order to set the human free.

The sociogenic implications for age were readily apparent in the case of Emmett Till. His lynching occurred during the US civil rights era, at a time when liberal personhood was expanding to include black Americans in civil, political, and economic life. At 14 years old, Emmett was both a juvenile—not a full legal person by virtue of race or age—and a presumptive adult who was a supposed sexual threat to white women. If a black boy's sociogenic adulthood is the stuff of white nightmares, and if the way black subjects experience their own life stages and lifespans is concealed from the white gaze, then age itself is symptomatic of the "thing" that covers black subjects like a shroud. Against the postwar era's anti-racist movements, from anti-colonialism to rights-based activism, black untimeliness tacitly emerged as an intractable problem. Thus, the radical analytical potential of age waited in the wings of Fanon's analysis of transatlantic blackness. The postwar break into a new moment of black liberation was itself shrouded with a temporal dimension that was neither regressive nor progressive, but rather untimely, insofar as established trajectories for alternative, counter-national temporalities. Amid US-based efforts to curb racial violence at home while the nation displayed a benevolent imperialist face abroad, Emmett's murder blasted the appearance of racial liberalism's progressiveness wide open.[35] With a glance into his casket, untimeliness looked like the removal of age.

Black Skin, White Masks and Emmett's murder touch upon a postwar paradox—"the black is not a man," as Fanon laments, but adulthood is shackled to the necks of black children—that the liberal humanist achievement of manhood cannot resolve. It is not enough for the black subject to gain the legal trappings of manhood. The inadequacy of such achievement is why I read the destruction of Emmett's face as an epistemic opening: The task is to avoid settling for the ostensible resolution that liberal nationalism offers. Black *manhood* is that ostensible resolution: It silently sutures black untimeliness to the hegemonic temporality of nationhood. However, such suturing does not actually resolve the temporal splitting of blackness and nationhood as illustrated in the divergence between the aims of black liberalism and the aims of more capaciously emancipatory black activism of the 1950s and '60s.[36] The first strain was manifest in the NAACP's agenda. Cedric Robinson reminds us that, from the 1930s onward, the organization

> pursued an agenda that reflected Black middle-class interests, political sensibilities, and cultural values. In its legal activism, for example, the organization concentrated on suits to end the exclusion of Blacks from professional and graduate programs in state universities and to equalize salaries and physical facilities in the all-Black primary and secondary public schools.[37]

The NAACP's pragmatic approach to liberal inclusion would have fraught outcomes in later generations, when scholars began entering the academy to develop knowledge projects about modern blackness while being disciplined within the liberal institutions in which that work was produced. As I argue, disciplining practices of only partially inclusive institutions were the impetus for doubt about the efficacy of adhering to liberalism's progress narrative. The turn that black literary studies makes toward slavery and temporality by the end of the twentieth century is thinkable as a reaction to the limits of liberalism's progress.

To follow a pragmatic vision of black liberalism—referred to here as an orientation combining participation in statist politics, liberal institutions, and capitalist expansion into the limited horizon of black liberation—was to move in sync with the dominant temporality of the nation. That synchronization, however, required black conformity to the standards of proper liberal subjectivity. For instance, to turn to another example from the 1950s, 15-year-old Claudette Colvin was arrested for defying segregation on a public bus in Montgomery, Alabama, in 1955, nine months before Rosa Parks would be arrested for the same act of defiance. Although Claudette belonged to the Youth Council of the NAACP, the organization chose to support the middle-aged, light-skinned and, thus, ostensibly middle-class Parks over the darker-skinned, teenaged girl, widely rumored to be pregnant.[38] The price of the ticket to organizational support, institutional inclusion, and state protection—the price of national synchronism—was communal disavowal of black subjects deemed to be out of time. The discursive production of black manhood conceals this disavowal, and the violent imperative for all black subjects to conform to the narrowly normative standards of proper liberal subjectivity and a linearly progressive temporality. That temporality, which the black liberal subject shares, combines the ontogeny of adulthood with the ideology of national progress to create the illusion that we are living under an umbrella of shared, unbroken time.

By the late 1960s and early 1970s, an emergent emphasis on black electoral politics and entrepreneurialism, which arose in the wake of statist efforts to dismantle leftist grassroots activism, allowed black liberalism to appear as a dominant and homogenous force that synchronically moved with the American state. The Black Caucus, constituted in 1971, strove for a unified agenda. In 1972, politicians and activists from across the wide spectrum of black political life gathered in Gary, Indiana, for the National Black Political Convention with the goal of building a "black agenda." Not only does the resulting document, the "Gary Declaration," proclaim that there is a black nationalist place at the "vanguard," but it ends with these words: "We stand on the edge of history. We cannot turn back."[39] The refusal to turn toward the past would be met with strong cultural reaction in the following decades, as black feminist writers and other black cultural producers such as Toni Morrison delved "deeper into historical concerns."[40] Still, the singular horizon of "nation time" named a black nationalist temporality that moved both within and alongside dominant nationhood. As literary critic Daylanne English argues, the "strategic presentism" of American black nationalisms—which is most saliently articulated in Amiri Baraka's poem "It's Nation Time" and in a slogan of the Black Panther Party, "seize the time," announced a collective will to challenge the way black Americans have been cast as belated in the dominant national imagination.[41]

Despite a person's nationalist sympathies, however, one never knows when one will be caught in the zone of untimeliness. At the edge of history, the events of the 1950s could have served as a usable reminder that untimeliness was a constitutive aspect of black life that no form of nationalism could systematically dismantle. Both Emmett Till and Claudette Colvin were non-childlike, non-adults to white segregationists and the NAACP alike. Their non-childlike, non-adult status had nothing to do with their actual ages, since childhood, like blackness, is the outcome of power-based social relations. Neither the white supremacist nor the proponent of black liberalism recognizes childhood at the intersection of blackness and economic dispossession, since childhood, when normatively manifested, signifies total worthiness of social protection. To think of childhood sociogenically is to imagine that it does not have an ontological existence that cuts it off from the historicity of racial capitalist domination. The black man is not a man, and the black person of any gender is not a child. So, Emmett and Claudette appeared to be something other than children. One was accused of whistling at a white woman; the other, as Monique Morris puts it, "was so incensed by the demand to give up her seat that she shouted. She resisted with her body."[42] The zone of non-protection in which Emmett and Claudette found themselves reveals how neither conformed to the temporality of liberal humanism, where childhood emerges as a protected status as a matter of law and custom. Although black subjects were relegated outside of the realm of childhood, they were not entirely included within adulthood, either. But exclusion from proper adulthood was culturally construed as the singular bane of black men.

By the 1970s, radical black feminists understood that the form of gendered adulthood that had become synonymous with western humanism and liberal personhood—manhood—would not get them free. For them, gender was the paradigm from which to analyze intersecting oppressions of the most socially vulnerable subjects under racial capitalism. At the same time, they realized that gender was a category that separated all black people from their collective interests.[43] Thus, to do away with the social divisiveness produced and reinforced by gender, I argue that black feminist thinkers tacitly turned to the conceptual potential of age. Age has provided black feminist and counter-nationalist cultural producers with a framework by which to critique a liberal humanist schema of time that privileges political-economic uses of development. As black feminists knew, if black men tethered their self-interests to the achievement of full liberal personhood and to the agendas of black liberalism and black capitalism in order to progress with the nation, then other black subjects—women and girls, single mothers, queer and transgender subjects of any age, the disabled, teenagers, the sick, the poor, the elderly—become increasingly untimely and are cast outside the realm of social legibility and protection. The awareness of untimeliness is evident in black feminist writings that dwell on improperly gendered childhood or on black female gender that does not conform to the hegemonic logic of age. As I argue throughout this book, such untimeliness contains the radical promise of a future world comprised of undifferentiated humanity. The under-recognized, yet lasting contribution of 1970s-era black feminism to black consciousness is the way it reestablished how time—as historical, social, personal, political—is represented through and as age, along with the possibilities for how age is thought at the intersection of blackness and gender.

When returning to radical black feminism's collective understanding that racial capitalism distorts black gendered age into something untimely, and thus inhuman, it becomes possible to see the sociogenic aspect of age, and to surmise that black age was undone with black enslavement. It also becomes possible to imagine, as many have, that the murder of 17-year-old Trayvon Martin in 2012 was the moment of danger that calls Emmett's flesh to mind in the twenty-first century. To view both the postwar years of the 1950s and the reactionary years of the 2010s through the analytical prism of untimely flesh reveals that in both eras, a social split arose between the potential of a radically inclusive humanism and the neutralizing promise of liberal personhood. The life and death of Trayvon evoked a tacit confrontation with this split precisely because he embodied the contradiction between the distortion of black age and the presumptive naturalness of age in general. The contradiction signified the problem of black claims to humanity.

On February 26, 2012, in Sanford, Florida, Trayvon was walking to his father's home, wearing a hoodie, after buying candy and iced tea from a local convenience store. A self-appointed neighborhood watchman, 28-year-old George Zimmerman, confronted Trayvon and, after a struggle, fatally shot the teenager in the chest. Zimmerman was not arrested or charged with a crime for several weeks; he claimed on record that he feared for his life. But as the days and weeks passed, the public demanded accountability. Millions called for Zimmerman's arrest, wore hoodies in protest, and pressed for prosecution.[44] Comparisons between Trayvon and Emmett abounded, since key among their similarities was innocent black boyhood.[45] However, an opposing narrative about Trayvon's age undercut the jointly constituted conditions of innocence and boyhood throughout the course of Zimmerman's 2013 trial. As Michael J. Dumas and Joseph Derrick Nelson explain, "Zimmerman's defense for killing Trayvon—and the public discourse surrounding the incident—centered on constructing the seventeen-year-old as an *adult man* with suspect movements, threatening physicality, and malevolent intentions."[46]

Suppose we take Trayvon's adulthood at face value. (Suppose this, even though Mamie Till-Mobley showed us that faces reveal complicated realities, especially when they violently go missing.) If Trayvon was an adult, then what *sort* of adult was he presumed to be? When Zimmerman saw Trayvon's "adulthood," what precisely was he seeing, besides blackness and maleness, a certain height and weight, and a hoodie? Like Emmett Till in 1955, Trayvon had not been taken for a man, a person with all of the social privileges and authority that proper manhood entails. As Fanon observed, having "woven [the black subject] out of a thousand details, anecdotes, stories," the white observer beholds something akin to age—not actual childhood or actual adulthood, but something untimely.[47] This untimely way of being in the social world is sociogenically woven into blackness and factors into the third-person consciousness that comes from having a negating presence appended to one's humanity. This negating presence manifests as a hoodie, a pregnancy, a whistling sound. In Zimmerman's defense, Trayvon was constructed as an "adult man" that was the monstrous inverse of Zimmerman's own adult manhood. In the struggle between man and monster, only one adult was deemed worthy of protection.

Just as Mamie Till-Mobley invited all the world to share in Emmett's untimely flesh, all black subjects can wear Trayvon's hoodie. Indeed, the hoodie, as a manifestation of human negation, represents black age. It matters that Emmett and Claudette and Trayvon were teenagers, and that their juvenility did not protect them. It matters that black men have been routinely referred to as "boys," that black children are viewed as adults. As hashtags of the late 2010s declare, #blackgirlmagic and #blackboyjoy matter. These phrases, like *black don't crack*, express that there is liberating potential in the reclamation age, which entails defining girlhood and boyhood on black cultural terms. Hashtags raise the question of what a framework that centralizes gender either reveals or obscures regarding the historicity of blackness. Imagine that the hashtags mentioned above are revised so that age, rather than gender, is shifted to the foreground. Since black "girls" and "boys" could be of any age as a matter of black colloquial reclamation, I imagine they would look like, #black___magic, #black___joy. In the open spaces, what becomes seeable, knowable, imaginable, about black life? The question about our modes of analysis and their relation to black historiography and historicity brings us back to the 1980s. In the post–civil rights era, the market for black literature grew, and the establishment and expansion of black literary studies in the academy took place.[48]

From Historiography to Temporality

By the late 1980s, black literary studies and black feminist thought were comfortably installed within the academy. But, as black feminist literary scholars discovered, the institutionalization of black studies in the academy came with forms of regulation that were reminiscent of the same nationalist heteropatriarchy that characterized black radical politics of the late 1960s and 1970s. As Roderick Ferguson argues, throughout that period, black feminists expressed how their subordination to black men by reason of a broadly held presumption that black men were superior agents of both politics and knowledge was, of course, sexist. But, if we have gained any insight from black feminist analyses of interlocking forms of oppression, we know that gender intersects with other kinds of social relations, including age. Ferguson writes, "Indeed, we can say that black feminism during that period represented a critique of a particular—albeit hegemonic—genre of black male affirmation that was predicated on slotting black women into the position of 'students' who, in the words of Angela Davis, were supposed to 'inspire' [their] men and educate [their men's] children."⁴⁹ Black feminists understood that the sexism of nationalist discourse entailed a separation between timely and untimely subjects that was representable in terms of age: men's "students" and men's "children" effectively existed on the same subordinated plane. Black feminists such as Michele Wallace and the members of the Combahee River Collective described their childhoods as nascent encounters with blackness's ungendered, non-developmental formation. Thus, by turning to the question of how the *temporality* of childhood was related to their black feminist politics, these writers—along with black feminist literary scholars working in the academy at the end of the 1980s—refuted the terms of writing black nationalism's historiography, which was the basis of an emergent form of black social regulation. Of black nationalism's historical discourse, Ferguson states, "nationalist historiography [. . .] is akin to its hegemonic Western counterpart in that both forms of historical writing represent the people on the condition that they remain silent."⁵⁰ Intensified interest in the stakes of who becomes the agents of black literary history and who is represented while falling through historical cracks marks the late 1980s as a key turning point for the trajectory of black literary studies. In this sense, the structure of feeling that permeated the black radical politics of the 1960s and 1970s, discernable in its hierarchical historiographical practices and mode of regulation, was present in the gender politics that shaped the course of black literary studies during the late 1980s. Who would write black literary history, and who would fall silent in the writing of it, was characterized as the difference between practitioners of muscular, rigorous "theory" and practical, feminine "criticism."⁵¹

The negotiation of differences between theory and criticism was part of a broader moment of the field's self-reflectivity in its interrogations of methods. By the 1980s, black literary studies, in relation to the deeper descent into "historical concerns" that black writers, such as Toni Morrison, were expressing in their literature, and a "diasporic turn" in the field of black history, turns to explorations of where the limits of historiography meet with temporality.⁵² As Stephen Best suggests, what I am calling the "historiographic-temporal turn" is engendered by the emergence of slavery as "the constituent object and metaphor in African American studies."⁵³ In a word, by the late 1980s, deeply delving into history meant focusing on slavery. Best offers 1988 as "an important turning point," and names the numerous, influential works that had been published by then, including Spillers's "Mama's Baby, Papa's Maybe." After this turning point, the enslaved past become a generative source of intellectual production. It becomes so because of a generative problem with which black studies scholars are endlessly confronted, which is the problem of archival loss, the impossibility of evidencing black subjectivity in the archives of European colonialism and transatlantic slavery. In the face of what the archive cannot say or prove, through the feedback loop between historiography and temporality—the experience of the past as present loss, the experience of the past as the present—we are suspended in a self-constituting relation with the past. Best provides a useful account of both the preoccupations of black studies over the last 40 years and its restrictive effect, which he refers to as "melancholic historicism." My aim is to focus on another aspect of the "1988" turning point that Best identifies. Black literary scholars were turning to the past, but the question of method pertained to the decidedly open question of which pasts, including recent ones, were deemed worthy of preserving, reconstructing, and retrieving, and for whom. In order to retrieve a moment of the field's development that captures another history of the turning point, while illustrating how the exclusionary humanism that underpinned (black revolutionary) nationalism haunted the field's historiographic concerns, I turn to 1987.

In 1987, an unfortunate exchange between black feminist literary critic, Joyce A. Joyce, and two prominent, black poststructuralist theorists, Henry Louis Gates, Jr. and Houston Baker, Jr., played out in the pages of the journal *New Literary History*. Gates and Baker provide responses that are equal parts vicious and erudite to Joyce's essay, which argues that poststructuralist frameworks are a mediating obstacle between black literature and black readers that obscures and hinders meaning.[54] By 1987, scholars whose analyses of black literature operated outside of poststructuralist epistemologies were associated with the feminized, less prestigious domain of criticism, while scholars who embraced the presumptively neutral and rigorous methodologies of continental theory—most notably, the pioneering Gates and Baker—gained professional prominence. The stakes of this gendered divide were historical: Some would be the masters of black cultural history and some would disappear in the writing of it. As Barbara Christian explains in her 1987 essay, "The Race for Theory": "I know, from literary history, that writing disappears unless there is a response to it."[55] Such disappearance, which was the result of deceptively neutral judgment of the past, is the basis for the recovery projects of the 1970s and '80s. And contemporary writing, notably by black women, is at risk of disappearing now. Listen to Christian's clarion call and imagine how Walter Benjamin's angel of history might sound: "If our emphasis on theoretical criticism continues, critics of the future may have to reclaim the writers we are now ignoring, that is, if they are even aware these artists exist."[56] The question of method, which ostensibly converged around a black gender divide, revealed deep concern over thinking historically about the present, for the sake of a future.

In their renunciations of poststructuralism's hegemony and institutional value systems that render both black feminist reading practices and textual objects irrelevant, Joyce and Christian express their sense of being cut off from a past and a future. Benjamin's angel, his key figure of historical consciousness, elicits that problem by being suspended in the historical present. Referring to Benjamin's "Theses on the Philosophy of History," and Jacques Derrida and Giorgio Agamben's elaborations of Benjamin's philosophy, David Scott suggests that the tragic suspension is paradigmatic of the late twentieth century's dominant temporality. I submit that what Scott refers to as the "untimely" disjuncture between time and history after the Grenada Revolution (1979–1983) is applicable to regulatory practices that discipline a contingent of black women in the academy during the 1980s. As Scott explains, once time is out of sync with history, "what we are left with are *aftermaths* in which the present seems stricken with immobility and pain and ruin; a certain experience of temporal *afterness* prevails in which the trace of futures past hangs like the remnant of a voile curtain over what feels uncannily like an endlessly extending present."[57] To wit, Spillers describes the experience of being stranded in the aftermath of a feminist movement and stuck with a "curricular object": "All of a sudden, it would seem, the conversation changes, and it is so sudden it is institutionally traumatic, and for some individuals it is traumatic. [. . .] In other words, there are women in this country today who legitimately wonder, what happened to their movement? But it went to the university."[58] The year 1987 indexes a critical moment when black feminist literary scholars understood gender as the means through which academic discourse deemed black women's discernments, approaches to analysis, and modes of inquiry to be irrelevant to the production of black cultural and historical knowledge. In the aftermath of feminism's disappearance outside of the academy, gender signified the out-of-jointness of reaching black liberalism's horizon, only to achieve a feeling of perpetual untimeliness. In short, gender made time itself noticeable.

As a category that made the experience of time conspicuous, gender—despite the occasional dismissals of feminism—served as an analytical framework through which to consider the human.[59] Indeed, gender's analytical power arises from the way it signposts how subjects are oriented in time on various scales. For instance, throughout the 1980s and into the present, black success looked like the achievement of a normative gender binary in which men are "entrepreneurs" and women "can be 'feminine' and sit at home."[60] The binary gender schematic signposts black success on two scales: It implies that black people are in synchronic movement with bourgeois motivations and, more broadly, it announces that black people are constituted through western humanist reproduction of gendered pairs.[61] Gender indicates how subjects are installed within historical temporalities.

In 1987, two major publications in black literary studies took black female subjectivity as an analytical starting point for their interventions in the writing of historiography. These works are Jean Fagan Yellin's groundbreaking biographical account of Harriet Jacobs, which confirms her authorship and hence, the facticity, of the 1861 slave narrative *Incidents in the Life of a Slave Girl*, and Toni Morrison's Pulitzer Prize–winning novel, *Beloved*, which reinvents a life for the historical subject, Margaret Garner, after the baby daughter she murdered during slavery makes a preternatural return. Both works enhanced gender's relation to temporality by emphasizing gender's relation to age.

Yellin once again encountered *Incidents in the Life of a Slave Girl* (1861) while developing a project about anti-slavery feminists. The narrative is a first-person account by Linda Brent, who we now know to be Harriet Jacobs. It chronicles her embattled girlhood as a slave who is forced to constantly ward off the sexual advances of her predatory master. She eventually escapes by hiding in an attic crawlspace of the home of her grandmother, Aunt Martha, for seven years, so that she can remain close to the children she had with another man. Yellin provided painstakingly researched evidence of Harriet Jacobs's previously unthought-of authorship, along with details about her life and milieu. Her recovery project brought under-considered evidence to bear on how we read and situate *Incidents* in the moment of its production, which expands the uses of gender as an analytic for the study of enslavement.

It also establishes Jacobs's enslaved girlhood as a historical problem. The conundrum through which Jacobs had to write—presenting the reality of routinized sexual violence while appealing to the Victorian sensibilities of her readership—rested on another conundrum, which is that a slave girl is not actually a "girl" in the socially conventional sense of that category. Along with Jacobs, white feminists of the nineteenth and twentieth centuries who were responsible for the publication of a slave girl's story also encounter that foundational problem. As P. Gabrielle Foreman reveals, Lydia Maria Child's editorial decision to have the narrative end with a final reference to Jacobs's "good old grandmother," along with Yellin's placement of the 1894 photograph of an elderly Jacobs on the frontispiece, reinforce a substitution of Jacobs the slave girl for the older and respectable Aunt Martha.[62] Thus, the narrative is bookended with archival and literary elements that point to the fungibility and indeterminability of black female age. An elderly woman is the slave girl. The slave girl is always already old. Girlhood does not exist in a narrative about it. Considering the absence of properly gendered age, the telos of freedom in the narrative is an aporia: It does not signify the achievement of bourgeois femininity in marriage, nor of manhood. If all the women are white and all the blacks are men, then what is the narrative trajectory for black females for whom age is fungible?

Before *Beloved* became "the paragon literary text" of the turn to slavery in black studies, Morrison published *The Black Book*, a recovery project of sorts, while she was still an editor at Random House in 1974.[63] The book captures ephemera of the enslaved past—newspaper clippings, postcards, images of torture devices—and is thereby a counter-historiographical record of the black image in the white mind and under-recognized black responses to that image. While working on *The Black Book*, Morrison came across the story of Margaret Garner, who, in 1856, crossed the Ohio River with her family to flee slavery in Kentucky. Upon imminent recapture, Garner killed her own baby daughter in an impossible attempt to save the baby's life. In the 1987 novel, Morrison reimagines the historical Garner as the fictional Sethe in *Beloved*, dwelling in that space of impossibility. The preternatural Beloved who returns is identified in terms of age: She was "crawling-already?" age when her neck was slit, and the entire span of her girlhood is absented from the text. She reemerges as "Grown. The age it would have been had it lived."[64] "It" is appropriate since, like in Jacobs's narrative, black gender in *Beloved* is a historical problem. "It" signifies the way Beloved is something other than human. She is the agential embodiment of the dead, the 60 million or more at the bottom of the ocean, in addition to being Sethe's crawling-already/grown-up daughter. By imagining psychic lives for which there is no archive, Morrison represents age as a figure of narrow and broad temporal scales. Age scores Beloved's lifespan, albeit with a widened crack where girlhood should be. Beloved manifests the age of slavery and the age of black modernity.

With gender as their starting points, the interventions that Yellin, Morrison, and Spillers make are illustrative of a shift in the means and methods for "making" historical time, which entails the writing of historiography and the envisioning of alternative ways of being historical. Age is always present, the concept for living (in) time, even when it is not as it seems. Just as historiography negotiates the balance between the evidentiary and the imperceptible, so, too, does age: It is a metaphor for a version of time that is both knowable and imaginary. Let us now turn from 1980s-era reencounters with slavery to a broader timescale, in order to consider how modern racial formation entailed epistemic obliteration of historical time, which was linked to discourses about human development. The lack of history and the untimeliness of age were jointly constitutive aspects of "blackness." This observation that blackness connotes historical lack and untimely age has led to the now commonplace interpretation of modern racial formation, which is that the primitive and the savage were akin to children, since the racializing regimes of colonialism and enslavement were patriarchal, and primitives and children ostensibly existed on the same plane of development in relation to patriarchal force.[65] But black embodiment expresses untimeliness in ways that exceed that adult/children binary. The black body has been constituted as a site of historical and human emptiness, which could be endowed with any meaning at all.

The Age of History

In order to think of black life in the aftermath of western modernity, it is critical to imagine that a centuries-long process of racialization has not only constituted blackness as the preeminent sign of non-value and non-humanity but also constituted blackness as a manifestation of untimeliness, existing in ways that run counter to dominant modalities of knowledge and reason. Even as blackness signifies the outcome of a historical process that has systematically validated the full humanity of some humans while dispossessing full humanity from others, blackness lays claim to an untimely version of time that exceeds, transforms, or reinterprets western modern rationality. That untimeliness signifies the unacknowledged endurance and reinvention of human life. I do not hypothesize a black humanism that is distinctive from but nonetheless analogous to an overly dominant white, western humanism that incorporates property as a constitutive aspect of its being.[66] Rather than thinking of untimely time in the liberal humanist terms of property—something private, that the possessive individual both claims and manifests—I think of it as uncaptured evidence of a radical alternative to liberal humanism. In what counts as our legitimate social order, untimely time is the unrecognized, undervalued, or disavowed residue—or, conversely and potentially, the beginning—of alternative humanisms despite the dominance of western reason and its epistemological projects. As such, untimeliness arises from what Achille Mbembe calls black reason, the "reason of unreason," the contingent rationalizations about blackness and black responses to such rationalizations that ostensibly operate outside of dominant modes of rationality.[67] Untimeliness has particular relevance for Enlightenment reasoning of what constitutes history and the presumed derivation of historical knowledge as that which arises from civilization's progressive development. Having been constructed as the exclusion from history, and inter-constitutively of the human, blackness comprises an alternative relation to time, and this alterity marks the possibility of making another, untimely history of modernity.

Since history only properly exists as history when it constitutes, reifies, and fortifies western humanism, I think of it as belonging to an assemblage of western epistemologies that together comprise what I refer to as "human time." That assemblage includes western modernity's epistemic structures of time—the developmental and evolutionary time of ontogeny and phylogeny, the political philosophical time of liberal humanism, and the overarching historical time of civilization. The very concept of age, which has been naturalized to such a degree that to speak of it at all requires a reliance on western modernity's knowledge and reason, is in fact the embodied consolidation of human time. Signifying and manifesting humanness overall, age expresses how humans exist in a hegemonic, timely temporality that operates on numerous scales which range from the individual to the universal. The human matures individually and in synchronicity with chronological, calendrical time. The human develops along with liberalism's teleology, so that one grows into being a fully developed liberal subject endowed with social, economic, and political obligations, along with social protections and privileges. The scheduling of rights, privileges, and protections is mapped onto a schema of biological, chronological, and social human development, so the precise numbers of lived years make up the schedule. But even within the realm of the human, a legal schedule of rights has failed to capture fully the maturation of anyone other than the liberal humanist subject par excellence, who is implicitly white, heteronormative, and male.[68]

Consolidation of western epistemic structures of time constitutes the human, and that consolidation simultaneously produces discourses about and seeps into the common sense as age. In opposition to this consolidation, we have the blankness of blackness which, as a form of racialization, supposedly exists without claim to time or the past. Consider Orlando Patterson's well-known concept of natal alienation. As a result of enslavement and in the aftermath of being removed from a legitimating social order, the slave is definable as "a socially dead person"; social death entails being cut off from one's own heritage and ancestors, and from a usable past.[69] A life alienated from human time, which is demonstrated in the dispossession of familial lineage and collective memory, ceases to count as human life. And yet, such alienation was not total, since the enslaved "reached back for the past," indicating that the problem was not that the enslaved possessed no past, but that attempts to access it "meant struggling with penetrating the iron curtain of the master, his community, his laws, his policeman or patrollers, and his heritage."[70]

Imagine that the iron curtain determines the dividing line between those who lay claim to the hegemonic time of sociality and those who live in the untimely realm of social dispossession. In *Black Age*, the iron curtain illustrates a division between age as naturalized a priori on the one side, and that which is unthought-of on the other. The curtain blocks the possibility of thinking of age as anything other than a commonsensical code word for human time. Even Fanon is cut off from what lies beyond the binary schema of Antillean children and European adults. We reach back for the past, *but the past is not actually behind us*. Age represents the past, which holds the promise of an alternative way of being in time, even though age is *right here* in the living flesh, constituting who we are now. Thus, the irony of an iron curtain that cuts us off from who we are is emblematic of how age operates as a figure of historical consciousness: Age is an experience of time so inalienable to us that it has been cut off from our sustained efforts to theorize modernity. Yet age is a key analytic for detecting the cracks in modern time. With it, we can further examine what exists in, but not of, the hegemonic side of the curtain, what is barely audible on the lower frequencies of the master's words, laws, history. On the lower frequencies is a past and a future that is already here.

Nonetheless, in Patterson's work, the iron curtain briefly represents the production of blackness as a form of racialization that lacks both history and humanity. Age functions as the condition of disavowal of the racialized eradication of historical time. It is important to link the broad historical connotations of age—the age of modernity—with other liberal, biological, and social connotations that reference an individual—the age of a person's lifetime. Since blackness has been conceptualized as fundamentally being without history and individuality, and thus without a conception of time as a distinctly human species, blackness signifies blankness on a smaller, embodied scale. Writ onto the broad global scale of western modernity, blackness is the sign of having no history; writ onto the smaller scale of individuated embodiment, blackness is the sign of having no age.

The conflation between negated time of history and negated time of lifespans is a commonplace aspect of Enlightenment reason. In one sense, history slides into the popular terms of life stages via anthropological knowledge of the nineteenth century. As David Theo Goldberg discusses, through scientific discourse, the notion of "primitive society" was created as the observable, measurable evidence of a primeval past, to which primitive subjects had a virtually unmediated relation. The primitive, having been a site of invention and scientific inquiry, transforms over time, and discursive connotations of history and age merge in their translated guises of the "primitive" and "child." Through this merger, "nonwhite primitives have come to be conceived as childlike, intuitive, and spontaneous; they require the iron fist of 'European' governance and paternalistic guidance to control inherent physical violence and sexual drives."[71] As this strange amalgamation between "childlike" qualities and adult-like violence and sexuality illustrates, racial capitalism required the separation and classification of human life for the sake of perpetuating systematically inequitable conditions for value extraction. More precisely, racialization entailed making humans who were on the dehumanizing end of value extraction age-malleable. Reproduction of blackness required more creative agility than a rigid child/adult binary could provide, even as such a binary became discursively dominant. Through racial capitalism, modernity ushered in the rise of a new age that was jointly constituted with blackness.[72] In that untimely new age, a black subject submitted to paternal authority amused the other with childish guilelessness, impressed, frightened, and sexually aroused the other by being a child with a fully grown body. As Goldberg rightly notes, "If the Primitive has no history at all, it is only because the theoretical standard-bearers of Civilization have managed first to construct a Primitive Subject and then to obliterate *his* history."[73] But in addition to this obliteration, another age was created and thus, the potential of an insurrectionary route toward another "history."

Political philosopher, John Stuart Mill, exemplifies that analogies between racialized others and normative children are ill-fitting. Still playing an administrative role in the East India Company while drafting *On Liberty* (1859), a treatise on the moral basis of social and individual freedom, Mill was quite certain that matters of liberty "apply only to human beings in the maturity of their faculties."[74] Of the free-thinking individuals who collectively work toward humanity's progress, he writes, "We are not speaking of children [. . .] we may leave out of consideration those backward states of society in which the race itself may be considered as in its nonage."[75] In Mill's time, "nonage" was a standard term for under-aged persons, also known as children. I suggest that it refers to the contradiction of being within and out of sync with dominant time, a condition that colonialism and enslavement foist onto their racialized subjects. In this contradiction, the uncivilized can be both "under full legal age," which implies legal personhood, and profoundly alienated from human time, on which the law relies.[76] Once the absence of civilization is mapped onto the co-constitutive absence of actual, developmental, and chronological age, nonage can be thought of through the crassly translated term, "no-age," which is at the etymological heart of the fifteenth-century, Anglo-francophone term. "No-age" suggests that one does not possess age.

We are not speaking of children, for as Fred Moten claims, "there are no children here."[77] Rather, in order to say a truer word about how age functions as a metonym for human time, it is important to recognize an essential aspect of its function, which is to disavow that uncivilized races had been dispossessed of their claims to time. In its inhuman form, "childhood" names a process for simultaneously including and alienating racialized subjects within a schema of human time. The key to endowing racializing regimes of domination with what seems to be inherent rationality and therefore legitimacy, the inhuman blankness of "no-age" and the human time of "nonage" *must appear to be the same thing*. Consequently, not only does age index a consolidation of hegemonic registers of timeliness—my concept of human time—it also marks a conflation between human existence and the non-human's political alienation. That conflation is founded on the violent dispossession of time that must be disavowed for human time to seem rational. Racialized childhood, then, does not refer to a life stage, but rather, to the seamless conflation of both humanity and human exclusion.

All the Females Are White, All the Adults Are Men

Fanon has had conspicuously little to say about the psychic life of the Antillean woman. After providing a lengthy analysis "on the psychosexuality of the white woman," Fanon briefly acknowledges that, of the development of "the woman of color," "I know nothing about her."[78] Lewis Gordon reads this as a pragmatic, rather than a conceptual or political matter. According to Gordon,

What Fanon means is that he lacks *clinical* knowledge of the *nègre* in the woman of color's fantasy life. The reason for this is obvious: racism and sexism are such that female mental patients of color would have been taken at their peril to a predominantly white male community of mental health workers. [. . .] Fanon, in short, had to rely on nonclinical information because of demographics of most mental health patients: white men, white women, and men of color.[79]

The exclusion of black women from the realm of clinical knowledge is attributable to their structural and institutional absence. But when the black woman does emerge as the subject of clinical knowledge in *Black Skin, White Masks*, we nearly miss it because she emerges, not as a woman—defined by virtue of having a fantasy life about male sexuality—but as a preternaturally elderly child. As I discuss in chapter 2 of this text, Fanon's mediating "antennae" have to fall before he realizes that he occupies the position of the adult in relation to a 73-year-old Antillean farm woman who suffers from dementia: "I condescend to her in my quest for a diagnosis."[80] Fanon does not tell us what she said; her irrational language is not worth repeating. Although she appears in Fanon's clinical archive, we know nothing about her. I want to think of this elderly woman's textual silence as being connected to other silences across colonial, transatlantic archives. As Saidiya Hartman asks in various ways across her body of work, how does one write historiography against the violence of the archive, which is frequently expressed as silence?[81]

Black feminists of the long 1970s attempted to fill epistemic and evidentiary silences that rendered their experiences unknowable with their own narratives of development. The title of a formative volume that marked the inception of black women's studies offers the aporia of black female maturation: *All the Women Are White, All the Black Are Men, But Some of Us Are Brave*. In the volume's opening essay, Michele Wallace describes how political consciousness arises from girlhood. As girls, Wallace and her sister transformed silken scarves into imaginary, long, straight hair; as Wallace knows, "the game was being feminine. Being feminine *meant* being white to us."[82] The game is illustrative of how black girls critique the temporal horizon toward which they move. A mimetic relation to femininity is not simply a developmental attribute of childhood, since there is no time in the future when black girls will grow into *being* feminine, as the title of the volume suggests. What constitutes a normative timeline of maturation for black girls when all the women "are white"? Without whiteness or maleness, under what circumstances can black females be adults? Of course, white women have been denied full adulthood, as feminist struggles for suffrage and equal rights indicate. Still, unlike black females of any age, white women have been socially endowed with girlhood, a human developmental status that entails protection as a matter of law and custom. As children, Wallace and her sisters appended scarves to bodies that lacked girlhood, which depended on the social conferral of white femininity. As children, they played at being girls, who could be women one day or, if not, then at the very least feminine subjects worthy of protection.

As if they heard the silences in Fanon's case study archive, the Combahee River Collective said the unspoken in their Statement: "The seemingly personal experiences of individual Black women's lives" are political and historical.[83] Black women's developmental lives are never completely individuated nor synced to the timeline of civic and national belonging. What is more, black feminist approaches to development account for the non-normativity of black gender. For instance, as mentioned in the Statement, "As children we were told in the same breath to be quiet both for the sake of being 'ladylike' and to make us less objectionable in the eyes of white people."[84] The imperative to be "ladylike"—to aspire for the femininity one lacks—is combined with an inhuman, objectionable something that covers black subjects of any gender like a bodysuit. Unlike the abnormal development that Fanon describes as the condition of the black Antillean child who grows up in contact with the white world, the Statement suggests that there is no version of Western modern society in which the black female subject grows up unaware of being ungendered. This aspect of sociogeny is a starting point that accounts for a modernity that shapes us all, and an untimeliness that cannot be avoided by remaining in the enclosure of a purely all-black world.[85]

As a counterpoint to the dispossession of age, Alice Walker invents a term of reclamation. "Womanist," which runs counter to the Eurocentric term "feminist," is a framework that makes age or embodied temporalities thinkable as a constitutive part of race and gender. Walker's 1983 essay collection, *In Search of Our Mothers' Gardens*, begins with a four-part, dictionary-like definition of "Womanist." The first and primary definition reads as follows:

> From *womanish*. (Opp. of "girlish," i.e., frivolous, irresponsible, not serious.) A black feminist or feminist of color. From the black folk expression of mothers to female children, "You acting womanish," i.e., like a woman. Usually referring to outrageous, audacious, courageous or *willful* behavior. Wanting to know more and in greater depth than is considered "good" for one. Interested in grown-up doings. Acting grown up. Being grown up. Interchangeable with another black folk expression: "You trying to be grown." Responsible. In charge. *Serious*.[86]

One outcome of non-normative racial formation is the ambiguity of age and life stages. Walker's womanism places "female children"—if not "girlishness"—at the conceptual center of black adulthood. Thus, Walker takes the racialization of age as the starting point from which to challenge a categorical understanding of "woman." In other words, in order for the black feminist or feminist of color to situate herself within a discourse that both produces and naturalizes gender as an integral part of being human, she begins with an unstable relation between "race" and "age." A fluid relation to the past, present, and future constitutes the womanist subject. She is at once the female child who can only be "like a woman" and the female adult for whom the mimetic relation to womanhood persists. Acting and being "grown up" are attributed to black femaleness across life stages, with performance sharing the status of a naturalized ontology.

In the fullness of Walker's analytical term, to be womanish is to inhabit a mode of being in which gender is a constitutive part of the fluid and dynamic meanings of racialized age. Gender obtains a fluidity that renders it non-binary, and without a stable teleology—toward rationality or reproduction—to codify it. "You acting womanish" and "You trying to be grown" are part of an ungendered afterlife that "womanist" is capacious enough to include. The anti-categorical definition of womanist is rife with refusals of linear temporality, of a telos that biological, chronological, cultural maturation promises. Female—and, implicitly, male—children and adults "want to know more," are "interested in grown-up doings." Wanting, desiring, acting, and being all are routes toward epistemological alternatives to the post-liberated, rights-bearing "adult." When linked to blackness, the fluidity of age and gender underscore "something else to be."[87] As an analytical framework for thinking of the untimeliness of black age, womanism manifests the Oceanic realm where "trans" meets "childhood."

The transness of womanism can be brought to bear on the recent rise of black girlhood studies, which retrieves young black female subjects from their liminal status beyond dominant historical narratives.[88] As Farah Jasmine Griffin puts it, "Perceived absences should not keep us from looking for black girls in the archive."[89] As the absences in Fanon's archive and the recovery of Harriet Jacobs show, archives might yield much of what we still do not know about the developmental lives of black girls and women. *Black Age* does not always presume that there is a knowable, retrievable subject—such as the black girl—that can be recovered through empirical methods. Rather, this book treats gendered life stages across lifespans as sites that reveal experiences of humanity that have been excluded from the normative domain of the human. It separates age from the empiricist domain of historicism, sociology, and ethnography in order to launch a critical inquiry into how age functions both as an effect of historical processes and as a metaphor of historical temporalities. I draw from all of these disciplinary domains in order to account fully for the epistemic co-constitution of blackness, gender, and age in the New World.

If, as Matt Richardson puts it, "Black bodies are unknowable under the schema of a two-gender system," then I would add that black bodies have been unknowable through the schema of linear, normative life stages and lifespans.[90] Ultimately, age points to the threshold of alternative humanity by thinking of temporality not only as it is related to history's teleology or wreckages, sweeping epochal or epistemic shifts, but as flesh. Spillers famously indicates this when she contends that the violent subjection of Africans crossing the Middle Passage has left "a kind of hieroglyphics of the flesh whose severe disjunctures come to be hidden to the cultural seeing by skin color."[91] In other words, *black don't crack*. Across time and generations, skin and age express something about our in/humanity that is unseen, unwritten, and unspoken.

Black age is a framework for epistemologically challenging what counts as human time and uncovering the infinite ways in which black life matters.

Chapters

Each of this book's four chapters focuses on figures that performs two functions: each reimagines the human as radical alterity and represents modes of mediation between past and present. By organizing this book around various figures of alternative humanism and historical mediation, I attempt to pivot continually between two argumentative gestures: the black body, to which inhuman meanings of gender and age have been attributed, appears as something other than—and differently—human, and the historicity of age reboots the way we interpret the historical past. Thus, each figure is an attempt to denaturalize the norms and categories we use for thinking how lives are lived throughout a lifespan. Further, my use of paired terms for most chapters is meant to evoke and critique the way western humanism reconstitutes itself through gendered binaries and pairings. Thus, by eschewing normative human pairs, this book imagines modes of alternatively human relationality. Such modes, as this book ultimately argues, is the basis for envisioning new strategies of protection that do not rely on normative schemas of gender and age.

Chapter 1, "Shape-Shifters and Body Snatchers," begins with "The Hug Shared around the World," a photo that had been widely circulated in 2014 and interpreted as a reassuring image in a time of national tumult. In it, a black boy, Devonte Hart, embraces a white police officer in the aftermath of a grand jury's decision not to indict another white officer who shot and killed the unarmed black teenager, Michael Brown. I situate this contemporary, over-exposed image in a cultural genealogy, which reveals that black boys are not seen *as boys* because black boy embodiment is socially imagined as shifting, in accord with white desires. Shifting connects Devonte's hypervisibility to little Harry's performances as a commodity in Harriet Beecher Stowe's anti-slavery novel, *Uncle Tom's Cabin* (1852). As I argue, hypervisibility, the shifting interplay between the visible and invisible, is linked to the shifting appearance of the commodity and its value, which Harry expresses through his "age-shifting" performances. Harry's performances of the commodity's relationship to white desires reveals that he and his mother, Eliza, exist on a horizontal, rather than intergenerational, plane of temporality, and thus "value" overrides differences between both gender and age. The logic of horizontal kinship is germane to Jordan Peele's 2017 film, *Get Out*, in which the shared dispossession of the black adult son and the black mother reemerged through a body-snatching act that leads to the recommodification, and untimeliness, of black embodiment. As I illustrate, shifting is thinkable in relation to the unseen social and historical forces that engender it, and the body snatcher is figurative of the unseen side of social domination. Together, the shape-shifter and the body snatcher mutually figure the condition of black hypervisibility, and a related condition of simultaneously seeing remnants of the discarded past within the shifting dynamism of the historical present.

Chapter 2, "Vampires and Relics," turns to speculative fiction to imagine what is historically irrecoverable or unknowable. This chapter argues that black girls and women have been represented as having an archival function, which is a cultural response to the irretrievability of black history. Black females on either end of the life cycle are represented as having a preternatural capacity to mediate between the present and the past. Two figures of such mediation, the vampire and the relic, call our attention to how black female age itself has been historically constituted to perform the labor of enchanting history. The vampire manifests a fleshy, counter-temporality, since her extremely long life allows to her account for the past in a manner that challenges the official or conventional historical record. Octavia Butler's last published novel before her untimely death in 2006 is the vampire novel, *Fledgling* (2005). *Fledgling*, along with Jewelle Gomez's 1991 black feminist vampire novel, *The Gilda Stories*, reimagine a counter-national dialectic between the past and present through the lives of black female, and queer vampires that appear much younger than their chronological ages. This chapter situates these young appearing, yet ancient, vampires as alternatives to the relic, the explicitly ancient figure of living history that provides audiences with an immediate connection to the past. The enslaved Joice Heth played the role of the relic for P. T. Barnum in 1835. Ernest Gaines's reimagined relic in *The Autobiography of Miss Jane Pittman* (1971) interrupts conventional narratives about temporality on which Heth's performance relied, which include historical time, chronological time, and national time. Through such an interruption, Gomez's, Butler's, and Gaines's work reinvent alternatively non-hegemonic versions of what living history means.

Chapter 3, "The Mass and Men," turns to fiction within historiography. In his significant 1959 work on US plantation slavery, *Slavery: A Problem in American Institutional and Intellectual Life*, Stanley Elkins argued that as a result of plantation slavery's "closed system" that locked the slave in a dialectic with the master, enslaved adult males—who Elkins presumes were paradigmatic of all enslaved subjects—were irrevocably infantilized. Denied the liberty to be men, the enslaved were reduced to being perpetual boys or, upon reaching seniority, elderly and ineffectual "uncles." This chapter begins with Elkins's argument in order to focus on its underlying premise, which is that both the land on which plantations were built and enslaved field hands were co-constituted to untimely effect. The co-constitution between "land" and "hand" that ostensibly clumps black males on either end of the life cycle—young boys and old men— into undifferentiated groups of non-developmental, non-adults has been commented upon in literature of the long 1970s. The decade marks a juncture when social historiographies on slavery converge with interest in contemporary conditions of black life in urban and rural spaces. Toni Morrison's 1973 novel, *Sula*, and Ernest Gaines' 1983 southern pastoral novel, *A Gathering of Old Men*, reveal redemptive responses to the static, homogenous, and overly generalized non-development of "Sambo" by drawing on the potential of the "mass," the collective that stands in for a singular and individuated personality. In *Sula*, the mass is comprised of the "deweys," who are three boys of differing ages and appearance that mysteriously become non-differentiated, perpetual boys. The deweys are a reclamation of the homogenous and inhumanly rendered stereotype of black childhood, "pickaninnies." Conversely, in *A Gathering of Old Men*, the titular collective of elderly, former field hands in Louisiana, attempt to redeem their manhood by speaking with individuated voices that convey a shared, lived history. As the many-in-the-one, the deweys and the old men beg the question of how black-male-age is situated in relation to the broad-ranging project of accounting for—along with the afterlife—of slavery in the post-civil rights era.

The final chapter, "Ghosts," argues that the conspicuously untimely age of ghosts is the key inducement that leads the normatively liberal subject to the haunting recognition that the time is out of joint. While each of the preceding chapters focuses on two complementary figures of black age, this chapter unfolds through exemplary pairings of an untimely ghost who haunts and the one who is haunted in normative, progressive time. Olaudah Equiano's 1789 slave narrative, *The Interesting Narrative of the Life of Olaudah Equiano, or Gustavus Vassa*, is the chapter's paradigmatic text that figures ghostly entanglements between timely and untimely black subjects. The unnamed sister from whom Equiano is separated during the First Passage is a ghostlike alter ego; I refer to her as the "Equiano Girl." As a fixture of Equiano's memory and a subject in her own right who is historically irretrievable, the Equiano Girl signifies melancholic doubt about the achievement of full maturity in a narrative that ostensibly affirms linear development and liberal individualism. Thus, the ghosts in this chapter have an untimely existence in the present in order to unsettle the presumptive progressiveness and completeness of historical time. In two ghost stories that bracket the emancipatory promises of liberalism's expansion in the twentieth century, Charles Chesnutt's 1898 short story, "The Wife of His Youth," and Toni Morrison's final novel, *God Help the Child* (2015), haunting is an embodying process that transforms the proper black liberal and neoliberal subject into alternative modes of being, which is expressed as age. To be haunted is to be transformed by and into the untimely alternatives to proper subjectivity, such as a middle-aged man who hovers between juvenility and adulthood, or a black woman who physically regresses into a little girl's body. To be haunted to be awakened to the history that is happening to us now.

Black Age concludes with a brief epilogue that asks how the history we have been awakened to in the second decade of the twenty-first century may lead us to an emancipatory mode of relationality. Girls, boys, the elderly, transgender and genderqueer adults and children, women and men of all ages, find no protective recognition through social logics that distinguish childhood from adulthood, one gender from another. Without hegemonic categories of gender and life stages to crisscross black lives, what modes of sociality become thinkable?

Devonte Hart hugging Sgt. Bret Barnum at a rally in Portland, Oregon on November 25, 2014. Photo by Johnny Nguyen.

1

Shape-Shifters and Body Snatchers

Whose little boy are you?
—James Baldwin, *The Fire Next Time*

Before his body became a part of the ocean, a tearful black boy had his picture taken, and the image circulated throughout news outlets and social media. The now-famous photo, dubbed by the press as "The Hug Shared around the World," is of 12-year-old Devonte Hart tearfully hugging police officer Sgt. Bret Barnum during a protest rally in Portland, Oregon on November 25, 2014. The protest was part of a nationwide response to a grand jury's decision not to indict Darren Wilson, the white police officer who fatally shot Michael Brown, an unarmed black teenager, in Ferguson, Missouri on August 9, 2014. Among the protestors, Devonte had been holding a sign that read, "Free Hugs."[1] In the photo, the boy is wearing a blue and white fedora and a caramel-colored leather jacket with cobalt blue cuffs. His right cheek is pressed against Barnum's chest; his face is contorted into a grimace as tears stream down. A blue-gloved hand clasps the back of Barnum's shoulder. Barnum, with the visor of his helmet disarmingly pushed up and his ungloved hands firmly wrapped around the boy's back, seems to be saying something soothing. The child's pained, tearful gaze looks off in the distance, not toward the viewer.

The image of black boyhood, of a black child who is gendered male, is key to the photo's force. Historically, black boyhood has inspired polarizing impulses comprised of affection and fear, each determined by whether black boys are childish or mannish, pet-like or monstrous. A genealogy of black boys as fascinating objects includes their status as the pets of eighteenth-century nobility, and an array of examples of black boys as entertainers that reach well into the twentieth century.[2] If the image of black boyhood has incited pleasure and fascination for mainstream audiences in recent history, then this may have to do with the tacit perception of black boys as freakish. As Lori Merish notes of the "midget," a performance category of the freak show and vaudeville, the black boy "unsettled, in a contained but dramatic fashion, the conventional boundary between child and adult."[3] Troubling the line between childhood and adulthood had been a commonplace conceit of black-boy performance throughout the twentieth century: As a six- or seven-year-old, Sammy Davis, Jr. performed as a "forty-four-year-old midget" on the vaudeville stage. Four decades later, Michael Jackson—a child who channeled the grown-man presence of Jackie Wilson and James Brown—was frequently referred to as a "forty-two-year-old midget."[4] Gary Coleman and Emmanuel Lewis, two black adolescents who starred in 1980s-era television sitcoms, were well-known for being much older than the young children they played on TV. All of these age-blurring performances were popular with the public.

Yet, seeing black boys *as children* saliently arose as a historical problem in the 2010s, and the photo raises the question of what "seeing" Devonte means. Thus, in the context of the present, the photo sets shifting meanings in motion. In this chapter, I think of shifting as a method for disassembling the pieces of a historical present to denaturalize it, in order to reveal how our perception of the present relies on what has been buried, unseen, and disavowed. It is a genealogical approach that requires actively *watching* for moments when the stable appearance of the present seems to waiver, when something disappears or crosses into another way of being, in order to reappear as something else. Watching for transitory, incoherent moments of shifting follows the interpretive spirit of what Tina Campt calls "listening" to the photographic image, a counterintuitive practice for discerning the black subject's nearly imperceptible reaction to a moment of exigency.[5] Like listening to the lower frequencies, watching for invisibilities embedded within a fleeting moment of shifting, the allusive in-between of disappearance and reappearance, entails a notable duration of attention. In this chapter, I watch for embodied, performative, connotative, and temporal moments of shifting across a range of cultural forms, including the photo of the famous hug. In all cases, the shift relies on black male hypervisibility, and in the case of the photo, on the condition of simultaneously seeing and not-seeing the black boy.

In the photo, the hug is the site of shifting between what the present moment affirms and disavows. One watches for the nearly imperceptible moment when, while shifting, affirmation momentarily melds with disavowal: The visuality of black boyhood is constituted in this space of seeing/non-seeing. Watch, and the embrace is paternalistic: Barnum is the authority figure who stands in for the missing black parent in the picture—the missing *black adult*—who should be caring for Devonte.[6] Paternalism shifts into desire for black infantilization, racial injury, and gratitude. Watch, and the embrace becomes unambiguously violent, signifying the carceral state and its early grip on black boys. And then, amid the Black Lives Matter movement, it shifts into national nostalgia: Devonte is the ungendered black subject who selflessly comforts white Americans in times of trouble, like the ostensibly elderly mammy and uncle in the mythic Old South. Through the shifts of social and historical connotation, Devonte is not a child, but an emblem of blackness as infantile, elderly, helpless, dutiful, and all of these. He is a figure of racial untimeliness, an embodied deflection away from the moment in history that was currently unfolding, and this racial untimeliness grants the photo its symbolic power.[7] While Barnum coherently maintains his moral, legal, and developmental superiority—as a father figure, the only adult, the state itself, the picture of white moral innocence—Devonte is the picture of incoherence. As I watch, he transforms into a son, a racial dependent of any age, an adult-like criminal, the elderly "help," and ultimately, an endless, timeless source of fantasy in the psychic life of whiteness. The photo begs the question: Is black boyhood seeable only when it is an age-shifting repository for white fantasy?

We begin with an overexposed image of a black boy as an illustration of how hypervisible blackness and the untimeliness of black age are thoroughly entangled. This chapter tracks the way this entanglement has been expressed not just in the stillness of the photograph, but also in the anti-slavery novel of the nineteenth century and contemporary film. Throughout this book, I explore untimely black age through cultural figures that elucidate facets of it in the afterlife of slavery. In this chapter, untimeliness is discernable as the appearance of shifting: Black embodiment appears to shift from one mode to another and, specifically, age appears to shift from one transitory moment to the next, as opposed to transforming over a long developmental or biological period of time.

But if age-shifting signifies an alternatively human temporality, one that is visibly present as instantaneous and transitory rather than developmental and linear, then I suggest that it be thought of in relation to unseen social and historical forces, modes of production that have led to the formation of modern blackness as a sign of social exclusion. Thus, this chapter's second figure of analysis is the body snatcher. Body snatching signifies violence masked when the black body appears as marvelously, magically, or spectacularly other than fully human, such as when a police officer claims to have seen an unarmed, 18-year-old black teenager instantly transform into a "demon."[8] The "snatching" of bodies is meant to be evocative of every phase of the transatlantic slave trade and conquest in the New World. It evokes past and currently routinized violence that is meant to protect the property rights of those who have been historically constituted as fully human. Blackness signifies ongoing expropriation of land, labor, bodies, and lives for the amusement and profit of others, even as the social freedom of black people has been achieved.[9] As a figure that exists in relation to the malleable and instantaneously altered embodiment of the black other, the body snatcher is figurative of the naturalized, well-established, and unseen side of social domination. Together, the shape-shifter and the body snatcher mutually figure the condition of black hypervisibility, and a related condition of simultaneously seeing remnants of the discarded past within the shifting dynamism of the historical present. Black male hypervisibility is a means for watching the shifting. Black embodiment and historical temporality come together at the shifting site of age, which is where we should train our eyes.

I locate the analytical potential of the shape-shifter in the black feminist imagination of the long 1970s, which is the context for how this chapter formulates untimely black age. Although I do not engage it here, Octavia Butler's speculative novel of enslavement, *Wild Seed* (1980), functions as the black feminist urtext that originally imagines the shape-shifter and the body snatcher as oppositional figures, locked in an immortal contest over the radically liberating potential of non-canonical humanism on one side, and unending conquest and enslavement on the other.[10] In Butler's novel, shifting is associated with a black feminist politic. This association complements a black feminist schema of development, from black girlhood to black gendered adulthood, which is encapsulated in a term I borrow from C. Riley Snorton, a "site of transition."[11]

Rather than taking black gendered adulthood as a coherent and stable point of temporal arrival, black feminists such as the members of the Combahee River Collective, Michele Wallace, and Toni Morrison identified black girlhood as a subject position from which to challenge the limits of knowledge and social action that spring from liberal humanism. Posited as the opposition to liberal humanism's privileged subject, who is white, male, self-possessive, and adult, black feminism of this era often turned to black girlhood in order to explore what an alternative humanism entails. As a result, black girlhood was formulated not simply as a discreet life stage that one moved through during sequential, linear development. Rather, as my engagement with Grace Hong's reading of Morrison's 1970 coming-of-age novel, *The Bluest Eye*, reveals, black girlhood marked a site from which one might transition into an alternatively human subject, having rejected the properly humanist conditions attributed to white male adulthood. As such, black girlhood was imagined as the site of a socially capacious political project, which could include black male subjects. I argue that black boyhood takes on a subjective role in the 2010s that complements the subjective role of black girlhood in black feminist projects that span from black feminism of the 1970s to the intellectual project referred to as "black girlhood studies" in the present day. While black feminists of the post–civil rights era imagined the terms of shifting into "something else to be," as Morrison puts it in her second coming-of-age novel, *Sula* (1973), black male age had been frequently fixed in liberal humanist terms of social and political action, such as individual possessiveness, resistance, and agency. Yet, in the second decade of the twenty-first century, black male gender became somewhat disentangled from the age-based, patriarchal meaning of "man."[12] Thus, black boyhood, devoid of adulthood's normativity, shares the subjective position of black feminist girlhood, a vestibule not for normative culture, but for something else to be.

With this social end in mind, we turn to a counterintuitive observation: black male age has been historically constituted as malleable. Shape-shifting, which is often age-shifting, is frequently brought about through historical modes of abuse that accompanied making modern blackness fungible. The ongoing challenge of "seeing" the black person who is conventionally gendered male lies not in the fixity of appearance but, rather, in the spectacular capability of shifting from one "thing" to another that black males across life stages are expected to have. Desire to *see* the black male body shift stems from the logic of commodity fetishism: The shift is part of the magical enchantment of the commodity that has been severed from its historical and social context. Severed from normatively linear, developmental time, the black male body age-shifts in accordance with the consuming public's needs and wants at any given time.

Once we can imagine black male age beyond the demands of liberal "manhood" and as situated within the subjectively capacious, black feminist formations of age, I turn to the nineteenth-century, antislavery novel best known for its reproduction of the black image, Harriet Beecher Stowe's *Uncle Tom's Cabin* (1852). I focus on the opening scene and watch how black male *age* and interracial feminine *gender* are constructed in terms of concomitant forms of value. Little Harry, an enslaved octoroon boy, has a fungible relation to his mother Eliza, a fetishized, white-appearing, highly valued enslaved woman. In Stowe's novel, not only does the four- or five-year-old Harry give his master and slave trader a rousing song and dance informed by blackface minstrelsy; he so skillfully imitates two elderly enslaved men that he appears to become each of them for a fleeting moment. I focus on the function of this second, age-shifting performance. Harry's capacity to shift into an adult, yet emasculated, version of black manhood explicitly, if temporarily, removes him from the social domain of normative childhood, and symbolically links his market value to that of his nearly white and highly feminized mother, Eliza. In short, age-shifting is the conduit to an ungendered "fancy" market for which both Harry and Eliza are soon after targeted. Harry's mimetic elderliness taps into white desire for black embodiment that shifts in terms of both racialized age and gender. Just as Harry seemingly transforms from childishness to elderliness and back again, Eliza, like those of the fancy girl category, vacillates between racial object and white feminine subject. Thus, in the brief scene that opens the most famous of abolitionist novels, age and gender are mutually constitutive aspects of black embodiment that shifts as a matter of market value and white desire. Harry's performance alludes to the fact that something is always at work behind the commodity's magical, spectacular appearance.

This chapter concludes by turning to Jordan Peele's horror film, *Get Out* (2017), which imagines black age in relation to the body snatcher.

Get Out depicts a white American fantasy in which the advancements of science and technology lead to the latest approach to social integration: the surgical merging of the white mind with the black body. In the nineteenth century, Harry's age-shifting performance prevents us from seeing him as a male child, and a different sort of shifting produces the same result for Chris Washington, the protagonist in Peele's film. Via hypnosis, Chris is transported to the moment in his childhood when he loses his mother. Forced to remember, he is suspended in the transitional space between his 11-year-old self and his current manhood: There is no developmental movement. Instead, the fearful, helpless child is conflated with the obligated, guilt-ridden adult. Chris's body is completely "snatched" at the moment of this age-conflation. Watching Chris shift from liberated manhood to boy-adult subjection, I see the threads of dispossession that bind him to his absent mother become visible. Harry is bound to Eliza by their mutual exclusion from the human. Likewise, Chris—the ostensibly free-willed, masculine adult—shares the condition of deprivation with a woman—an unfree feminine subject—who disappears. Age reveals how the precarity of his freedom is bound to her social disappearance.

Which brings us back to the unseen burden and responsibility of Devonte, the boy in the photo. Ultimately, both the shape-shifter and the body snatcher are figurative of a historiographic condition, which is the alternatingly possible and impossible task of retrieving something that has been lost in the making of the current culture. While the "hug" photo went viral, there was the evidence of things not seen: Devonte's two white adoptive parents, Jennifer and Sarah Hart, routinely abused their black, adopted children. As we now know, Devonte and his five siblings were in the family SUV when Jennifer Hart drove the vehicle off a cliff along the Northern California coast, into the Pacific Ocean. In a confounding act of bodily theft, three of Devonte's siblings were confirmed to be dead. As of this writing, Devonte's body has not been found. Presumably, it is now a part of the ocean.

But for a fleeting moment in the twenty-first century, Devonte was a spectacle of black pain, vulnerability, and forgiveness, even as we did not know for certain why the boy was crying. Looking at Devonte, the question that follows James Baldwin's account of his Harlem boyhood ascends: "Whose little boy are you?" This question resonates in this chapter as one that asks how the black male child, and more broadly, how the black ungendered subject who lives in the afterlife of slavery as a malleable spectacle, might be reconnected to a history that accounts for black humanity. From the wayward paternalism of pimps in the slum who hasten the final days of childhood, as Baldwin recalls; to the foster care system from which Devonte was adopted; to various phases of the slave trade; to the ongoing expropriation and disposal of black lives, the question pertains to the abuses of disconnection, and the recovery of claiming and having claim.[13] For a brief moment in time, a black boy was right here, right in front of us. How did we lose him?

Shifting: Black Gender and Sites of Transition

There is something about the photo of Devonte and Barnum, locked in an embrace of commingled affection and domination, that makes the time seem strikingly out of joint.[14] It captures a specific historical moment of our recent past, and yet it makes the experience of being in historical time, the temporality of the second decade of the twenty-first century, noticeably incoherent. The moment, like the photo of the crying boy that captures it, seems entangled with a presence that is neither clearly benevolent and progressive, nor openly violent and regressive, and yet both. It resembles James Baldwin's disoriented sense of time in 1968, when Medgar and Malcolm and Martin are dead, when white hippies and black revolutionaries share the newness of the moment and the streets of San Francisco, but missed each other in their sight lines nonetheless. Like Walter Benjamin's angel, who faces the past as the winds of progress push it toward a future it cannot see, Baldwin describes the problem of historical temporality as a hindrance of sight: "One may say that there are no clear images; everything seems superimposed on, and at war with something else. There are no clear vistas: the road that seems to pull one forward into the future is also pulling one backward into the past."[15] It is this superimposition of contending forces, the pull of a not-yet-attained future and an unfinished past, that comprise the photo's actual content.

If the mainstream media interpreted the photo as hopeful, it was likely because it represented an imaginary resolution to the traumatic, deadly encounter between Michael Brown and Darren Wilson: Now the black teenager is remorseful rather than wretched, now the officer is gentle rather than violent. Yet, to imagine that Devonte's youth is the occasion for staying with the trauma, rather than overriding it with a false narrative that trades in the emotional vulnerability of a child, is to remain watchful of the historicity of black age. Age mediates between what the photo ostensibly communicates, which is racial resolution, and the lingering historical problem of fully reconciling blackness to the exclusionary terms of liberal humanism, such as consent and the freedom to choose. Watching Devonte's tears fall, one wonders whether he could have chosen not to choose this hug with a potentially dangerous stranger. The limits of choice and consent have been historically applicable to black subjects of any age.[16] We return to the question of consent in the following chapter. As a mediating presence, black age opens the closure of the hug, like a wound.

For black boyhood, there are no clear images, and this point helped define the meaning of black disposability in the second decade of the twenty-first century. If one way of (not) seeing the black boy is through the liberal humanist terms of consent, then another, related way is through western humanism's violent visuality, which Frantz Fanon influentially critiqued.[17] The shooting deaths of black boys such as 17-year-old Trayvon Martin and 12-year-old Tamir Rice reveal that black children generally, and boys specifically, are seen through a distorting social lens. Black boys are more likely to be perceived as older than they are and, as a result, are more likely to be held to adult standards of responsibility and deprived of protections that are customarily and legally reserved for children.[18] Like an emblem of Fanon's formulation of sociogeny, in which white fears and fantasies trap black subjects in dehumanizing and alienating personas, Trayvon's hoodie trapped the teenager in his shooter's distorted vision. "Look, a Negro!" The appellation could refer to a black person of any age and gender. The white child who calls this out in Fanon's famous anecdote never appears as an embodied subject and is as evanescent as the whiteness of a white world. Captured in the white gaze as a "Negro," Fanon is aware of his over-embodiment, his body as a racial object that can only occupy space without the potential of being absorbed by the civilized, human world.[19] While looking at the photo, one might see Devonte as a figure of racial fixity: He is fixed in place by an embrace that he, a black child among white adults, had no choice but to choose. And the condition of his being captured by a stranger's camera is the same brazenly dehumanizing distortion of vision that had been superimposed onto Michael Brown's body.[20]

As Fanon and other theorists of the black diaspora have elucidated, blackness names a category of social existence that has been formed through exclusion from a dominant mode of western humanism. It names an alternative "genre of the human," to use Sylvia Wynter's term, which falls outside of the hegemonic boundaries of age, and at the same time defies conformity to a socially normative gender binary, on which western humanism relies.[21] Historically formed as non-binary, black gender shifts. I think of shifting as an analytical figure as related to what C. Riley Snorton terms "transfiguration." In his essay, "Transfiguring Masculinities in Black Women's Studies," Snorton critiques "black male feminism," an intellectual project that ostensibly deconstructs black masculine subjectivity through its engagement with the analytical insights of black feminist thought. Despite a political and intellectual commitment to black feminism, the "male" in "black male feminism" implicitly maintains the foundational, social, and anatomical coherence of gender and sex. Conversely, blackness, gender, and sex are all co-constitutive of what Hortense Spillers calls the flesh, the product of modern slavery and, in effect, an alternative humanism, as Snorton notably argues elsewhere.[22] Transfiguration is the conversion of a supposedly coherent maleness into a radically capacious position in which a multitude of feminist subjective possibilities arise. Snorton proposes an analytical "site of transition" in which to "exert theoretical pressures on the category of maleness, itself—to allow it to destroy itself—and in so doing to allow black feminisms [sic] radical inclusivities to reemerge."[23]

Since the "male" of "black male feminism" overwhelmingly implies the normative, patriarchal, adult power of "men," I suggest a site of transition in which to put pressure on the presumptive *adultness* that is a constitutive part of categorical maleness. It is significant that Snorton's critique draws our attention to the 1990s. In an era when the black male body had become hypervisible in a global marketplace for US culture; when 1970s-era black nationalism resurged, most saliently in the hierarchical gender politics that underpinned the 1995 Million Man March; and when the wealth and iconicity of black athletes and entertainers sharply contrasted with the invisibility and dispossession of black men in prisons and "the inner city," black male feminism was but one strain of a broader scholarly effort to theorize black manhood.[24] If "male" was a wedge that stubbornly broke into the fluidity of "black feminism," then this indicates that by the 1990s, "black manhood" had become an analytical site of contradiction. Patriarchal pasts competed with anti-misogynist and anti-homophobic—in a word, feminist—futures that could only be partly imagined. Such epistemic contradiction (an under-examined commitment to "manhood" on one hand, freedom from black gender essentialism on the other) led to the theoretical inertia that Snorton describes. Yet, some work in "black manhood studies" recognized such inertia or fixity as a constitutive aspect of properly liberal black male adult subjectivity, and as a topic of analysis. Such work grasps the impetus of Snorton's call for transfiguration, even if it does not ostensibly trade in a trans critique.

In one of the most notable efforts in this regard, the co-edited 1996 volume, *Representing Men*, Marcellus Blount and George Cunningham begin with an overview of the problem: "Beginning in the 1960s, and certainly codified by the mid-1970s, gender became a specific and explicit site for discussions of the 'state of the race.' Under various generic topics—'black male-female relations,' the 'crisis of the black family,' and the 'conspiracy to destroy black men'—*the stabilizing of the gendered male self* and the reconstruction of the true black man are among the defining obsessions of contemporary racial discourse."[25] If the black male self was discursively, representationally, and ideologically "stabilized" from the black nationalism of the 1960s and 1970s to the neo-conservatism of the 1980s and 1990s, then this is due to the presumption that male *adulthood* necessarily mediated between blackness and national belonging. All of the generic topics listed above suggest that the achievement of proper liberal personhood, which entails adulthood, was the only horizon toward which black people of all genders could move. Liberalism, a sociopolitical philosophy foundational to US nationhood, encompasses a concept of equal personhood: All persons are equally endowed with individual freedom, rights, and protections. Yet, historically, full personhood has been the sole province of the white, male, adult, possessive individual. Because of presumptively social, cultural, and anatomical proximity to the normatively patriarchal subject, black manhood is the most aspirational figure of such movement toward full personhood. And yet, the paradox to which Blount and Cunningham allude is that compulsory liberal personhood requires fixing masculine gender within the alienating shell of patriarchal manhood. Blount and Cunningham's edited volume is a key example of a project that turned to the analytical insights of black feminist and queer studies in order to free black male gender from the nationalist and patriarchal constraints of manhood, so that it might "cross boundaries" into and share common epistemological ground with other modes of black gender. I suggest that a critical move toward this realization relies not only on returning to black feminism's counter-nationalism, but more specifically, to a critique of hegemonic age and life stages to expound on the capaciousness of black gender.

If black (male) feminism failed to transition and reimagine the revolutionary capaciousness of black gender, then this failure lies in its disregard of black feminism's recognition of the non-categorical potential of age. Snorton usefully notes that "the authors [of the Combahee River Collective Statement] make clear their commitment to a black feminist politic that does not leave out Black men, women, and children."[26] It is a politic that holds black genders and ages together. And in this chapter, the shape-shifter manifests a site of transition that analytically squeezes presumptive adulthood out of black "men," so that we might retrieve and reimagine an alternative humanism on the basis of black untimeliness, on the zero degree of blackness ungendered and dispossessed of human time. Recall this moment in the Statement, which I have briefly discussed in the introduction: "As children we were told in the same breath to be quiet both for the sake of being 'ladylike' and to make us less objectionable in the eyes of white people."[27] Black girls were told that the achievement of racial respectability requires silence, as if silence is the only available route to an otherwise closed off resemblance to being a "lady," and thus to simultaneously achieved female gender and female adultness. But the very emergence of an overt black feminist politic—a political space in which, as Snorton puts it, "gendered bodies [. . .] *talk very precisely* about how they enter black feminist theory and practice"—reveals that "to be quiet" is to conceal the untimely and capacious potentials of black embodiment.[28]

Among the clearest examples of how black age was at the nexus of slavery's historiography and black feminist consciousness during the

1970s can be found in Michele Wallace's 1978 work of cultural criticism, *Black Macho and the Myth of the Superwoman*. As Wallace's discussion goes, the black man's mythical overrepresentation at the center of black racial politics arises from a widely held presumption that enslavement had been exceptionally injurious to black men. The black man was not "permitted to fulfill his traditional role as a man."[29] Touted as having explanatory power for black male disempowerment in the present, black masculinity that has been robbed of *adulthood* stems from Stanley Elkins's influential 1959 work, *Slavery: A Problem in American Institutional and Intellectual Life*, which asserts that enslaved black men were trapped in an artificial plantation boyhood until their elderly years, when the role of "boy" suddenly switched to that of "uncle." I return to Elkin's work in chapter 3.

Wallace points out that the cultural politics of black nationalism enabled contemporary black men to invent a chauvinist myth about black male adulthood precisely by treating the gap between childish boyhood and avuncular elderliness as an unimpeachable historical fact. Yet, such a gap, as it appears in the era's historiography about slavery, should be taken as a historical problem, rather than a sign of facticity. Why should a patriarchal, gender-normative "man" inevitably emerge in the afterlife of conditions that supposedly produce such a gap between "boys" and "uncles"? How did the enslaved perceive their own lived experiences at the nexus of gender and age? If black age has historically been a site of invention, and if the social meaning of black gender arises from inventive measures that comprise the meaning of black age, then Wallace suggests we turn to the historical record with an openness to inventive possibility. Pairing the abuses of enslavement with the reclamation of the enslaved, Wallace submits that the untimeliness of ungendered black flesh goes by various names: "Yes, black men were called boys. Black women were also called girls. But the slaves thought of themselves as 'mens and womens.'"[30] In a black feminist critique of a stringent gender binary that is comprised of "black macho" on one end and "the superwoman" on the other, the double plural of "mens and womens" belongs to an invented social grammar. Each category is ample enough to let the other become an embodied part of it.

Just as the authors of the Statement drew from their socialization as black girls to invent a more capacious social category of black adult gender into which black children could grow, Toni Morrison's girlhood observations similarly became the engine of invention. In relation to the apparent absence of any book like her first novel, *The Bluest Eye* (1970), during her own girlhood, Morrison explained that the organization of books in her hometown library physically displayed what are generally implicit developmental and subjective absences: "In those days, children's books, the fairytales, were on the bottom shelf where you could read them. And the next shelf was Faulkner, or Tolstoy. There was no YA, Young Adult; there was no transition, *physically*. They just put all the fairytales down there, and then they got serious."[31] There was a physical, visible absence where a site of transition, a material shift from one developmental stage to the next, should have been. This particular schema in which kid's stuff is permanently relegated "down there" while the canon of western civilization is so lofty that children—black girls like Morrison and black people of any age—cannot reach it fixes racial hierarchy in place, even as it seems to represent a natural, developmental division between "adults" and "children." The literary silence about black girlhood, which Morrison's first novel fills, pertains to the implicitly unthought-of connection between transition and development: How does a black girl transition, *physically*, into an "adult"? Grace Hong's materialist reading of Morrison's first novel indirectly responds to this question by waging a critique of the possessive individual, a normative subject who is "white, male, and property owning" and, implicitly, adult.[32]

Hong focuses on property as the basis for the social constitution of both a normative self-possessive subject and its other, the excessive, disposable, dispossessed black subject. As Hong reveals, the coming-of-age story in Morrison's *The Bluest Eye* plots the development of three early-adolescent black girls (an unnamed narrator, her sister Claudia, and their friend Pecola) through their encounters with the exclusionary terms of property relations. As Hong uncovers how the myriad forms of dispossession with which the girls are routinely confronted (such as the dispossession of proper domesticity, its privacy, protections, and route to social and historical belonging) form black alterity in the novel, we also see how adulthood is a site of both property and dispossession. Pecola Breedlove is the most dispossessed and distanced from the terms of normative social belonging, and as a result of this distance, she becomes the least able to successfully reach the next shelf, or, in terms of the novel's metaphors, to develop from a planted seed into a blooming flower. This stunted development is a condition she shares with her impoverished parents. Hong notes, "As subjects for whom 'choice' or the exercise of will is [. . .] rendered impossible, the Breedloves are forever immature. Cholly and Mrs. Breedlove's parental authority over their children is taken away by the state, for example, while Mrs. Breedlove is infantilized by her employers, who call her 'Polly.'"[33] Excluded from possessive individualism, there is no transition into normative adulthood, a metonym for homogeneous, property-owning citizenship, physically.

Yet, Morrison's first novel of development also alludes to a counterhumanist site of transition. Black girlhood is the subject position from which to explore the space of exclusion from proper subjectivity for its liberating possibilities. Black girlhood is a space of radical refusal, as when Claudia refuses motherhood as the only horizon of proper adult subjectivity toward which the well-meaning adults in black girls' lives encourage them to move. As Claudia believes, "Motherhood is old age."[34] She destroys the white, blue-eyed baby dolls she is given as precious gifts. Claudia is interested neither in hastening the end of her own childhood through aspirations of a future motherhood nor in the totems of white female preciousness that affirm her own lack of value. Instead, she has an alternatively imagined community in mind: "I was interested only in humans my own age and size."[35] It seems that by this Claudia simply means "children," but it is significant that she refuses to identify such humans in the terms of a normative social category. Being neither in her "old age" nor a baby, her disorienting encounter with inanimate dolls confirms that dispossession of proper subjectivity entails falling outside of proper age categories, as the Breedloves do. In terms that are not gender-specific, which implies that properly social gender arises from the property relations of domesticity, Claudia's reference to an ironic version of humanity—expressed in the objectifying term, "size"—resembles the categorization of human cargo during the transatlantic slave trade and the subsequent interstate trade.[36] Such an ironic assertion that an alternative humanism is formed in the exclusion from normative liberal humanism suggests that the possibilities for development, and transitioning from the present into the future, is split. On the one hand, black children can aspire to become fully human one day, to reach the top shelf in Morrison's library, by reproducing the standards of proper subjectivity. In other words, one can imagine one's own futurity through the properly domestic status of motherhood. On the other hand, there are humans of no specific gender who interest Claudia, whose futures have yet to be invented. They perhaps share a kinship of condition with two similarly aged girls of Morrison's second coming-of-age novel, *Sula*: "Because each had discovered years before that they were neither white nor male, and that all freedom and triumph was forbidden to them, they had set about creating something else to be."[37] In other words, black girlhood signifies a radically inclusive space in which dispossession is the condition of possibility for transitioning into an alternative subjectivity, and indeed an alternative humanism. Yet, the plot of *The Bluest Eye* gets underway only after Claudia acknowledges that the story we are about to witness follows the former trajectory. She communicates this through her own transition from a subject who refuses so deeply that she is capable of transferring her wish to destroy baby dolls to actual white girls: "my shame floundered about for refuge. The best hiding place was love. Thus, the conversion from pristine sadism to fabricated hatred, to fraudulent love."[38] In this way, Morrison's first novel alludes to an alternative space of transition in order to make all the more poignant how futile and fraudulent attempts to reach the next shelf within the boundaries of exclusion can be.

As Claudia's expressed interest in "humans" of a certain age and size suggests, the absence of physical transition that Morrison overtly discusses as a cultural problem is also a historical one. Morrison's spatial model for transitioning finds elaboration in recent work that turns to shape-shifting as a figure for black embodied movement through space and time. In the dominant white gaze, shifting signifies abuse, as when the black boy seems to instantly transform from child to adult. But contemporary black feminist scholars offer performative reclamations of the shape-shifter's flexible, moveable embodiment. Aimee Cox's ethnographic study conceptualizes "shapeshifting" as the "social choreography and performance arts practices" that allows black girls and young women to maneuver through sometimes hostile, sometimes apathetic, spaces of non-recognition.[39] For Cox, shape-shifting as choreography and performance reveals how young black women and girls enact refusals of static, dehumanized identities that the social world, which deems them unfit for citizenship, attributes to their bodies. Similarly generative, Uri McMillan's concept of the "avatar" is a useful induction to performative shape-shifting and acts of crossing over.[40] McMillan produces a social history of black women's performance art that spans from the nineteenth through to the twenty-first centuries. The performance artists of his study explore the objectification of black female embodiment as "objecthood" through their invented avatars. With malleable objecthood as their chosen medium, McMillan describes how "avatars' shape-shifting qualities [...] index the slipperiness of time itself. [...] time (like avatars themselves) recurs, reverberates, and exceeds artificial distinctions between the past and the present."[41]

In a sense, both Cox and McMillan turn to liberal humanism and its categories—citizenship and self-possessive subjectivity—in order to reveal how its epistemic boundaries might be crossed on the way toward an alternative humanism and something akin to freedom. Drawing from black feminism's counter-nationalist legacy, both scholars turn to performance as a method for both self-possession—"staying in the body," as Cox explains—and self-invention, which both operate outside of the desire to achieve (male) adulthood. Indeed, black age is figurative of a site of shape-shifting in both studies: Cox explicitly focuses on the lives of black girls and young women, while age and objecthood are linked in McMillan's discussion of Joice Heth, a figure to whom I return in the following chapter. Figured outside of proper liberal subjectivity, I suggest that the shape-shifter is analytically applicable to the maneuvers of black male age.

So far in this discussion, I have been focusing on how black feminism's analyses of gender are keyed to the ideological dimensions of age. But the link between age as a social category of study and feminist, humanistic scholarship is not particular to black feminism. On the contrary, scholarly interest in ideologies about children and childhood in particular is rooted in feminist inquiries about nineteenth-century sentimentalism, domesticity, and motherhood, as Karen Sánchez-Eppler notes.[42] In order to work toward an account of nineteenth-century cultural politics that no longer relies on a conventional gender binary, or predictable social categories in general, Sánchez-Eppler proposes we make an analytical turn to age:

> Age offers an interesting corrective as a way of approaching cultural analysis, because unlike gender, or race, or even class, *age is inherently transitional*. We may know that none of these other categories are absolute, but they still retain some experiential boundedness. Childhood, in contrast, is a status defined by its mutability—a stage inevitably passed through.[43]

To think of age as "inherently transitional" is indeed to gain a useful analytical tool for the study of social life. In addition, this insight raises questions about when, under which circumstances, *any* of the aforementioned categories could be said to be experientially bounded, including age. If, as Spillers has argued, modern blackness had been formed through the *ungendering* of the black body in transatlantic slavery, and that flesh simply seen as blackness and thus simultaneously *unseen* as the sign of such violence, then black *gender* is also inherently transitional, passing in and out of a normative social register. The duration of black gender's mutability need not be simultaneous with or superimposable onto any single life stage such as childhood. Rather, the intersections between various social sites of transition raise a useful analytical question about how the embodied experience of time is figural as age. Further, recognizing how social categories act as a route to an experience of time that could be anything—transitional, permanent, shifting, recurring, something to be possessed or reclaimed—requires an intersectional framework that accounts for how such categories have been mutually constituted.

In the following section, I work toward such an account. If black boyhood is no longer fixed within liberal humanism's developmental teleology, which posits a proper subject—white, propertied, male, adult—as the top shelf of all human existence, then there is room for different modes of maneuver. In the following, an enslaved boy maneuvers through an age-shifting performance that is, in effect, a means to express the untimeliness of being a commodity. Such untimeliness dissolves the generational hierarchy between "parent" and "child" and the gender distinction between "mother" and "son." Thus, the performance enacts numerous transitions across age and gender, which are all conditioned by the white, desirous gaze.

Black (Boy) Magic: *Uncle Tom's Cabin*

Harriet Beecher Stowe's 1852 novel, *Uncle Tom's Cabin*, has become synonymous with a catalogue of racial types it gave names to: Tom, the meek and pious slave; Eva, the sanctified, white, middle-class child.[44] Chloe is the archetypal "mammy," and Topsy is the comical, insensible epitome of the "pickaninny" that endured into the twentieth century. Tom, Eva, Chloe, and Topsy all have garnered critical attention for how they congeal racial discourses about blackness into intractable stereotypes. I turn to *Uncle Tom's Cabin* because of its highly influential role in reproducing images of blackness that endure into the present, and to underscore that such images frequently entail an account of age. Indeed, the wide circulation and familiarity of the racial stereotypes that Stowe's novel helped to popularize suggest that racial characterization tout court relies on the logic of uneven, racial age.

For instance, while explaining the cultural work that Tom's seeming lack of sexuality does for maintaining the social order, Spillers reveals how Tom's untimely age exists in (at least) two registers. Ostensibly, Tom has the artificial infantilism that has been conventionally attributed to blackness overall. It is this falsely natural condition of being childlike that makes his intimacy with Eva palpable. Yet, if one were to wonder for too long about why this adult male slave has been scripted as little Eva's companion, then a secret to Tom's age emerges: He is "a potentially 'dirty old man,' 'under wraps.'"[45] In a sense, Spillers lays out the abusive photo negative of black reclamation implied in "black don't crack": On the surface lies untimely immaturity, but "under cover" exists an actual maturity that remains unseen. Such insights into the abuses of black age are endemic to the criticism on black representation in Stowe's novel overall. The comedic Sam and Andy who help Eliza escape are "little more than bumptious, giggling, outsized adolescents," according to Richard Yarborough, and actual black children—to the degree that the novel makes a distinction between juvenile and adult black characters—are "frequent sources of humor for Stowe."[46]

And, perhaps most obviously, Tom himself has age-shifted over time. He incrementally became older within the static temporal frame of the narrative in which he was situated, shifting interpretations of the source material in stage and film adaptations notwithstanding. Tom goes from being an enslaved man of prime age—with "prime" indicating exchange value rather than a specific number of years lived—to the sentimental, elderly uncle figure of the *Tom* stage shows that ran throughout the rest of the nineteenth century, and into the *Tom* films of the early twentieth century.[47] Like the "crack" between what lies on the surface and what is concealed, this manner in which Tom ages is also exemplary of black untimeliness. It is a cultural, social, and historical process that parodies a natural biological process since the character progressively ages over linear and progressive time. In fact, Tom's age reflects the transformation of his function as a commodity: Age evolves from being an explicit category of labor capacity in the slave trade, into an index of an array of shifting motivations for the commercial consumption of blackness in the north, before and after emancipation. By the end of the nineteenth century, Tom's agedness was figurative of sentimental loss and the long-ago.

Yet, *Uncle Tom's Cabin* reveals that racial untimeliness is unevenly attributed across what Yarborough calls "full-blood and mixed-blood blacks."[48] This is to say that "fully" black characters like Sam and Andy are endowed with a racial essence that sharply distinguishes them from white characters in the novel, and generally this is not the case for the interracial characters who enjoy the humanizing attributes of whiteness.[49] The observation dovetails into the critical importance granted to how the racialization of childhood is represented in the novel. Topsy and Eva comprise the racial chiaroscuro of nineteenth-century childhood: They are counterpoints that illustrate how the cultural politics of childhood "innocence" fractured along divergent racial reasoning during the Victorian era, as Robin Bernstein argues.[50] More broadly, Stowe's depictions of the child, as Caroline Levander suggests, are illustrative of how the child has generally been deployed to produce racial logic that lies at the foundation of the nation. Thus, the child upholds an unbridgeable gulf between the racially superior Saxon and the enslaved African, even as the novel rhetorically conveys proximity between the two.[51]

But the child is also a conduit for intra-black affiliation. Although Topsy is the apparent exemplar of the "performing black child" that continues to live well past the nineteenth century, as Tavia Nyong'o suggests, the mixed-blooded Harry is the first child to perform in *Uncle*

*Tom's Cabin.*⁵² Coincidentally, Topsy repeats Harry's musical performance later in the novel.⁵³ We tend not to think of Harry as a performing "black" child because he is the nearly white, very young, generally inconspicuous son of the novel's white-appearing and heroic enslaved couple, Eliza and George Harris. By dint of his racial amalgamation, Harry is neither wholly inviolable like Eva, nor wholly disingenuous like Topsy, but is rather a transitional figure. I say "transitional" as opposed to "transgressive," which may seem readily apparent, especially given a later episode when both Harry and Eliza cross-dress in order to enact another crossing, this time to cross Lake Erie into Canada. To be enslaved, and to be black in the afterlife of slavery, is to be constantly confronted with the Law that constitutes black embodiment as the transgression of human boundaries, which include the social boundaries of gender and age. As the term hypervisibility connotes, such transgression is spectacular, even in the ironic case of racial passing, which carries the possibility of seeing blackness in the absence of it. Yet, rather than think of Harry against and through a boundary of human inclusion, I focus on his status within ideologies that heighten the visibility of a few social types in the cultural commentary about Stowe's novel—the pickaninny, the beautiful mulatta, the innocent white child—in order to discern how he shifts between these types, and what such shifting reveals about the lower frequencies, the invisibilities, of black social life.

As Sophia Bell argues, Harry shares the same representational function as other white-appearing, enslaved boys in Stowe's novel: Their racial amalgamation muddles the line between residual acceptance of corporal punishment and the era's kinder, gentler, sentimental approaches to disciplining both children and slaves.⁵⁴ Thus, Harry's racially mixed status is a site of fluctuating, transitional ideologies about nineteenth-century childhood and discipline. Neither the violent whippings that Topsy inexplicably believes are good for her nor sentimental influence alone are adequate measures for managing Harry. And neither measure secures his safety. Harry is in danger the moment he appears in Stowe's novel. Indeed, long before Augustine St. Clare and his cousin Ophelia have a debate over the management of the wayward and unfeeling Topsy, little Harry has already been sold into the domestic slave trade.⁵⁵ Thus, unlike Topsy, the quintessential heathen who is miraculously brought to submission, Harry is a model of sentimental childhood who is threatened with intensified enslavement from the beginning. Of course, this threat is the needed impetus for Eliza's memorable act of maternal heroism. Determined to prevent her son's sale, she whisks him away, leaps across the frozen Ohio River and into a way station of the Underground Railroad. But, while the emotional value that Eliza (and Stowe's readers) confer onto little Harry makes him legible as a normative child by the emerging cultural standards of the time, when the proper role of children was to satisfy adults emotionally, Harry's opening performance is distinctly non-childlike in the normative sense.[56] As a transitional figure, Harry shifts between the idealized object of familial love, a pet-like slave, an authentic "negro" of any age, and older black men who actually exist. In other words, he is a wish-fulfilling marvel. Harry's power to express fluctuating social desires of white men and women alike during the antebellum era is indebted to how the enslaved child integrates the enchantment of the racial commodity with the aesthetics of minstrelsy and sentimentality. Minstrelsy and sentimentality make up the aesthetic structure for seeing the commodity as a source of pleasure.

Thus, pleasure is key to how black age is represented at the start of the novel. The white patriarchal gaze, which opens *Uncle Tom's Cabin* and frames Harry's performance, imposes a dimension of desire onto Harry that is just as determinative as Eliza's maternal love, which is the reason for Harry's existence in the novel. In the desirous, white patriarchal gaze, Harry is a commodity that shifts between normative categorical boundaries of age and gender. As a result of this shifting, he holds a lateral status with Eliza, the sexually desirable, female adult, rather than a cross-generational relation to her as a socially legitimate mother. Thus, the novel unwittingly begins with the "horizontal" mode of relations that the enslaved formed in the exclusion from the "vertical" schema of the patriarchal family, in which one generation confers property to the next.[57] *Uncle Tom's Cabin* does extend something akin to familial legitimacy to the Harrises—Eliza is married, and she and her son take George's name. Additionally, Stowe bequeaths to her black characters what Lori Merish calls "sentimental property relations," which entitles them to family-like intimacy with the people and things in the master's home, while downplaying the fact that they remain excluded from actual property relations.[58] Yet, in the opening scene, Harry stands before two patriarchal figures who emphasize that the property relations that are intrinsic to "family" are denied to both Harry and Eliza. Thus, unlike the redemptive mode of kinship that the enslaved created irrespective of biological relations, horizontal kinship here is comprised of the shared condition of being commodities. Harry's age-shifting imitations of older, decidedly emasculated black men is the condition of possibility for his Oceanic non-differentiation from Eliza, the novel's general investment in her patriarchal motherhood notwithstanding.

Stowe's novel begins with a problem. Genteel Kentuckian Mr. Shelby is in debt, and the sale of his slave, Tom, is not enough to cover it. Mr. Haley, the crudely rendered slave trader, suggests that Mr. Shelby "throw in" a "boy or gal" to make up the balance. A "boy or gal" functions here as filler, much in the way that small-bodied women or children were used to tightly pack slave ships of the Portuguese and British slave trades. As a result, a broad modern history of commoditizing racial age infuses the scene. This logical linkage between size, age, and value endures throughout the antebellum domestic trade; enslaved children of either gender under the age of ten were of generally equal and minimal value.[59] (Imagine the proto-black feminist, Claudia, signifying on this history nearly a century later in Morrison's first novel.) We are introduced to Harry directly after Haley links age to commodification, and as it happens, he is a mixed-racial beauty: "There was something in his appearance remarkably beautiful and engaging. His black hair, fine as floss silk, hung in glossy curls about his round, dimpled face, while a pair of large dark eyes, full of fire and softness, looked out from beneath the rich, long lashes, as he peered curiously into the apartment."[60] No sooner does Harry appear than he is told to perform. I cite the following scene at length in order to track the variations of his performance.

> "Hulloa, Jim Crow!" and Mr. Shelby, whistling, and snapping a bunch of raisins towards him, "pick that up, now!"
>
> The child scampered, with all his little strength, after the prize, while his master laughed.
>
> "Come here, Jim Crow," said he. The child came up, and the master patted the curly head, and chucked him under the chin.
>
> "Now, Jim, show this gentleman how you can dance and sing."
>
> The boy commenced one of those wild, grotesque songs common among the negroes, in a rich, clear voice, accompanying his singing with

many comic evolutions of the hands, feet, and whole body, all in perfect time to the music.

"Bravo!" said Haley, throwing him a quarter of an orange.

"Now, Jim, walk like old Uncle Cudjoe, when he has the rheumatism," said his master.

Instantly the flexible limbs of the child assumed the appearance of deformity and distortion, as, with his master's stick in his hand, he hobbled about the room, his childish face drawn into a doleful pucker, and spitting from right to left, in imitation of an old man.

Both men laughed uproariously.

"Now, Jim," said his master, "show us how old Elder Robbins leads the psalm." The boy drew his chubby face down to a formidable length, and commenced toning a psalm tune through his nose, with imperturbable gravity.[61]

Shape-shifting shares the logic of concealment with the commodity. Through mysterious, imperceptible means, one form of being shifts into another. From the beginning, *Uncle Tom's Cabin* draws a connection between the exchange value of enslaved people and enslaved people's ages, thus rendering black age as exchange value. As a result, Harry enters the scene, first and foremost, as a commodity. Before I address the minstrelsy on display, let us focus on the performance of age-shifting across the extremes of male age.

Taken within the context of Mr. Shelby's unsettled debt, his demand that Harry shift between very young childhood and elderly adulthood has the effect of making opposite ends of the life cycle appear as equivalent categories within the logic of exchange value. During the domestic slave trade that spanned the 1830s to the 1860s, the average sale values of enslaved children younger than ten years old and the average sale values of the elderly and superannuated were low in comparison to those of enslaved adults in their prime, since high mortality rates and serious illness on each end of the lifespan were devaluating factors.[62] With age as exchange value in mind, Shelby demands to *see* the magical ways in which his monetary problems might be solved. Meanwhile, Haley sees an objectified body enchanted with any given number of market-driven fantasies. Harry's "flexible limbs" are like the legs of Marx's enchanted table that not only stand on the ground; as part of the commodity, they appear capable of dancing just for you.⁶³ They are as illustrative of being a fetishized object as of being an active child. Just as Harry stands in for an ungendered boy-gal, his age-shifting transformations imply a nondevelopmental leap from childhood to old age, which is the storied outcome of plantation slavery with which the black men of Wallace's era took umbrage. Never possibly a "man," Harry is both "boy" and "uncle."

If Shelby wanted to see the instant transformation of age, he was not alone. Antebellum traders instantly transformed the ages of the enslaved while preparing them to be sold for the market. According to Walter Johnson, traders "shaved men's beards and combed their hair, plucked gray hairs or blackened them with dye," with the latter forms of grooming to make them appear younger than they were.⁶⁴ Practices for preparing human commodities on the way to and in the New Orleans slave market entailed artificial staging techniques that led to the coerced performance of black age, which undercuts the conceit that black age is naturally malleable enough to become nearly whatever the market requires. William Wells Brown's anti-slavery novel, *Clotel*, published a year after *Uncle Tom's Cabin*, illustrates this tension between the performance and authenticity of black age. Since "few persons can arrive at anything like the age of a negro, by mere observation," Dick Walker, a slave trader, advertises the sale of "a prime lot of able-bodied slaves" who are "between the ages of fifteen and twenty-five," even though some are actually much older.⁶⁵ The much older enslaved men not only have their gray whiskers shaved and their aged skin oiled. They are also coerced into telling prospective buyers that they are as young as the trader wants them to be. The performance of black male age is a key site of ideological divergence between Stowe's novel and Brown's. While Harry effortlessly makes a circular transformation from young to old and back again and demonstrates that age is whatever the slave market demands, Brown's novel displays the work—and violence—that goes into making old men into new commodities. These men know that this process, and their coerced participation in it, intensifies their self-alienation, and unlike the unspeaking Harry, they are able to say so.⁶⁶

When Harry first appears as a wish-fulfilling fantasy, he is absolutely alone, with nothing but "Jim Crow" standing in for his given name. He appears to be as alienated as the enslaved in the domestic trade and all phases of transatlantic slavery, having been far removed from their origins and personal histories.[67] A fetishized commodity, Harry exists in temporal suspension, between a past from which he has been removed and a historical moment that has not yet occurred.[68] Alienated from normative social and property relations, both Harry and Eliza share this temporal condition, expressed in this scene in the marketing term, "fancy." As Edward E. Baptist argues, two registers of the fetish, elaborated in Marxist and Freudian thought, are applicable to the white-appearing "fancy maid" of the antebellum slave trade. Women and girls sold in the fancy trade were often salable for high sums of money. Through a jointly constituted economic mode of abstraction that relies on forgetting the commodity's origins, and a sexual mode of partially remembering rape and coercion that is the productive source of "white" slaves, the white men who traded and bought slaves made a fetish of white-appearing enslaved women.[69] I suggest that Harry is similarly fetishized, and the structure of this fetishism emerges through the divergent roles that Shelby and Haley play in this scene. The two men share the same cultural desires and watch Harry through the same cultural lens. Yet, as we will see, Shelby, who is aligned with the novel's dominant abolitionist stance, represents historical disavowal, while Haley reveals a partial recollection.

As we have seen, Harry performs equivalent exchange value between the very old and the very young. The disappearance of "manhood"—the prime of masculine adulthood—is less a matter of anatomical or social *gender* than a matter of *value*, which is literally expressed as age. This logic reemerges in a manner that flips the gender/value relation, so that gender now seems to be the dominant category of consideration. Just as Harry has sufficiently impressed Haley, who emphatically offers to settle Shelby's debt if Harry is included in their transaction, Eliza, like Harry, unexpectedly walks into the room. The two are granted nearly the same introduction: "There need only a glance from the child to her, to identify her as its mother. There was the same rich, full, dark eye, with its long lashes; the same ripples of silky black hair."[70] But, unlike the child, Eliza is endowed with the signs of proper, adult femininity—the well-fitting dress, the slender hands and feet. She and Harry leave, and Haley emphatically offers to buy her because, unlike the boy-gal Harry, her value is *high*. Although Eliza is never referred to as a "fancy maid," nor is "fancy" explicitly mentioned in the assessment of her value, it is strongly implied in Haley's claims about the "fortune" Shelby can make in New Orleans by selling such an attractive slave. Shelby flatly refuses to sell her, and Haley returns to his original interest in buying Harry, thus making a strikingly awkward transition from the woman to the child: *Harry* is now the fancy item. Even Shelby is surprised by this sudden turn of reason, as if Haley is revealing too much: "What on earth can you want with the child," he asks, because the boy-gal has little value.[71] In response, not only does Haley mention a fancy market for the first time. He also makes a clumsy attempt to resolve the incoherence between Harry as a highly valued "fancy" slave, and Harry as the "common negro" entertainer we have just seen. A friend of Haley's "wants to buy up handsome boys to raise for the market. Fancy articles entirely [. . .]. They fetch a good sum; and this little devil is such a comical, musical concern, he's just the article."[72] As Johnson notes, "The traders' daily business was to shape the real people they had in their hands to reflect the abstract market they had in their heads"; Haley shapes the child he had in his sight.[73] Now deemed to be worth more than he was when he first appeared, Harry is distinguishable from old Uncle Cudjoe and Elder Robbins because he, unlike they, is endowed with potential value. Granted the proximate value to whiteness that "fancy" connotes, Harry is now able to move through linear, developmental time—to be "raised" for something—as opposed to the circular transformation he just performed.

Considering the fancy market, Harry's minstrelsy is an example of what Bernstein calls racial innocence: It is the scene's deflection away from the explicit sexual desire that suffuses the commoditization of both Harry and Eliza. Both are constituted as commodities though the same psycho-sexual structure, and gender is the means by which the scene makes an ideological swerve away from the possibility that both Harry and Eliza are compelling for the same reason. Swerving away, the scene introduces us to a boy rather than to a girl, who spectacularly calls our attention to other enslaved males. The swerve is the reason that Topsy, the only enslaved girl under the age of ten, is as black, and wicked, and singular as she is. But most pertinently, the masculine culture of black-face minstrelsy is a crucial part of the deflection.

Performative shifts between racialized age—white manhood and black infantilism—were a key component of blackface minstrelsy. Being a "negro" with natural musical ability, Harry need not be an actual child. The performance of black expressive and comic forms of culture was always already a performance of the inherent naivety of blackness. As Eric Lott maintains, the conceit that black comedy was inherently childish explains the pleasure of minstrelsy. When a white blackface performer succeeded in momentarily appearing to be a black person, white audiences enjoyed the chance to "indulge in lost moments of childish pleasure evoked by the antics of children, or 'inferior' people who resembled them."[74] If the basis of this pleasure was the presumptive infantilism of blackness itself, then the blackface performer's momentarily concealed adulthood established a transitional space between black infantilism and white maturity, a space in which white pleasure was produced.

But such a transitional space produced more than simply pleasure. As David Roediger explains, for white working-class men of the northeast who performed on the early minstrel stage and comprised its audience, "childhood" was the subtext of Jacksonian republicanism's infuriating contradictions, capitalism's denial of full adulthood to white, working-class men. Childhood was a site of desire and shame, and the metaphor for helplessly living in a time of cultural and social flux. Although both Lott and Roediger refer to the early development of blackface minstrelsy during the 1820s and 1830s, the emotional charge that the aesthetic form held for white men seems present in a scene about economic loss and intensified reliance on slavery. Shelby and Haley are watching an embodied manifestation of their partially unconscious desires for a temporal existence that can only be spoken of in terms of enslavement, such as an ideal, infantile sense of wholeness. It is the temporal existence of a never-ending, artificial childhood that must be disavowed and transposed onto blackness. Shelby and Haley watch Harry and see in the little boy the freest version of their own white male adulthoods. If Harry has a relation to normative "manhood," this is where it lies.

Harry is a spectacle, and Jacqueline Rose reminds us that, "Spectacle always signifies money." This axiom sufficiently links Harry's performance to the subject of Rose's commentary, the eternal boy of fin-de-siècle English theater, Peter Pan.[75] The many reproductions and figurative rebirths of Peter Pan into our own time have merged the conceit of an eternally innocent child with the ostensible innocence of the commodity that magically flies with no strings attached.[76] Similarly, the enslaved child who suddenly appears when a debt must be reckoned, apropos of nothing, and performs for the explicit benefit of a planter who owns him, the slave trader who buys him, and for white, middle-class readers of the northern states is a thing of magic.[77] Harry's age is the key to his status as a commodity because it acts as the nexus between three developments of the antebellum era that, when taken together, express how age was considered to be an effect of black inhumanity within the white cultural imagination: sentimentality, blackface minstrelsy, and the domestic slave trade. Each of these developments were productive sites of cultural logic that contributed to the counter-normativity of black age.

Yet, if we focus too closely on the spectacle, we miss a transition into something else: an alternative schema of kinship forged in the condition of being fungible. Whose little boy is Harry? Why, Eliza's. They exist in the same suspended temporality; he shares her condition and she, his. Although the novel attempts to conceal Eliza's non-possessive status by rendering her in terms of white femininity, and although the opening scene uses gender to differentiate the woman from the child, Harry's malleability—his transformations from superannuated male to fancy object—reveals Oceanic flesh that binds him to a black mother. He shifts because black age structures the ideological dimension of owning slaves: For Shelby, you can love the child who is not a child, maybe even *because* that boy-gal is not a child. For Haley, based on reasons that are halfway conscious and halfway repressed, you could love seeing something that shifts into whatever you want. Because they are indecipherable, there are no clear images of black boyhood, and in the 2010s, the explicit abuses of black age come roaring back.

Disappearing Acts

We began this chapter with a look at how second-wave black feminists addressed the limits of liberal humanism by critiquing adulthood as an inextricable and exclusionary part of proper liberal subjectivity. Black manhood, as an aspirational subjective position that includes all the agency and entitlements of possessive adulthood, was a necessary target of black feminist critique. Thus, although *gender* was the ostensible site of critique, it served as the analytical tool for dismantling a humanist hierarchy that *adulthood*—the supreme achievement of all modes of development—signified. As I have been arguing, gender without this particular concept of adulthood is the epistemic space for emancipatory maneuvering, even when the "emancipatory" nature of such maneuvers amounts to nothing more than a gesture toward a historical reality that has not yet arrived, or toward a not-yet-recognized means of connection between subjects forged through the terms of humanist exclusion. In my reading of *Uncle Tom's Cabin*, I watch where space might open for an alternative humanism to emerge from out of the conditions of objectification, where Harry and Eliza might make a lateral reconnection.

In the antebellum era, Harry's beautiful and beloved boyhood is an ideological cover that masks his status as a commodity and encodes him as a member of the family as opposed to what he really is, which is property. Legitimated acts of body snatching are the condition of possibility for boys like Harry to appear before a white audience. Further, the black body's exchange value supersedes the social significance of gender. Yet, through the ideological work that conceals how blackness is constituted as property, "gender" emerges as the overburdened category that pertains to every facet of black social life, as Blount and Cunningham have suggested, and separates black subjects from each other. Stowe's racial sentimentality nearly separates Harry from Eliza with the gendering term "fancy," until the ungendering logic of the market rudely intrudes. Like the "male" in "black male feminism," "gender" is the socializing partition that separates the very young male child—who is indistinguishable from very young female children in terms of value—from the mother, even though he legally shares her condition and she, his.

As Hong mentions of the Breedloves, non-possessive people are "forever immature." If immaturity is just another word for dispossession—a condition shared between mother and son—then in the afterlife of the slave market, *disappearance*, of either the mother or the son, genders and separates members of the dispossessed black family. Recall the photo of Devonte. He clings to an enforcer of the law, but he had a black mother once. Her name is Sherry Davis. The criminal justice system in Texas separated Devonte and his two biological siblings from Davis, even though she wanted to maintain custody of her children. Subsequently, Protective Services had taken them away from their aunt, Priscilla Celestine, who petitioned to adopt the children in an unsuccessful effort to retrieve them from foster care.[78] Both Davis and Celestine are absent when Devonte becomes a household image. More precisely, their disappearance from the frame of kinship is the reason Devonte appears. An enduring logic of black bodily value and fungibility shores up a schema of appearance and disappearance that evokes a gendered separation between mother and son.

Yet, at the same time, the schema is incidentally, strategically, and tragically baked into contemporary responses to anti-black violence. Think of Camille Bell and the seven other mothers who formed the Committee to Stop Children's Murders amidst the disappearances of predominately black boys in Atlanta, Georgia from 1979 to 1981, and more recently, the Mothers of the Movement, comprised of seven women whose children, including Trayvon Martin and Michael Brown, have been killed by police brutality. The fact that we so often need to be reminded that not all of the victims of the so-called Atlanta child murders or of the state violence that sparked the Movement for Black Lives were boys or children suggests that *disappearance*—of girls, women, men—endures as part of an ideological structure that conceals horizontal modes of black kinship, connection, and identification, and insidiously communicates that such non-hierarchical togetherness cannot exist.[79] In the case of the famous "Hug" photo, the condition of possibility for seeing the black boy is the *mother's* disappearance. If dispossession is what it means to be "immature," then I watch her disappeared presence in the spectacular image of the crying black child. (S)he did not choose to enter this embrace.

I conclude this chapter with a consideration of Jordan Peele's 2017 horror movie, *Get Out*, as an example of how the black contemporary imagination illustrates disappearance and economies of snatching.[80] The film treats black boyhood in the terms I have just discussed: as constituted through a gendering separation between mother and son that occurs when one disappears, and that conceals their shared condition of dispossession. I remain watchful for a space where the black woman, the black boy, ungendered and untimely, might reconnect with each other, and what gestures toward such reconnection look like.

As a basic summary of the plot reveals, the film is an allegory for the magical enchantment of enslaved objects. Chris Washington (played by actor Daniel Kaluuya), a black photographer living in New York City, is about to take a trip upstate to meet the parents of his white girlfriend, Rose Armitage (Allison Williams), for the first time. As they drive to the Armitage estate, they hit a deer, which lays dead in a wooded area by the side of the road and foreshadows a key revelation: Chris's mother similarly died in a hit and run when he was just 11 years old. Rose's father, Dean Armitage, is a neurosurgeon, and his wife Missy is a hypnotherapist. Without Chris's consent, Missy hypnotizes him and exploits a repressed memory—an 11-year-old Chris waits for his dying mother, who never comes home—in order to make him suggestable enough to sink psychically into a realm of total immobility. "The sunken place" is a dark, oceanic nowhere to which Chris's voiceless, suspended consciousness is relegated within his own body, which he no longer controls. As we soon learn, the Armitage family is running a covert, commercial operation that relies on the theft of black people, whose bodies are auctioned off to elderly, wealthy white customers looking to extend their lifespans indefinitely. By agreeing to visit Rose's family, Chris unwittingly participates in his own three-part theft. The psychic route to the sunken place is the second part, and the third is a surgical procedure called the Coagula, which installs the white consumer's mind in the purchased, inert, and controllable black body. In a silent backyard auction, Chris is sold to a blind art dealer who appreciates Chris's photography so much that he wants the physical means to see as Chris sees.

Get Out cites the cultural politics and genre conventions of postwar film, when "invasion" and "integration" were two sides of a Cold War–era coin that each signified, in different ways, the looming question of who counts as human. Although it begins with the same integrationist premise as the 1967 Sidney Poitier vehicle, *Guess Who's Coming to Dinner*, it more distinctly evokes Jack Finney's 1955 science fiction novel and the 1956 film, *Invasion of the Body Snatchers*, in which an alien species covertly and insidiously replace human beings with unfeeling replicas that collectively drain the earth's resources before moving on to other conquerable planets. In this unwittingly ironic, allegorical reversal of modern European expansionism, the replicas of humans, also known as "pod people," are historically and physically new. In the novel, the face of one is described as vaguely unformed: "It's not—immature, exactly. [. . .] it was formless, characterless. [. . .] it wasn't marked by experience."⁸¹ The relationship between blackness and immaturity is obvious, but recall the "newness" of older enslaved men's bodies that are shaved and oiled in preparation for the domestic slave trade. "Integration," on the other hand, names a postwar social project that relied on the disavowal of slavery. It required black people to socially reemerge as proper liberal subjects, separated by gender and age. Whereas "integration" relies on the disavowal of slavery, "invasion" speaks to what, precisely, is being disavowed. As Walter Johnson notes, the antebellum slave trader's powers of invasion represented a kind of necromancy: "The magic that could steal a person and inhabit their body with the soul of another—the forcible incorporation of a slave with the spirit of a slaveholder's fantasy."⁸² The trader was responsible for conjuring whatever the white world wants through the objectified body of the enslaved. Thus, before a body could flex its flexible limbs and dance, it is stolen and rendered inert, as Chris is during the movie's two modes of invasion, hypnotherapy and neurosurgery. In a word, "integration" names the liberal logic behind Chris's ostensibly rational and free-willed decision to visit the Armitage family. But "invasion," which combined magic with secular science, is the mechanism behind the making of the modern episteme.

From the beginning, invasion is attached to the film's racial schema of age, in which whiteness is encoded as elderly and on the brink of extinction. The Coagula procedure is an attempt to avoid the dreaded end of Man with modern reason. It relies on medicine and a Darwinian-like logic of natural selection, in which the evolution of the species relies on forcibly incorporating black bodies with the fantasy of whiteness. The biopolitics of age first emerges when Chris's friend Rod, a TSA agent, mentions that he was reprimanded for "patting down an old lady." Rod is black, and one imagines that the "old lady" deemed undeserving of such routine indignity is white. Rod's claim that, "The next 9/11 is gonna be on some geriatric shit," indicates that gender, a means of concealing age as value, is a deception. He flips the focus from gender to age. As we saw regarding the enslaved in the antebellum era, age was exchange value. Here, in the context of the whiteness of Man, age—like whiteness itself—is property.⁸³ Whiteness is saturated with age, and this deep saturation that occurs over historical, evolutionary, cultural time is another connotation of elderliness in this film. If, as Kobena Mercer explains of the horror genre, "Women are invariably the victims of the acts of terror unleashed by [. . .] the monster as nonhuman Other,"[84] then *Get Out* reorganizes this conventional schema of horror (if not terror) to uncover the connotation of age as racial value. "Women" share the same condition of "men" in the revelatory auction scene, which is old age. The "nonhuman Other" includes all manner of racially inappropriate subjects, such as Rod and the imaginary, Orientalized people who are implicitly the actual terrorists. Also, outside of the categorical framework of "old lady" are black women. Recall how the authors of the Combahee River Collective's "Statement" knew from a very young age that they could only ever bear a mimetic relationship to "ladies," which required their silence. This silence is associated with the disappeared presence of the black mother.

The clearest route to the sunken place is trauma, the temporality often associated with the afterlife of slavery. And the traumatic event, which is unspeakable, is the child's separation from the mother. As Chris explains to Dean and Missy, his "dad wasn't really in the picture," and since he never mentions who raised him after his unnamed mother died when he was 11, Chris's backstory serves to indicate that he is tragically orphaned and left alone. In a sense, the profound absence of Chris's mother simply intensifies the social illegitimacy historically associated with black motherhood from enslavement onward. The black "matriarch," the formidable head of the black family who has no actual power, pathologically bequeaths to her children nothing but illegitimacy, according to the 1965 "Moynihan Report" and discourses across the ideological spectrum since then. Having been dispossessed of both (white) patriarchal family and (black) maternal illegitimacy, Chris—like the unsupervised Harry—is primed for the invasiveness of the neo-slave market.

Trauma, the experience of dispossession that is unassimilable as memory, robs Chris of the volition to interpret and speak of his own personal history on his own terms. This may seem like an apt metaphor for the way all phases of the slave trade—from the First Passage to the continental coast, to the Middle Passage, to the domestic trade—severed the enslaved from their personal histories. Yet even the older men in *Clotel*, having been sold and shaven and greased and coerced into *being* 10 or 15 years younger than their actual ages, remembered how many planting seasons they had lived through. Trauma is not simply the temporal metaphor for the unfinished experience of enslavement—the experience that alludes your possession of it as memory and thus possesses you, that holds you as captive to your involuntary, repetitious responses to it. Rather, trauma names the effect of disciplining the proper liberal subject in the afterlife of integration. To enter the film as his own man, someone suitable enough to bring home to the family, Chris must remain silent about what must be disavowed. He encounters the gaslighting coercion to be silent the moment he begins to speak: "Did you tell them that I'm black?" According to Rose, she has not. Indeed, why would she mention it?

Since the past is not only structurally outside of recall, but transformed into that which must not be recalled, Missy is able to manipulate how Chris understands what he now involuntarily remembers through hypnosis. He involuntarily remembers where he was when his mother died: The film cuts away from the present to the past. We view Chris from behind. He is an 11-year-old child, sitting cross-legged on his bed in his bedroom, watching TV. The image on the TV screen is an illuminated blur. The scene is awash in blue, the edges are blurred, and the only sound is of the rain outside. Back in the present—in the convivial setting of Missy's cozy home office—Missy asks about the whereabouts of Chris's mom: "She was coming home and she wasn't home." The impetus for leaving the home was her obligation to "work," and the temporal suspension between destinations—about to arrive and has not arrived—is where Chris is located in the primal scene of his trauma. In this suspension between futurity and its non-arrival, which is also a suspension between boyhood and proper manhood, arises a question about Chris's personal responsibility. Missy asks, "And what did you do?" To which Chris replies, "Nothing." Missy repeats this, to reinforce its inadequacy. She continues: "Did you call anyone?" To which Chris answers, "No." Rather than let the fact stand, or criticize it outright, Missy leads Chris toward his own self-judgment by asking, "Why not?" To this, Chris explains what the childhood version of himself thought: "I don't know. I just thought that if I did, it would make it real." Rather than create distance between the past and the present, which in effect is the distance between Chris's childhood and adulthood, Missy uses this opportunity to conflate the two life stages. She does this by holding the 11-year-old Chris to adult standards of action, and insisting that this is how Chris, then and now, understand what happened: "You're so scared. You think it was your fault." At this point in the hypnosis, Chris becomes paralyzed, and Missy demands that he sink into the sunken place.

Historical disavowal leads to a reinterpretation of the past that shores up a neoliberal present, in which black subjects are held to the standards of full adult citizenship. They are held punitively responsible for meeting the obligations of citizenship without equal protections and entitlements. Just as Chris's mother is obligated to work outside of the home, which leads to the temporal suspension between the will-be and the is-not, Chris is similarly obligated to act. As the 11-year-old Chris waits at home in this temporal suspension, it is unclear how much he knows about what happened. He tells Rose, presumably for the first time, that he found out only later that his mother was still alive after being hit by a car, and that she could have survived, had anyone been looking for her. Thus, the traumatic event is re-experienced not as it "really was," but rather, as Chris's woeful negligence, as a miscarriage of responsibility.

Having sunken from his childhood bedroom into utter darkness, the adult Chris, still tainted from the blue of the primal scene, continues to slowly sink into nothingness. The vague, illuminated TV screen that 11-year-old Chris watched has been replaced with another, small, screen-like image, which is how Missy now appears to Chris. Floating in space, Chris seems to be screaming, but he is inaudible. He appears to be flailing, but he remains suspended. As *Get Out*'s most evocative image, the sunken place figures the black condition as one defined by profound social alienation and futile temporal suspension between almost arriving at something—a future, social inclusion, the achievement of humanness—and having not arrived. This might be where the film illustrates the Oceanic, the non-differentiation that forms modern black subjectivity, where the social categorical distinctions of age and gender dissolve.

Yet, the Oceanic, and its emancipatory potential for connection, is elsewhere. The screens that are present in both the moment of the traumatic event and the sunken place suggest that mass visual culture is the aspirational route to social inclusion. When the adult Chris holds the childhood version of himself responsible for negligent inaction, he does so by noting that he sat passively, "just watching TV." While the child Chris watches representations of social life, visual versions of social inclusion that one might achieve in only a mimetic sense (like "lady"), in the safety of *a home*, the sound of rain from *outside* invades the room. To be sure, the blue tint that connotes rainwater colors everything, conflating the domestic inside with the realm of dispossession or, "out of doors," as eviction is termed in *The Bluest Eye*. This relation between being a child who is protected by domesticity, and being a part of wild, outside space is precisely what the sunken place signifies. Still tainted in blue, adult Chris yells uselessly toward Missy's image on a tiny screen. The beautiful, well-kept home he sat in just moments before are now part of the tiny image. If mass visual culture, with its ideological power to subject us into being proper men and women and adults and children, was the fatal distraction that kept a young Chris from searching for his mother, then being sent to the sunken place is the retribution he does not actually deserve. Like his unnamed mother who dies alone outdoors, Chris is similarly condemned to a living death in the nowhere space of a body that is no longer his. Still, this is not where the two reconnect.

Rather, the unnamed black woman who we can only refer to as "Chris's mother" is the shape-shifting presence that determines what and how Chris sees. A photographer, Chris watches, and captures fleeting instances of her. As such an instance, she is captured in Chris's black-and-white photos. In the foreground of one, a black woman in a white halter top exposes her pregnant belly; nearly no other part of her body is in the frame. The belly is emblematic of what Alys Weinbaum calls the "reproductive afterlife" of slavery.[85] But she also is the rain outside in the primal scene of loss, she is the deer that died after being hit by a car, and in the embodiment of Georgina, the black woman whose body Dean's mother occupies, when she too is left unconscious on an outside road. All of these moments evoke some aspect of the traumatic event that inextricably links Chris to his mother in the present: It was raining on the night Chris's mother died; she was hit by a car; she died alone outside, left unconscious on a roadside. A constitutive part of a psychic structure of identification, Chris's mother shifts as a matter of

Chris's own shifting registers of knowing and being in a "post-racial" world. Shape-shifting is figurative of what cannot be apprehended all at once, since to see it is to discern a shift from one register of human existence to an alternative one, and to watch an ontological process of not-quite-arriving. For a moment, I watch for Sherry Davis in Devonte's remorseful face. I watch for the shift from the spectacle of pain to the black boy we did not see. In the next chapter, we encounter another spectacle, the preternaturally aged black woman, and listen to what she says when she speaks.

2

Vampires and Relics

These undecipherable markings on the captive body render a kind of hieroglyphics of the flesh whose severe disjunctures come to be hidden to the cultural seeing by skin color.
—Hortense Spillers, "Mama's Baby, Papa's Maybe: An America Grammar Book"

In 1835, P. T. Barnum began his career as an exhibitor with the purchase of the black female slave, Joice Heth. As Barnum and his collaborators headlined, Heth was 161 years old—old enough to have nursed the future father of the nation, George Washington, which she supposedly did. Heth's unique role in history was a centerpiece of the exhibit: According to Benjamin Reiss's rich account of the Barnum-Heth tour, she spoke "of swaddling Washington, of the future general's favorite gray horse, of the menacing presence of the redcoats."[1] Such historical anecdotes, along with Heth's nearly preternatural longevity, "put many visitors in a reflective, even nostalgic frame of mind."[2] Barnum recalls his reaction to Heth, who he exhibited as a human curiosity until her death in 1836, in his 1855 autobiography: "I was favorably struck with the appearance of the old woman. So far as outward indications were concerned, she might almost as well have been called a thousand years old as any other age."[3] Although the act had transformed over time—eventually to purport that Heth was an automaton, and not human at all—the initial attraction for Barnum and nineteenth-century audiences was the unearthly, uncanny quality of her age.

That a black body "might almost as well have been called" any impossible age indicates how modern blackness has been constituted outside of the realm of the human. Age, in this context, is a key analytic for rethinking the limits of the human and its temporality. The Barnum-Heth exhibit, which belongs to a broader context of transatlantic enslavement and its afterlife, is simply one example of how this limit is manifested. As a performance and spectacle of a "commodit[y] who spoke," Barnum's exhibit of Heth might be considered alongside canonical slave narratives that figure the question of lifespans in terms of objectification and subjectivity.[4]

Frederick Douglass's Narrative (1845) and Harriet Jacobs's Incidents in the Life of a Slave Girl (1861) posit age as a conceptual challenge borne out of the racialization of the human. Narrative begins with an explanation of how the slave could have been called any age: "I have no accurate knowledge of my age, never having seen any authentic record containing it. By far the larger part of the slaves know as little of their ages as horses know of theirs, and it is the wish of most masters within my knowledge to keep their slaves thus ignorant."[5] Douglass describes an informal practice of relegating chattel outside of the time of Western modernity—the time of documentation and print culture—and, simultaneously, chronological time. In an attempt to extend liberal humanism to include the enslaved, Douglass implies that a precondition of personhood is the temporality of human development. Alternatively, Jacobs pinpoints an inextricable link between race and gender in the universalization of Man by gendering the process of aging in order to endow enslaved females with girlhood. She alludes to routine sexual violence that denies girlhood to the enslaved: "Even the little child, who is accustomed to wait on her mistress and her children, will learn, before she is twelve years old, why it is that her mistress hates such and a one among the slaves."[6] Indeed, the Barnum-Heth exhibit was predicated on the freakishness of a black female who was so old that her youthfulness seemed too distant, inaccessible, or impossible to consider. As Uri McMillan puts it in his work on the performances of the "ancient negress," Heth typifies "the ancient black female witness to history."[7] Through Heth, the exhibit demonstrated that national history lives.

Within the purview of slavery's historicity, the denial of liberal humanist normativity makes blackness appear untimely in one of two ways: It appears to have the object status of an ancient relic, or it signifies something "inherently childlike" irrespective of chronological age.[8] In other words, blackness does not simply appear as any impossible age. Rather, it often appears as extremely old or as incongruously infantile. This chapter focuses on two figures that illustrate how these divergent forms of untimeliness have been expressed as black age, which is the embodiment of historical time: the vampire and the relic.

At once supernatural and historical, the vampire and the relic comprise both exclusions of western humanism and potentials that arise from racially non-normative relations to time. While commenting on the centuries-long project of establishing "Blackness" as a signifier of categorical exclusion from western humanism, Achille Mbembe reminds us of Michel Foucault's description of "monsters and fossils," temporal concepts within the epistemic development of natural history. While the monster, in Foucault's words, "provides an account, as though in caricature, of the genesis of differences," the fossil "permits resemblances to subsist throughout all of the deviations traversed by nature."[9] Of this, Mbembe suggests, "On the great chart of species, genders, races, and classes, Blackness, in its magnificent obscurity, represents the synthesis of these two figures."[10] The conflation of monsters and fossils, two versions of in/human development, evokes the untimeliness of black age. On the one hand, Heth's extreme longevity expresses a monstrous divergence from normative biological development: She is an organism that does not die. On the other, she manifests the survival of prior deviations. Either possibility could have arisen from "questions about the biological differences between the races" that the exhibit prompted.[11] Yet, unlike my figurative use of vampires and relics, monsters and fossils are wholly confined within the phylogenic meanings of western man.

Alternatively, the vampire and the relic force us to reckon with the contingent social status of bodies as flesh-and-blood organisms, as artificial contraptions, as simultaneously living and dead. As all of these things, they express a dynamic relation between humans and nonhumans, and comment upon the endless production of human "history" itself. Thus, not only are the vampire and the relic denaturalized alternatives to monsters and fossils. They are also Oceanic analogies to two more familiar figures of plantation slavery that join race and gender into mutually constitutive categories of untimeliness: mammy and jezebel.[12]

If Douglass implies that the route to a full humanism, and subsequently, entry into liberal personhood, is normative age, then Heth's exhibition and Jacob's narrative reveal how gender complicates such a straightforward course. McMillan argues that Heth evoked a structure of feeling on the part of white viewers that he refers to as "mammy memory," or sentimentality for erstwhile wet nurses who tended to them as children.[13] Yet, such affect ironically illustrates that enslaved female subjects who provided child-related labor underwent an age-based transformation in the white cultural imagination, from being any age at all to becoming consummately elderly. As Kimberly Wallace-Sanders suggests, black women referred to as "mammies" were not necessarily old.[14] On the other end of the age dichotomy, jezebel's youth did not include "girlhood." As "a slave girl," Jacobs eschews the convention of naming herself in the title of her own narrative, a hallmark of liberal personhood. As P. Gabrielle Foreman notes, "'a slave girl' occupies the linguistic space which one would expect to be filled by Linda Brent," Jacobs's pseudonym, which itself conceals the author.[15] "A slave girl" signals the problem that Jacobs was forced to write around, which is the dispossession of "girlhood" for the enslaved. Such dispossession is what "jezebel" names.[16]

Heth's body and Jacobs's "linguistic space" are two key instances that draw our attention to age as a constitutive part of gender and the human. In ways that trade in the strange and unconventional—Heth's decrepitude, Jacob's empty signifier—both prompt us to notice, albeit tacitly, that age is a constitutive part of blackness and gender and is thus where a historical problem resides. This requires a reconceptualization of "age" as an outcome of what Hortense Spillers refers to as "flesh": During the Middle Passage, captive subjects had been violently transformed into "that zero degree of social conceptualization," and excluded from the social order of the New World.[17] As I argue in this book, the black body was not only ungendered during this process as Spillers claims, but also made to appear untimely. Unlike mammy and jezebel, which, like the monster and fossil, exist for the perpetuation of Man, the vampire and the relic return us to this aspect of untimeliness. They allow us to focus as much on black lifespans as on black femaleness, which mammy and jezebel raise as the primary problem. As supernatural and in between the human and inhuman, the vampire and the relic denaturalize the concept of age, and thus, allow us to see it anew.

This chapter's point of departure is the Atlantic Ocean. It begins with the Oceanic origins of the vampire, its reclamation of time in the face of human dispossession and concludes with the national and counternational uses of the relic. As figures of the eternal, they reboot our queries about how the past of New World enslavement is related to the present and future. We turn here to the question of how to recognize ostensibly undetectable forms of temporal relatedness. We will contend with the entanglements of the fictional and the historical, since black-gender-age appears as an amalgamation of fact and fiction. In pursuing such queries and methods, this chapter evokes the problem of the archive of transatlantic slavery, which the Oceanic lifespans of black female age express.

Contemporary fiction is a key site for the exploration of how race, gender, and age converge to obscure whatever is true about "her." As Saidiya Hartman discusses in her essay, "Venus in Two Acts" (2008), narrative is a site where history combines with fiction, which she explores through a heuristic she terms "critical fabulation."[18] As Hartman explains about her production of "recombinant narrative," it is that "which weaves present, past, and future in retelling the girl's story and in narrating the time of slavery as our present."[19] In "two acts," Hartman first accounts for the violent encounter with the archive of transatlantic slavery, in which she discovers a myriad of unknowable black "Venuses." At times, each is bestowed a different name: "A flagellant and a Hottentot. A sulky bitch. A dead negréss. A syphilitic whore."[20] She then turns to a particular "Venus," one who appears in the margins of another black female's death aboard the *Recovery*, about whom Hartman has written elsewhere.[21] The "girl" about whom Hartman speculates is "knowable" only through the fantasies inscribed onto her. I reimagine "Venus"—a black female signifier of what is historically irretrievable—in another two-act schema that stages the potentials of both loss and reclamation expressly in terms of Oceanic lifespans. The vampire comprises a first act, which addresses the foreclosure of black femaleness from the social logic of liberal humanism; the relic comprises another, which addresses the task of historical retrieval itself. Neither figure is "capable of resuscitating the girl,"[22] as Hartman concludes, or black femaleness of any age. They can only express what our fantasies of resuscitation look like.

The vampire is an icon that instantiates the notion of a fleshy counter-temporality. Although Octavia Butler was best known for her science and speculative fiction of the 1970s and '80s, the last novel she published before her untimely death in 2006, *Fledgling* (2005), is vampire fiction. Jewelle Gomez's *The Gilda Stories* (1991) reimagines the conditions that Joice Heth supposedly experienced through a counter-national dialectic between the past and present. The vampire is a vehicle for the exploration of consent, which has racial, gendered, and age-based logics. Through this exploration, the vampire makes manifest questions of how the black female subject is presently situated in the context of liberal humanism: She is presumed to be a consenting subject, even when the condition of "consent" is choicelessness. Thus, the vampire, which is consummately autonomous, and conventionally engages in non-consensual acts of extraction, is the figure through which the present state of freedom in relation to black-female-age is cast as a historical problem. Unlike the version of living history that Heth was made to perform, Butler's and Gomez's vampire novels interrupt conventional narratives about temporality—which include historical time, chronological time, and national time—in order to explore Oceanic narratives, such as "artificial childhood" and "immortal girlhood." Through such an interruption, the vampires that Gomez and Butler invent explore alternatively non-hegemonic versions of what living history means.

Along with the vampire, this chapter returns to the legacy of Heth's function as an ancient conveyor of history through the related figure of the relic. The human relic, like the vampire, is monstrous. If "artificial girlhood," as we will see, evokes the manner in which blackness was constituted as a category of fearful-yet-sexually-alluring, adult-like children, then "artificial immortality" evokes the equally atrocious way white dependency on blackness keeps the dead alive among the living. Artificiality notwithstanding, the status of the relic relies on the real. The relic is revered for its realness, as the actual-yet-enchanted remains of the bygone. Thus, the relic turns our attention from speculative fiction to genres that trade in historical veracity, such as oral history and autobiography. In Ernest Gaines's novel, *The Autobiography of Miss Jane Pittman* (1971), the titular character is a 110-year-old black woman who recounts her life story for an interviewer who "teach[es] history."[23] The narrative begins in 1862, a year before the Emancipation Proclamation is issued, and ends 100 years later, in the current moment of 1962, when civil rights campaigns are underway. As a black reclamation of both the relic and a history of emancipated black life, Gaines's novel conflates black female agedness with black historiography: If Heth was a garish "commod[y] who spoke," then Jane Pittman is the talking book we wish we had, the elusive evidence of black existence that survives.

The vampire novels addressed here explore Oceanic lifespans with speculative flights of fancy just before and after the turn of the twenty-first century. During the last quarter of the twentieth century, Gaines's reimagining of the relic occurs when conventional methods of historicism are central to the work of retrieving lost evidence of black life. The revisionist historiographies of plantation slavery that proliferated during the 1960s and '70s attest to this.[24] Yet, the task of reading historical time through black age and lifespans prevents me from following a linear temporal schema, in which conventional historicism of the late twentieth century gives way to fanciful speculation in the twenty-first. Speculative-historical impulses range from Gaines's reclamation of the "ancient black female witness to history," to Alex Haley's wish-fulfilling genealogy in *Roots* (1976), and Octavia Butler's time-traveling neo-slave narrative, *Kindred* (1979). While Haley resurrects a paternal African ancestor who establishes an unbroken chain between the pre-enslaved past and the present, rendering the Door of No Return, in Dionne Brand's cartographic re-imagining of it, suddenly available and wide open, Gaines and Butler figure the im/possibility of returns and survival through black womanhood. Of *Kindred*, Butler notes that she chose to have a present-day black woman transported to the antebellum South because a black man would never have survived: "So many things that he did would have been likely to get him killed."[25] Taken together, the vampire and the relic explore how black female age has taken on an archival function through abusive and liberating presumptions about who is likely to survive. Figured as the vampire and relic, the black female body—old, young, neither, both—is a site of speculative historiography, of epistemic renewal and preservation. She manifests an unfulfillable desire to make direct contact with the past. Thus, she turns our attention to the Ocean.

The Vampire

Theorists from across the black Atlantic have situated gender as a key analytic for exploring the historicity of racialization that the category of the human contains.[26] Frantz Fanon's *Black Skin, White Masks* (1952) holds the status of a foremost text that examines the psychic life of colonialism, and thereby explores the experience of living in proximity to the concept of Man. Fanon famously asserts that "the black is not a man,"[27] thus marking a double exclusion of racialized masculinity. As Michelle Rowley claims, this formulation of humanism's exclusions "provides unique insight into the philosophical problem of absence that confronts black women."[28] Black feminist scholars of the United States and Caribbean, particularly Spillers and Sylvia Wynter, have made notable contributions to addressing this absence in transatlantic terms. However, many critics have noted the way Fanon dismissively posits black womanhood as being complicit with colonial racism in *Black Skin, White Masks*.[29] The most prominent example of this appears in the second chapter, which addresses "the relations between the woman of color and the European [man]."[30] This chapter primarily focuses on Mayotte Capécia's 1948 novel, *Je Suis Martiniquaise* (*I Am a Martinican Woman*). Fanon's reading of Capécia's text argues that black female sexuality is constitutive of colonialist racism, and that for black women—of which Capécia is representative—white masculinity is the constant object of desire. As he puts it, "in a word, the race must be whitened; every woman in Martinique knows this, says it, repeats it."[31]

Yet, in the first chapter Fanon describes how his own psychic complicity with the colonial humanist project plays out through gender, tacitly revealing recognition of black female exclusion as a problem. Having claimed that "[a] white man addressing a Negro behaves exactly like an adult with a child,"[32] Fanon explains:

> I myself have been aware, in talking to certain patients, of the exact instance at which I began to slip.... Examining this seventy-three-year-old farm woman, whose mind was never strong and who is now far gone in dementia, I am suddenly aware of the collapse of the *antennae* with which I touch and through which I am touched. The fact that I adopt a language suitable to dementia, to feeble-mindedness; the fact that I "talk down" to this poor woman of seventy-three; the fact that I condescend to her in my quest for a diagnosis, are the stigmata of a dereliction in my relations with other people.[33]

With regard to the ease with which the question of the human in Fanon's work invites neglect of gender difference, Anne McClintock notes that

"Women are [. . .] effectively deferred to a nowhere land, beyond time and place, outside theory."[34] The discursive manner in which black womanhood conjures its own erasure through what every black woman supposedly "says" and "repeats" is interrupted upon the encounter with this aged farm woman. In this "language suitable to dementia" resides the "nowhere land" where usual pathways to the concepts of humanness or colonial agency—implicitly forged through gender difference—break down. This woman's age—her 73 years and the disability/possibility that attend them—exposes an impasse that leaves the philosophical dualisms of race and gender inadequate and allows Fanon to be uncharacteristically self-reflexive about his own "slipping" in this moment. This "slipping" can be characterized as an inability—if only a momentary one—to maintain a dialectic in which Fanon provisionally occupies the subject position of the (white/masculine) "adult," while this 73- year-old (black) woman occupies the status of a "child." Age interrupts how "the fateful chiaroscuro of race is at almost every turn disrupted by the criss-crossings of gender," and thus demands an account of historically contingent subject positions that can surpass the logic of static binaries.[35]

The vampire is an ideal figure for animating this "slipping," and illustrating how race, gender, and age have been mutually constituted across the Atlantic Ocean. One might speculate that Fanon's lost "antennae" not only collapse but are submerged in deep social meanings of the circum-Caribbean that adhere to black female agedness in particular ways. According to Giselle Liza Anatol's comprehensive study, the Afro-antecedent of contemporary black literary representations of the vampire is the folkloric *soucouyant*, an elderly, supernatural figure of terror. She is a "frightening old hag, skin-shedder, bloodsucker, fly-by-night."[36] As Anatol argues, the contemporary vampire narrative is an outcome of New World colonialism and enslavement, and of the cultural exchange between African and European folk traditions. For instance, during the nineteenth century, "ideologies of race led to a predominance of images of monstrously racialized—and often feminized—bodies" that constitute our vampiric inheritance, which black women writers such as Nalo Hopkinson, Edwidge Danticat, Gomez, and Butler revise.[37]

The soucouyant, who both precedes and elaborates on a process in which bodies become monstrous through oceanic crossing, instantiates an oceanic metaphor of liminality. She is "an old woman [. . .] the figure of abjection, hovering in that liminal space, that border between 'us' and 'them,' and also between life and death."[38] However, through embodiment, the oceanic is imaginable as more than an abstraction. As Omise'eke Natasha Tinsley submits, oceanic histories of how "Africans became diasporic" indeed contain actual experiences of embodiment, of "Africans [that] became fluid bodies under the force of brutality" and that, like the ocean, "became liquid, oozing."[39] Together, Anatol and Tinsley advance an approach to conceptualizing the vampire as a heuristic with which to treat histories of New World colonialization that were forged both figuratively and literally through blood and skin. Thus, the ancient myth of an old hag who sheds her own skin resonates in a colonial context, where skin is routinely shredded from actual bodies and blood is drawn: "the slow and tortuous draining of [. . .] literal blood through punishing beatings or the depletion of [. . .] 'life-blood,' or essence, through the agonizing and humiliating existence of slavery would have been perceived as much more horrific than the prospect of death," and thus more likely to become the terrifying substance of lore.[40] The vampire is a blood relation, "*historically* and *materially*,"[41] to the ocean, African diaspora, to fluid modernity.

While Anatol and Tinsley richly theorize how blackness and womanhood have been mutually constituted through colonial and anti-colonial discourses about gender normativity, or how black queer desire is constitutive of the embodied experience of the Middle Passage, I suggest that such work can be further enriched by bringing the under-theorized concept of age to the fore. The soucouyant is aged, but upon colonial encounters, what did it mean for a black body to embody "age"? For African bodies forcefully removed from their social context, oozing like the ocean beneath the ships, with skin that bled or broke, creased or sagged or too taut to do either, did "age" retain a social meaning? When "feeblemindedness" signified the negation of white adult rationality rather than something endemic to aged bodies, did "age" become a concept as supernatural as blackness itself?

Clearly, the vampire can be thought in relation to other figures of black embodiment. Spillers's 1987 essay, "Mama's Baby, Papa's Maybe: An American Grammar Book," aptly illustrates how the black body is defined through racializing violence that dispossesses it of social meaning and situates it in static time. Spillers speculates that the captive black body is "ungendered" through the violence of transport across the Atlantic, and thus carries the potential of a non-differentiation of gender. According to Spillers, distinct subject-positions of gender were inapplicable and irrelevant for Africans transformed into commodities during the slave trade. However, I submit that her theorization of black dehumanization can easily be applied to age as well as gender. Bodies relegated outside of the New World social order can be neither male nor female; instead, males, females—and, I would add, children, adults, the elderly—were "taken into 'account' as quantities" and as taxonomies of commercial value.[42] With this dispossession of gender—and life stages—in mind, the distinction she makes between the "body" and the "flesh" limn "captive and liberated subject positions."[43] The body is the undifferentiated vessel of commercial value, upon which a vast array of cultural meaning can be imposed over time; the flesh, which comes before the body, is "that zero degree of conceptualization that does not escape concealment under the brush of discourse, or the reflexes of iconography."[44] The conceptual term of Oceanic lifespans indexes that for which Spillers makes theoretical room but never names: While crossing the Atlantic, African subjects are both ungendered and unaged.

As "Mama's Baby" argues, the central problem with reaching a potentially liberated, non-normative subject position is temporal: "ethnicity" is the condition of being trapped in stasis, of being unchanged in a temporality that transcends historical time. As Spillers states, "'Ethnicity' . . . freezes in meaning, takes on constancy, assumes the looks and the affects of the Eternal."[45] Thus, the condition of modern blackness is being caught between two irreconcilable temporalities: that of a preexistent patriarchal social order to which one can never completely belong, and other possibilities that have yet to be invented in the future. This imagined future is where the vampire enters: She is a vehicle for imagining what this future invention might look like through age, which splits between the categories of the human and racial temporality. Alexander Weheliye comments on how the functions of gender and sexuality seem to split between the normative realm of Man and the aberrant realm of blackness: "In the same way that black people appear as either nonhuman or magically hyperhuman within the universe of Man, black subjects are imbued with either a surplus . . . of gender and sexuality or a complete lack thereof."⁴⁶ "Maturation and youth" can function as substitutes for "gender and sexuality" to further index how blackness is constituted outside of the norms of the human.

Joice Heth is an example of Oceanic lifespans, given that she is trapped in the context of conquest. The aged black body is caught between nonhuman time and national time. The Barnum-Heth exhibit was to represent the black body as if its non-humanity and nationalist identity were reconciled. Barnum's commercial endeavors and sentimental audiences required reconciliation between inhuman stasis and a homogenous emptiness in which national belonging could exist. Not unlike the way Heth supposedly carried baby Washington, Heth's aged body supposedly carried a historical moment that had been lost through national progress for which audiences were nostalgic. In other words, nonhuman bodies carry national time. However, one might reframe Joice Heth's performance with Spillers in mind to consider a temporal schema in which Heth not only exceeds the time of patriarchy, and thus becomes a spectacle of decrepitude, but also signals some other "time," beyond that of Man, which might exist in the future. In such a future, we may claim "the monstrosity" of black womanhood borne outside of a patriarchal order, which includes the spectacularly decrepit woman who experiences historical time in non-normative ways.⁴⁷

Artificial Childhood in *Fledgling*

The vampire is monstrous. It is a figure that is either immortal or long-lived as a matter of convention. The *Oxford English Dictionary* notes that "in the original and usual form of the belief, [the vampire is] a reanimated corpse," or the very manifestation of the previously forsaken and awakened dead. In other versions, the vampire reanimates the historical past while living over a course of numerous centuries, or as consciousness comes to stand in for a redemptive relation to the past from the standpoint of the present. *Fledgling* and *The Gilda Stories* are useful representations of this redemptive relation.⁴⁸ The vampire genre can so easily reject an inert historicism, that empty, homogenous time where battles over the conditions of social life have already been either lost or won. Ostensibly, speculative genres, such as Afro-futurism, take up the past in order to imagine what might be in the future, while the vampire genre represents a past in relation to the present. However, generic boundaries and temporal investments become fluid within a larger project that renders modernity's social categories unfamiliar. Anatol claims that *The Gilda Stories*, which concludes in 2050, is removed "from afro-futurist work, which typically addresses the correlations between race and technology in futuristic settings" and is closer to "soucouyant stories that harken *back* in time to folktales."[49] Gomez's vampire narrative may harken back to folktales, but it also resembles another genre of the past, the neo-slave narrative, since it begins in 1850 from the point of view of a fugitive slave. According to Ashraf Rushdy, "the neo-slave narratives' major unifying feature is that they represent slavery as a historical phenomenon that has lasting cultural meaning and enduring social consequences" which, I argue, includes the meaning of black age.[50] Yet, the vampire figuratively extends concerns about the past into the future. Ultimately, the novels addressed here imagine the constituting of social meaning across the past, present, and future. Thus, they crisscross boundaries between Afro-futurism, vampire fiction, ancient folklore, and the neo-slave narrative.

Octavia Butler's 2005 novel, *Fledgling*, opens in the aftermath of catastrophe. Readers learn that someone "awoke in darkness," but "who" remains uncertain. Unknown to herself, and to the audience, this anonymous person reflects, "Somehow, I had been hurt very badly, and yet I couldn't remember how."[51] The rupture that separates this present moment of darkness from the past is the impetus for our attempt to retrieve what existed before. The catastrophe is an invitation to consider a temporal break, and it is after that break that we begin.

Shori Matthews, who appears to be an African American girl of about ten years of age, is the lone survivor of a fire that destroys her community. She awakens with a traumatic head injury and amnesia. Over the course of the novel, Shori gathers information about herself, the fire, and her dead family. She learns that she's a member of a vampire species that calls itself Ina. Although she looks like a human child and is in fact a juvenile among the long-lived Ina, Shori has lived for 53 years. She is the outcome of her family's pioneering experiments in genetic engineering. While a majority of Shori's genes are Ina, she has also inherited human DNA from a black woman, who is one of her four biological mothers. Her human genes account for her dark skin and unusual ability to function in daylight. Thus, Shori is a manifestation of the old adage about black skin and age—"black don't crack"—since the protective melanin of her skin is sutured to the now-unrelated, deceptive youthfulness of her appearance. Not only does the novel's plot suture dark skin and deceptive youth together through the figure of Shori. It also raises in high relief the contradiction of protection and abuse that is embedded in "black don't crack": The protective element in dark skin has been transformed into a highly visible signifier of otherness and the impetus for a profound denial of protection. "Blackness" and "youth" are brought together in a manner that is simultaneously familiar and unfamiliar, in order to situate anew these overlapping terms in relation to conditions of "protection" and "endangerment." Shori embodies the contradiction. One racist and xenophobic Ina family, the Silks, is responsible for setting the fire that killed Shori's family, as they attempted to kill Shori herself. The entire final third of the novel chronicles the Silks's trial, organized by a council of their Ina peers for their xenophobic crimes. Shori is vindicated, and presumably will pass her distinctively human traits to her descendants, which would genetically alter the Ina well into the future.

Melissa J. Strong has noted that *Fledgling* "invites readers to imagine blackness as a signifier of humanness."[52] The novel does invite this association, if perhaps ironically: The nameless black woman who donated her DNA is a minor plot point. More precisely, her absent presence is a signifier of a historical problem, which is the status of black humanity in the modern western world. If a "recombinant narrative" recombines the past, present, and future in order to address a current historical problem, such as the inhumanness of black age, through an understanding of historical time as dynamic, contingent, and unfinished, then Shori embodies the "recombinant" in two ways. First, as the progeny of a black woman who is mentioned but largely unaccounted for in the novel, Shori is the embodiment of "blackness" as the ongoing erasure of facts with which the novel is complicit and, paradoxically, which it troubles: The black woman's previous role as human DNA donor is reanimated in the present-day conflict over Shori's social status among Ina. Second, since a primary definition of "recombinant" specifically refers to the recombination of genetic material in progeny, Shori is the actual embodiment of this process: Her dark skin makes an erstwhile black woman's embodiment more salient than the normative whiteness of her Ina ancestry, while projecting a future in which Ina will be black. Shori is the genetically recombined embodiment that makes "blackness" show up as both a developmental throwback and a sign of futurity.

For a moment, let us focus on the absent black woman, who is described as both a "human woman who donated DNA" and a "black human mother."[53] These descriptions evoke a range of concepts—socially detached genetic material, liberal self-possession that being a "donor" suggests, and motherhood—that surprisingly pertain to the life and death of Henrietta Lacks, a black woman who, for decades, had remained unknown and is associated with immortality.[54] As James Doucet-Battle notes, Lacks is often described as the "matriarch" of her uncompensated and historically disenfranchised black family. The term "matriarch" functions as a disavowal of the Lacks family's ongoing dispossession. Relatedly, the discrepant terms used for Shori's unnamed "mother" have a revealing function similar to Doucet-Battle's analytical term, "bioethical matriarchy"; both reveal that "racialized and gendered forms of exchange aris[e] from the absence of consent or of obligational precedents for reciprocation."[55] Since we know almost nothing about Shori's DNA donor/biological mother, aside from the fact that she was black, the question of how historical precedents of obligation in the absence of consent factored into her exchange, donation, or motherhood looms large. We do know that her DNA outlived her own mortal life. As Lacks's cancer cells illustrate, the black body can be broken apart, so that the resulting separate parts are granted separate timelines of their own. Mere parts of the black body are allowed to live, which is the afterlife of being transformed into flesh.[56]

Shori bridges, rather than conflates, the inhuman logic of black immortality and the liberal humanist logic of the autonomous individual. Something must be disavowed and forgotten in order for Shori to appear as the liberal individual. Her black human mother facilitates such disavowal and forgetting. In addition to the lengthy legal process where Shori's injuries are addressed, consensual agreement is a part of the novel's investment in a liberalism that inadequately addresses the catastrophe of history. Robyn Wiegman's thoughts on consenting agreements that underpin reproductive technologies strongly resonate here:

In this new economy of the body, the contract serves to secure the ideology of liberal personhood as that which, precisely, differentiates the past from the future. It is this differentiation that functions to place liberal personhood within the progress narrative of modernity, transforming the violence of "bodily theft" under slavery into the seemingly benign social relations of autonomy and choice that the contract is made to speak.[57]

All we know about Shori's mother is that she donated DNA, and in the novel's silence about the details and preconditions of this donation, we presume this was her choice to make. But "in this new economy of the body," consent itself is a matter of forgetting. Consent serves as an entryway into matters of possessive individualism, property, and choice; since this entryway separates the past of enslavement from the post-liberated present, not walking through it is a benign non-choice. The connection between the speculative genetic engineering in the novel and historical theft is nearly lost because Shori's mother "consented."

As Spillers's work demonstrates, if there is something liberatory about signifying a black woman as the mother of invention, it is not to be found in liberal personhood. But despite the novel's tendency toward liberal, or as Karla Holloway has stated, neoliberal ideology, *Fledgling* invites us to imagine the conditions of historical retrieval.[58] In conventional vampire narratives, the vampire can realize the potential within the present to redeem the losses and seemingly trivial relics of the past, yet Shori is unable do this. Her loss of memory marks the novel's foundational problem. The novel begins, "I awoke to darkness. I was hungry—starving!—and I was in pain. There was nothing in my world but hunger and pain, no other people, no other time, no feelings."[59] *Fledgling* may indeed invite readers to imagine blackness as a signifier of humanness, but these opening lines paradoxically problematize how humanness is constituted in the first place. In the beginning, there is profound hunger and pain, but what is attributable to the category of human—a social order and temporality—are absent. Shori's waking in darkness can be interpreted as metonymical—not of blackness as humanness, but of blackness as the exception of modern Western humanity. Shori's profound separation from the social order as she awakens in the burned ruins of her family's compound evokes what Orlando Patterson has termed the "natal alienation" of being completely separated from history, the social death of slavery.⁶⁰ Once Shori learns that nearly everyone in her family and community has been killed, she wonders how the Ina honor their dead. She wants to honor them, but she can't remember how.⁶¹

Fledgling illustrates how the neo-slave narrative and vampire fiction open deliberations about the living past. And through its vitality, the past shapes speculations about the future. One of the most obvious and provocative aspects of Butler's vampire and her embodiment of time is the ambiguity of Shori's age. I turn to age as the temporality of personhood, since it is through the category of age that the novel engages the historicity of racial formation. In this regard, Butler's final novel makes a recursive gesture toward her earlier novel, *Kindred*.⁶² *Kindred* reorganizes time in order to simultaneously narrate black existence in the antebellum South and in California during the US bicentennial year.⁶³ The novel *Kindred* is an example of speculative fiction that explores the historicity of the present through the simultaneity of slavery and a liberated present. As a result of traveling back in time from California in 1976 to various years that span, roughly, between 1811 and 1836, Dana—a black woman—makes contact with a white, slaveholding ancestor who lives not only in a distinctly different time period, but also in a distinctly different temporality. Rufus Weylin lives in early nineteenth-century Maryland and grows from infancy into adulthood over what is for him a timespan of two decades. For the 26-year-old Dana, the same time period is roughly one year. As she periodically re-encounters Rufus in the past to protect him from danger (thereby to ensure that he will procreate), she appears to be older than her ancestor, in much the same way that Joice Heth was much older than baby (Founding Father) George Washington, of whom she spoke of nursing. Indeed, the comparative agedness Dana and Heth share in relation to their wards emphasizes a combined racialized and gendered aspect of the labor they produce as caregivers. In addition to comparable agedness, both Dana and Heth take on the look of temporal stillness. If Heth's erstwhile girlhood is utterly unimaginable—if part of what she performed for the public is this impossibility of black female youth—then she manifests a version of comparatively older yet static age that Rufus also attributes to Dana. As he claims, "But Dana, you're saying while I've been growing up, somehow, time has been standing still for you," to which Dana replies, "It hasn't stood still. [. . .] I'm sure my last two visits here aged me quite a bit, no matter what my calendar at home says."⁶⁴ While both Rufus and George Washington have "been growing up," black women are temporally restricted, forced to witness and foster this growing. Thus, it is up to Dana to assert that, despite appearances of aged stasis, time moves for her, touches her, changes her. Or, quite simply, her age is imperceptibly related to time, despite what calendars, "history," or her own body might suggest.

This exploration of age in *Kindred* culminates in *Fledgling*. Whereas the mysteriousness of time travel overshadows the equally odd fact that Dana is older than her ancestor in *Kindred*, *Fledgling* explicitly invites readers to consider the strangeness of how aging works. Vampire fiction invites us to consider how age, race, and gender are mutually constituted. As the novel explains, Ina are required to have symbiotic relationships with humans or "symbionts," which includes sex. The first person to encounter Shori after she awakens is Wright Hamlin, a 23-year-old white man, who becomes Shori's primary symbiont and sexual partner. Since Shori appears to be 10 or 11 years old, pedophilia comes to mind even as we are aware that Shori is an adult. But why is Shori, the only surviving black Ina, both young and old at once?⁶⁵

Shori's ambiguous maturation leads to the question of how age is a meaningful pivot between moments of transport across the Atlantic and maturation statuses attributed to those enslaved in the New World. Definitions of a "child" vary throughout the slave trade and across time. For instance, during the seventeenth century, Portuguese slavers tied the definition of "child" to the arbitrary matter of size, which directly correlated to how many bodies could be packed onto ships and how much trade contractors would be taxed for each body.⁶⁶ In an overview of the literature on children enslaved in the New World between 1500 and 1865, Gwyn Campbell notes that the distinction between "child" and "adult" was inoperable for enslaved US populations: "Random evidence from the nineteenth-century 'slave' advertisements in the United States is difficult to interpret, given the tendency of slave-owners to categorise [sic] all slaves as socially immature."⁶⁷ The relegation of all slaves to the ranks of quasi-childhood was part and parcel of the Enlightenment-era tendency to distinguish reasoning subjects from irrational beings. An outcome of the delineation between rational and physical beings is a schema in which the former would have control over the latter. As conceptions of maturation were folded into political notions about civic and social participation, enslaving "adults" required the relegation of adult slaves into the symbolic realm of childhood, the contradictions of this relegation notwithstanding:

> The artificial "childhood" of adult slaves fundamentally contradicted their imposing physical presence among whites. These grown "children," male as well as female, were—powerfully contradictorily—both sexually alluring to their masters, and thus potentially also threatening, as well as all too physically able to defend themselves against, or retaliate for, the abuses that these intensely emotional contradictions provoked among whites.[68]

Perhaps the "childlike Negro," an intractable stereotype, stems from what Spillers has called an initial *"theft of the body"* from a "socio-political order" prior to arrival in the New World.[69] With regard to what happened after arrival, a large body of scholarship published from the late 1950s onward has focused on whether adult slaves were able to resist "infantilization" through their relationships with slave masters.[70] We will return to black infantilization in the next chapter.

Pertinent to a reading of *Fledgling* is less the denial of rational adulthood status to fully mature slaves than the "intensely emotional contradictions" that attend notions of human growth. The artificial childhood of blackness—the way race and age are mutually constituted—is a technology of power, used to contain the uncanny, incoherent outcomes of making slaves. And yet, those outcomes, which sometimes appear as a series of contradictions, exceed the rationalizations that were created to contain them. Together, rationalization and the emotions that exceed it shape the psychic life of coercion. *Fledgling* plays with this dynamic by exploring reversals: Shori's adulthood is contradicted by her appearance, which Wright describes as "a lovely, elfin little girl."[71] But it is Shori who binds Wright to her by taking his blood. He tells her, "I can't leave you. I can't even really want to leave you."[72] But I would claim that the fantasy of reversed coercion through intimacy evokes what Sharon Holland calls the erotic life of racism, or the afterlife of making slaves and masters. *Fledgling* taps into what Campbell describes as the experience of masters who were simultaneously aroused by and afraid of this new species of children they have created. We are invited to consider such an emotional contradiction, even if the novel's ostensible investment is in symbiosis.

Like a neo-slave narrative, *Fledgling* signifies what it is to awake in darkness, after a catastrophe. Douglass starts his 1845 *Narrative* with an iteration of what it means to awake in darkness—that temporal rupture that bears ramifications not only on a grand scale but also at the very ordinary level of the quotidian: "I have no accurate knowledge of my age." The vampire, not as a signifier of humanity but as a metaphor of living in proximity to the human, opens imaginative possibility for how and when the past and present make contact and inform each other. Perhaps Shori's amnesia is a red herring. Her embodiment, the sort of peculiar body that it is—child, adult, neither, both—makes Douglass's condition of being in the dark about his own age resonate in the present. As a recent study entitled, "The Essence of Innocence: Consequences of Dehumanizing Black Children" notes, "individuals [. . .] see Black children as more like adults or, more precisely, to see them as older than they are."[73] Black existence is perceived as a non-differentiated expanse of time, with no distinct life stages and no innocence. At the same time, black girlhood and adulthood are squeezed together into a homogenous, artificial life stage of vulnerability. As Monique Morris notes, this "age compression" "stripped Black girls of their childhood freedoms and [. . .] makes Black girlhood interchangeable with Black womanhood."[74] Since Shori figures "black girlhood" as a historical problem and a site of humanist dispossession, we now turn to a version of the vampire that transforms this racial-gender-age category as the condition from which the redemptive imagination takes flight.

Immortal Girlhood in *The Gilda Stories*

The Gilda Stories begins with the chapter, "Louisiana: 1850," in which a black girl has just escaped her enslavement in Mississippi. She has fatally stabbed a white overseer who attempted to rape her while she hid in an abandoned farmhouse. Gilda, a vampire who runs a brothel, discovers her. Gilda rescues "the Girl"—the only name used for the fugitive slave—and brings her to the brothel, where she lives for the next few years, though remains off limits to the clientele. Gilda's companion Bird, a woman who had been renounced from her Lakota family of origin, becomes the Girl's primary caregiver and educator. Eventually weary of living, Gilda decides to end her preternaturally long life; by this time, the Girl has matured into full adulthood, and Gilda decides that she is ready to take her place. She facilitates the Girl's transformation into a vampire and leaves the Girl to take both her name and place at Bird's side. In the remainder of the novel, the "new" Gilda lives in various communities across chronological time: for instance, "Yerba Buena: 1890," "Rosebud, Missouri: 1921," "Off-Broadway: 1971," and eventually "Land of Enchantment: 2050." What unifies each episode are matters of care: Gilda develops intimate relationships with individuals, finds companionship in queer and feminist communities, maintains an ethics of equitable exchange with humans from whom she feeds, and is bound to Bird psychically and emotionally, since they are physically separated for most of the novel. As a vampire, Gilda's growth is ethical and political if no longer physical and biological.

Both *The Gilda Stories* and *Fledgling* begin with either the condition of being roused from a dreamlike state or being fully awakened. These metaphors of dreaming and waking stand in for a particular philosophy of history.[75] A dialectical relation between past and present is akin to the fleeting remembered moments of dreams, which inform the awakened consciousness of the present in an urgently political way. By the time we encounter the Girl in an 1850 Louisiana farmhouse, she has already "surrendered to this demanding sleep hemmed by fear."[76] Yet, she is neither fully dreaming nor fully awake. Instead, she perceives something as if it has not yet occurred—something fearful—which, simultaneously, has already occurred, and in the current moment, is occurring. The Girl is in the farmhouse, and there is a sound:

> In the dream it remained what it was: danger. A white man wearing the clothes of an overseer. In the dream the Girl clutched tightly at her mother's large black hand. [. . .] In sleep she clutched the hand of her mother, which turned into the warm, wooden handle of the knife she had stolen when she ran away the day before.[77]

The Girl uses the stolen knife to stab the overseer in "real time" but, just as present as the knife is the hand of a now-absent mother. The hand and handle, along with her mother's "urgent voice"—"Get up, gal, time now, get up!"—all shape this particular moment of crisis that compels the Girl to save herself.[78]

I focus on the novel's opening representations of "girlhood" because the category is a crucial lens through which to read the entire novel and its concern with a historical problem about the human. This particular memory of the Girl's mother and the various ways in which she provided parental care to her daughter is a significant analog to "the Girl" as a glaringly anonymous placeholder for social status. Together, the conjured existence of maternal care and the allusion to childhood suggest that the crisis of the encroaching overseer is simultaneously a crisis of what Wilma King calls the "stolen childhood" of the enslaved. As King notes, "Social customs rather than age alone determined whether one called bond servants 'boy' or 'girl'" during the nineteenth century.[79] The novel calls the fugitive bondservant "the Girl" as a way of marking a splitting of meanings from which chronological age is the point of departure. For the overseer, a proxy for the force of slavery, "girlhood" is a life stage circumscribed by protections of law and custom, and therefore inapplicable to black bodies. To him, "the girl was young, probably a virgin he thought, and she didn't appear able to resist him."[80] This is to say that black bodies can be young, virginal, or impossibly old, and still fall within the realm of girlhood, which is largely a categorical term for particular modes of labor or forms of availability attributable to female bodies.

Just as Heth appeared to be of an infinite age, black girlhood can also take on a supernatural quality, since it can be "young" and "virginal" though not synonymous with childhood as defined by law and custom. In the absence of legal and social protection, "girl" and its concomitant social meanings circulate in the Girl's reveries: "I'ma put these biscuits out, *girl*," says her mother; "The *Girl* ran to the stove" in response.[81] When her mother says "girl," she means it as a form of black familiarity, as a colloquialism for addressing other females irrespective of age. Conversely, through the reveries of a mother who performs all manners of supervision within the limiting confines of bondage—she holds her daughter's hand, combs her hair, imparts wisdom for serving and surviving the masters—the Girl experiences herself as a child, in relation to a protective adult. This understanding of childhood is predicated on recognition of the human, which modern processes of racialization posit in hierarchical terms. This reference is a part of a broader transformation illustrated in the text: "girl" moves from a taxonomic marker of non-humanity, to a colloquialism for black female familiarity, to "Girl," a proper name for a subject. What facilitates the transformation of meaning is a substitution of the liberal apparatus of law for a cultural function of care, and maternal care especially. In the remainder of the novel, a cultural ethics of care endows the vampire with humanity, rather than liberal legalism or categories of the human, including age.

As vampire fiction, *The Gilda Stories* blasts open a historical-political problem of who gets to age along a human lifespan. It is through the heavy underscoring of "Girl"—a subject who is somehow not a girl by law and custom—that we arrive at the problem anew. Gomez's novel imagines "girlhood" as the starting point for broaching the question of the human as the precondition for personhood, which places it in conversation with feminist concerns of the antebellum era. As Corinne Field argues, black and white feminists understood chronological age as a political instrument, and therefore as a conduit to liberal personhood. Although the overarching focus was on women's attainment of adulthood status, Harriet Jacobs provides a famous example of what stolen girlhood entailed for the enslaved: "Soon she will learn to tremble when she hears her master's footfall. She will be compelled to realize that she is no longer a child."[82] Field suggests that "Jacobs invoked chronological age, not because white women underwent a clear transition to adult independence based on age but because describing the extreme youth of enslaved girls subject to sexual abuse was a means of arousing the sympathy of northern readers accustomed to viewing girlhood as a stage of life characterized by sexual purity."[83] Jacobs appeals for black females to have a girlhood that is socially, if not legally, intelligible. Although Jacobs and the white, bourgeois women who were her readers may have converged around the political efficacy of chronological age, they would have likely done so for opposite reasons: Although white women struggled for legal adulthood, black women had never been accorded an inalienable girlhood "as a stage of life" characterized by sexual virtue, legal and social protection. In this way, chronological age is a point from which racialized female temporalities diverge.

By taking such a divergence seriously, we can begin to consider this departure in terms that do not reify the ontologies of Man, with one temporality advancing into a future while the other remains always present and non-developmental. "Adulthood" and "girlhood," in this case, are not proxies for orientations within Western historical politics of development. Rather, such a divergence might be thought of in terms of the way women activists either uncritically embraced or sharply critiqued the terms of liberal personhood. In this way, adulthood signals investment in and inquiry of the privileges of personhood. Alternatively, girlhood signals another set of interests, which include the problems and preconditions of what constitutes gender/age. Thus, by focusing on the "sexual purity" of girlhood, Jacobs opens a space for inquiry of its connotations and preconditions, which include a differentiation of gender and lifespans of which "blackness" has been dispossessed. Gender and lifespans lead to sexual virtue, which leads to the possibility of consent. Hartman puts it this way: "If [. . .] virtue designates a racial entitlement not accorded to the enslaved, then consent is nullified not only on the grounds of one's civil status but also on the basis of presumed sexual predilections, which in the case of slave women come to be defined by default."[84] Consent, then, ironically marks the outcome of a series of social preemptions mapped out over racial time. Or stated another way, "consent" signifies a historical trajectory of negation or dispossession. It is this negative version of consent that forecloses *Fledgling*'s cursory treatment around the way Shori's mother contributes DNA.

In Gomez's and Butler's novels, vampiric ethics highlight the problem of consent with all of its irony. This is the case even as *The Gilda Stories* substitutes an emphasis on consent for one on exchange. As the first Gilda explains: "We draw life into ourselves, yet we give life as well. We give what's needed—energy, dreams, ideas. It's a fair exchange in a world full of cheaters."[85] What is left unspoken is the absence of consent: A vampire decides from which person it will feed, determines which thoughts are "needed" from what it discerns about a person's psychic life, and then instills those in an exchange. It is sensible to read this non-consensual dynamic as Miriam Jones does—as an "oversight" in the novel's overall vision of equally beneficial social life.[86] However, I argue that the omission is constitutive of the dispossession that black femaleness signifies, and that the novel takes as its speculative starting point.

Key elements of the novel's establishing scene in 1850—the nearly accomplished rape, Girl's lack of humanness, personhood, girlhood, and thus protection—are reframed through the new Gilda's supernatural ability. However, having enhanced abilities is not the same as obtaining liberal personhood and protection. Rather, the ability to facilitate exchange has the textual effect of continuously underscoring the negation and dispossession that "consent" marks. In other words, the absence of consent and "the law's negation of the captive will" continue to emerge as an ongoing problem of freedom in subsequent decades and centuries.[87] In this way, freedom is incomplete, despite the novel's surface positivism around fairness and mutuality. Throughout the novel, Gilda registers this incompleteness: in one instance, she solemnly affirms the universality of "our shared life, our shared humanity."[88] In another she explains that "The past does not lie down and decay like a dead animal . . . It waits for you to find it again and again."[89] There is no ideal social contract between equivalent, possessive individuals that withstands this recursive quality.

Recursiveness is what immortality comes to mean in *The Gilda Stories*: It is what waits to be found again and again at the site of a black female body that is simultaneously young and old, and neither of these. The Girl's transition into adulthood coincides with her induction into a vampiric life. The implicit realization of black girlhood's impossibility breaks into the monstrosity of self-creation outside of the social order, which can never be entirely addressed through the normative subject positions "woman" or "adult." Immortality signifies a reworking of stasis, which is the temporal condition of what Spillers calls "ethnicity," and the version of history Heth's black, decrepit skin carried.

The Gilda Stories redirects the uncanny dynamic of aging in Heth's performance. As Reiss writes, "in a white bourgeois culture that emphasized manliness and virility, it placed a decrepit female black body on center stage; it was not often, after all, that a slave woman was asked questions about sacred national history in public."[90] Presumably, Heth would not have been granted the opportunity to discuss "sacred national history" had she not been seen as a spectacular, physical vessel that contained such history. She was placed on center stage as an object that dispensed a history belonging to national citizens. Alternatively, Gilda is a former slave who also becomes living national history, without the indignity on display. Indeed, the secrecy of the vampire is a response to the exhibition of the black body. By the end of the novel, vampires like Gilda are routinely hunted, which is the risk of being public. While Heth's decrepit female black body starkly contrasts with the purity and innocence of baby Washington, Gilda is forever young. More pertinently, her youth/age is not situated in relation to the normative age or temporality of other lives.

Although the novel ostensibly organizes historical time in a linear progression that extends from a past into a future we should have some investment in, the present time and place of each chapter is recursively yoked to the past: At various moments in the present, Gilda is reminded of the dead and almost forgotten. Her enslaved mother's face and hands, a Fulani heritage with origins that extend before Gilda's birth, return to her decades and centuries later.

The vampire taps into the cultural commonsense about the opaqueness of black age in order to re-articulate the way we view the past. Gilda does not float through homogeneous empty time as someone who will remain young forever. Rather, the fragmented past—an enslaved mother's hands, and before that, Fulani and Lakota lives—continually reemerges, shapes the present, and anticipates a future.

The Relic

We have just considered the stories of "two girls" who, like contemporary echoes of Hartman's "Venuses," manifest untellable histories. As vampires, Shori and Gilda embody living history: Untimely, and through immortality, they place inert aspects of the past in a dynamic relation to the present. They also raise the question of consent, which is at the heart of the problem of writing (liberating) historiography. The dead cannot consent either to the violence of slavery's archive or to our romantic attempts to resurrect them and make them whole. In "Venus in Two Acts," Hartman wants to defy the violence of the transatlantic archive in order "to tell a story about *two girls* capable of retrieving what remains dormant—the purchase or claim of their lives on the present—without committing further violence in my own act of narration."[91] This task requires a new historiographical method that destabilizes the status of archival evidence, and uses creative elements of narration to enliven what remains dormant in "a ship's ledger [. . .] or in an overseer's journal," or "in a traveler's account of the prostitutes of Barbados."[92] As the impetus for new inquiries about how to write historiography against the grain of the archive's violence, Hartman's "two girls" themselves have an archival function: Neither one of them "vanish[ed] into the heap of obscure lives scattered along the ocean's floor"; both are "immortalized," one in a speech related to her death in 1792, and the other in Hartman's own experiments with restorative narration.[93] Thus, both continue to "live" as evidence of a story that cannot be told.

Perhaps this is why, in a speculative flight of fancy, Hartman evokes the relic. "Picture them: The relics of two girls, one cradling the other, plundered innocents."[94] On the slave ship, the *Recovery*, not only did "two girls" die in an actual sense. "Girlhood" had been removed from their existence. With the sparse evidence of their lives in the archive, the two "girls" are immortalized as "relics," the embodied remains of what no longer exists, and yet what brings us in closer proximity to what is now absent. Picture them: two captives, ungendered and untimely, who have an archival function as relics, which is to generate new inquiries about what happened on the *Recovery*. Their archival function is endlessly generative; it constantly reproduces the absence, inadequately filled with new ways of telling an untellable story.

As Barnum's "ancient relic" illustrated, black bodies can be recruited in the service of being any age. Yet, as the vampire shows, black subjects bear the fleshy potential of invention and redemption that arises from embodying non-normative temporalities. The vampire, a reanimated corpse, is figurative of how this abuse and repossession of age are schematic of our encounter with the historical record of slavery: The vampire figures how impossibility and actuality, fact and fiction, constitutes the flesh-and-blood aspect of a past from which we are estranged, and yet, paradoxically, of which we are caught in the afterlife. In the interstice of living and death—in the reawakening that the vampire manifests—is where a redemptive relation between the past and present resides. The vampire is the flesh-and-blood manifestation of "history," and as such, in the interstice between life and death, is the reanimated reminder of what it means for black people to have "any other age" inscribed in the flesh.

The relic, like the vampire, also exists in the interstice between life and death. A secular definition of the relic that emerges in the modern era, according to the *Oxford English Dictionary*, is "Something kept as a remembrance, souvenir, or memorial; a historical object relating to a particular person, place, or thing; a memento." This is applicable to the exhibition of Joice Heth, as is Alisa LaGamma's definition, which refers to the practices of various global traditions: "Relics intimately identified with revered individuals have been preserved so that they remain a concrete presence following these individuals' passage into the afterlife. [. . .] exceptional individuals have been honored and invoked to intercede on behalf of the living through such vestiges of their being."[95] As a presence that mediates between the "exceptional individual" who has died and those who currently live, the relic itself is ambiguously inert and alive. Its inertness appears to concretize that which would otherwise appear as ephemeral, contingent, or contested, which includes how significance is attributed to events of the past.

"History," the official record comprised of the lives of "exceptional individuals"—Founding Fathers, rather than female captives—is magically delivered to the living through a passive mediator, so that "history" may intervene on behalf of the living. As a mediating presence, the relic is both a concrete go-between and that which produces the illusion that the dead and the living are making an immediate connection. Thus, the relic offers an occasion for a broader consideration about historical mediation. In so doing, it determines how the conditions of "mediation" and "immediacy" demand that the living constantly negotiates with the relic itself. Under the pressure of such negotiations, the concretized connection between the relic and past begins to crack.

The relic prompts an encounter with the aged black female body in order to ask how such embodiment mediates between the past and the present, and additionally, between historical veracity and speculation. McMillan discusses how both registers of mediation occur at the site of Heth's performance as an object, a conveyor of national history. Her body was presumed to manifest the "facts" of racial difference; as McMillan puts it, the exhibition "granted adult white spectators permission to become pseudo-scientists. [. . .] Heth's deteriorating body was made available to witnesses for examination of discernable clues of her extreme old age."[96] However, what these spectators were actually seeing was a projection of their own cultural construction of the mammy figure. Thus, Heth's avatar—her performative persona of an object—obscured visual access to the "facts" of blackness, and instead made visible a living piece of fiction.[97] I want to emphasize that the prior invention of flesh was the condition of possibility for this entanglement between truthful "scientific" time—the racialization of biological evolution and development—and white cultural fictions. In other words, age itself represents a combination of fact and fiction, which is malleable enough to appear to be as ancient as Heth or as youthful as Shori. This combination, which prompts a dynamic relation between dispossession and reclamation, is precisely what Oceanic lifespans names.

Conjecturally, encounters with Heth's Oceanic lifespan complicated the way her body provided white spectators with immediate access to a valued, bygone past. While "mammy memory" partly informed what spectators did (not) see when gazing at her decrepit body, Heth's body also had the unintended effect of detracting from a direct experience with young George Washington and his milieu. The human relic, like the vampire, is monstrous. If "artificial girlhood" evokes the manner in which blackness was constituted as a category of fearful-yet-sexually-alluring, adult-like children, then "artificial immortality" evokes the equally atrocious way white dependency on blackness preternaturally keeps the dead alive among the living. Heth did not embody another figure of the ocean, the zombie, which returns from the dead in order to fulfill its own demands.[98] Rather, as a relic, the ancient black woman is denied the capacity to die. Instead, she must constantly work at preserving and conveying sacred aspects of national history. She cannot die because the need for her productivity has no end.

On some level, Barnum must have been aware that Heth's body could have been a historical problem rather than evidence of scientific fact. Such an inkling arises in his autobiography, when he ostensibly addresses claims that the exhibit was a hoax. He overemphasizes the way Heth provided immediate access to history. He describes a moment in which she demonstrates her precise knowledge of olden hymns, and then asks, "If Joice Heth was an impostor, *who* taught her these things? and how happened it that she was so familiar, not only with ancient psalmody, but also with the minute details of the Washington family? To all this, I unhesitatingly answer, *I do not know*."[99] Ironically, her ostensible realness is where the monstrosity lies; audiences may have enjoyed this seemingly direct access to lost information, but they did so with ambivalence. According to Reiss,

> No single view of Heth ever held in this exhibit. Instead, as she traversed the spaces of premodern and modern culture, half-alive and half-dead, shaking hands and being stared at, telling a story of freedom that excluded her, she elicited an unsettling mixture of disgust and envy, degradation and exaltation, objectification and wonder.[100]

Thus, artificial immortality entails an unsettling contradiction: While preternatural black female agedness has been constituted against normative schemas of verifiable, national time—such embodiment signifies exclusion from history—contradictorily, the ancient black female delivers to a white audience seamless contact with history. If, for the white viewing public, close encounter with Joice Heth prompted the unsettling awareness that one was experiencing a jarring rift between human and inhuman timelines, then artificial immortality casts in high relief the strikingly divergent logic between inhuman embodiment and national history. Yet, the function of the relic is to conceal the fiction of history: Her old age is needed to make the fiction real.

The status of the relic relies on the real. The relic is revered for its realness, as the enchanted remains of the bygone. The relic turns our attention from speculative fiction to genres that trade in historical veracity, such as oral history and autobiography. Recall the 1993 best-selling oral history, *Having Our Say: The Delany Sisters' First One Hundred Years*, chronicling the lives of Sarah and Elizabeth Delany, who were 101 and 103 years old at the time of publication, respectively.[101] As journalist and editor Amy Hill Hearth notes in the preface, "Their story, as the Delany sisters like to say, is not meant as 'black' or 'women's' history, but American history. It belongs to all of us."[102] But Mary Helen Washington calls our attention to the vexed circumstances that transform the personal stories of two individual black women into "our" property. Of *Having Our Say*, and Hearth's contribution as the person who interviewed the Delany sisters, she writes, "The racial difference between subjects and interviewer is never mentioned in this book, yet the entire history of black storytelling in this country, from nineteenth-century slave narrative to the 1930 WPA interviews of ex-slaves, has been dominated by the issue of the white presence and white reception of the black person's story."[103] In other words, *Having Our Say* is illustrative of how black storytelling is a site of negotiation between the black achievement of self-possession, which is a precondition of the personal narrative, and ongoing dispossession, as "the white presence and white reception" suggests.

The relic evokes the fraught territory that exists between self-possession as a sign of achieved humanity, and the intractable objectification entailed in making (former) non-humans speak. In other words, the relic is an embodied mediator between the nominal liberation of the present and the ever-enlivened subjection of the past. Aged black femaleness constitutes this mediating body, and as a result, elderly black women are easily figured as conveyors of public stories. The storytelling function, and the problem of un/freedom it raises, is manifested in the relic's aged female body. If the Delany sisters spoke in the afterlife of Joice Heth, whose story "belonged" to a white national audience, then in the context of black life, black female agedness troubles the relation between being and telling for others. In the context of black national history, to which we now turn, the relic illustrates, rather than obscures, the trouble between historical mediation and the widely desired illusion of making immediate contact with the past. There are political, epistemological stakes to historical mediation, not least of all for the subject who has been constituted as the mediator. In the context of black life, the relic tells us so when she speaks.

A Book Who Spoke: *The Autobiography of Miss Jane Pittman*

Like Butler's *Kindred*, Ernest J. Gaines's 1971 novel, *The Autobiography of Miss Jane Pittman* (hereafter referred to as *Autobiography*), expresses longing for an alternative historiography that somehow delivers an immediate, non-mediated encounter with the past. If Hartman attempts to craft a written narrative that reanimates the dead, and Butler places a contemporary black woman directly into the horror of enslaved life, then Gaines attempts to make his book speak.[104] In the novel's brief "Introduction," we learn that Jane Pittman is approximately 110 years old when she tells her life story to an unnamed "teach[er of] history" in 1962, who records the interview over several months. This prolonged interview occurs after years of Pittman rebuffing the interested teacher, about whom nearly no details are given. He is not to be reckoned with. He is a placeholder for a scholarly, intellectual, and activist community that wants to retrieve lost history without transforming the outcome, and thus he reveals his ambivalence about historiography. When Pittman's caregiver, Mary, asks why he needs Pittman's oral history—"What's wrong with them books you already got?"—the hopeful interlocutor responds, "Miss Jane is not in them."[105] This establishes a reorientation from the veracity and fullness of the written record, to the aged black female subject who manifests such historical veracity and fullness as lived experience, memory, embodiment, and language.

By not disclosing the racial identity of the history teacher, the introduction downplays the potentially problematic aspects of mediated black storytelling that Mary Helen Washington describes. After the first few introductory pages, the teacher, tape recordings, and transcription are nowhere mentioned in the narrative. Instead, the interviews become the condition of possibility for a seemingly unmediated oral history, which expresses Gaines's desire to capture living history. Of Pittman's story, Gaines notes in 1974, "I wish I didn't have to write it; I wish no one had to write it. [. . .] It's too bad that we don't have tapes of those older people talking, so we could listen to this without ever having to read it. That *is* one of my aims—for them, in their folk way, to tell what happened."[106] Unlike Toni Morrison's 1992 novel, *Jazz*, in which the book itself imagines a vital intimacy with the reader whose hands, eyes, and mind enliven an imperfect narration of the past, *Autobiography* imagines older people unfettered by stifling white presence and response. In the brief introduction, the interviewer accounts for a process that includes Pittman's memory lapses, contributions of other elders close to the Louisiana plantation on which Pittman lives, and his own failed attempts to control the narrative.[107] In the outcome, the history teacher, as editor, attempts to deliver a subject—much like Hartman's attempt to retrieve two lost girls on a slave ship—who belongs to a community, and has an intimate relationship with detailed, quotidian aspects of history. Thus, he attempts to capture an "essence" of the past: "What I have tried to do here was not to write everything, but in essence everything that was said. I have tried my best to retain Miss Jane's language."[108] This recombinant essence stretches the generic conventions of "autobiography" toward a reclamation of the relic. In the end, the history teacher thanks all the elders who contributed to Pittman's story: "This is not only Miss Jane's autobiography, it is theirs as well. [. . .] Miss Jane's story is all of their stories, and their stories are Miss Jane's."[109] Pittman's voice is the narrative, which not only contains collective historical experience, but also, in its "folk way," caresses the listening ear, fills our current-day imagination with an immediate, aural presence. Jane Pittman, not historiography, conveys such desired historical immediacy.

Setting his novel entirely in Louisiana, Gaines maps a historical period that begins when Union soldiers ride through the plantation of Pittman's youth in 1862 and ends with the onset of the twentieth century's civil rights era in 1962. The novel is divided into four books, with the first two—"The War Years" and "Reconstruction"—representing the end of the nineteenth century, and the latter two—"The Plantation" and "The Quarters"—accounting for the first half of the twentieth century. If the first two sections implicitly illustrate how black femaleness becomes a relic, the latter two build toward a political model of the singular, black masculine leader.

At the start of the narrative, we encounter Jane Pittman when she is an enslaved girl of approximately ten years old, and her name is "Ticey." The Confederate army has ridden into the plantation yard. Ticey hands a gourd full of water to each of the soldiers, but, as the old woman recounts, "they didn't even see little old black me. They couldn't tell if I was white or black, a boy or a girl. They didn't even care what I was."[110] While this unseeing is attributed to the soldiers' extreme fatigue, it also marks a mode of protection for Ticey: to be the walking embodiment of negated social signification is to avoid the unwanted notice of the slave "girl," who is dispossessed of childhood. Such a start to the narrative presents Ticey as an ungendered, untimely precondition for Jane Pittman, the ancient black female who carries black history: Ungendered and untimely, her body is vacated of social meaning, and available for witnessing, for carrying memory.

When "girlhood" arises as a category for Ticey to consider, it is as an elusive ideal that is conflated with freedom itself. After the Confederate soldiers depart, the Union soldiers arrive. One of the soldiers, Corporal Brown, has a conversation with Ticey, during which he bestows upon her the gift of girlhood: "I'm go'n call you something else 'sides Ticey. Ticey is a slave name, and I don't like slavery. I'm go'n call you Jane [...]. That's my girl's name back there in Ohio. You like for me to call you that?"[111] This, being "the prettiest name [Jane] had ever heard,"[112] becomes a talisman that provides her with something akin to freedom, which is normative femininity, and along with it, the presumed protection of white "manhood," the only normative adulthood there is. She claims "Jane" along with the corporal's last name. When her mistress berates her for not responding when called, armed with a feminine signifier, Jane is defiant: "I raised my head high and looked her straight in the face and said: 'You called me Ticey, My name ain't no Ticey no more, it's Miss Jane Brown. And Mr. Brown say catch him and tell him if you don't like it.'"[113] "Mr. Brown" is figurative of long-denied, normative inclusion into a patriarchal social order, which includes national citizenship and familial belonging. Named after his "girl"—who could be either his daughter or his lover—Jane attempts to walk from Louisiana to Ohio in search of him during the following year, after emancipation. When patrollers murder the group of ex-slaves with whom Jane traveled, she takes guardianship of Ned, the only other survivor and a boy of approximately four or five years. With Jane in charge, the two children walk through fields and swamps, encountering vaguely benevolent, bemused, or harmlessly hostile adults along the way who warn that their goal of reaching Ohio—with its promise to fulfill "girlhood," protection, full personhood, freedom—is ill-fated. As children, they are metaphors of black national freedom in its infancy: They walk in circles, free to fend for themselves without preparation or resources, free to imagine another world while remaining stuck in Louisiana.

Jane's post-emancipation childhood is clearly laden with adult-like responsibility. If Frederick Douglass's first narrative offered one iconic transition—"You have seen how a man was made a slave; you shall see how a slave was made a man"[114]—then the opening of *Autobiography* allows us to see how a "girl" is made a relic. Despite her pursuit of girlhood, Jane is most saliently a substitute for Ned's adult mother. On more than one occasion, adults assume that she is Ned's mother, to which she responds with evidence somehow not discerned: "I can't be his mama because I ain't no more than 'leven or twelve."[115] Nonetheless, this impossible maternity allows for a divergence of developmental timelines between Jane and Ned. Jane's pursuit of girlhood and normative childhood comes to an end when she and Ned settle down on a Louisiana plantation, so that Jane can earn a living. Objecting to the fact that women laboring in the fields earn more than she is offered, the 11- or 12-year-old Jane declares, "I'm a woman."[116] Tacitly, this relinquishing of a girlhood that was never fully granted allows Ned to survive and progressively develop into his manhood. He refers to Jane as "Mama." Jane's role is to preserve Ned's life, which is destined to ignite the embers of liberation at the turn of the century, and then to preserve Ned's legacy in her narrative. Ned's eventual status as a race man, which is portended by the flint and iron he carries as a small child, is fully expressed when he returns to the plantation after soldiering in the Spanish-American War. Taking the last name of "Douglass," after the era's still-prominent race leader, and wearing "his uniform everywhere he went,"[117] Ned attempts to establish a school, which leads to his assassination. Ned's life and death are paradigmatic of the way Jane Pittman is situated in relation to the men whose lives bear historical significance. In the case of Joe Pittman, Jane's erstwhile husband, she survives so that his name lives on, too.

As Butler realized while failing to write a black man into the past, black women are more likely to survive. This speculative capacity of black femaleness is the bedrock of the relic's figurative existence. If "Ticey" was emptied of signification at the beginning of the narrative, this "zero-degree of signification" reemerges in the figure of infertility. As we learn, "Slavery has made [her] barren."[118] Jane Pittman, like Joice Heth, is capable of maternal surrogacy, since each is an invented persona that generates living history. Joe Pittman dies while attempting to break a wild horse, but conjecturally, the death is partially due to Jane's inability to bear his children, and more generally, his need to "prove he is a man."[119] Just as Jane foresees Ned's death in a dream, so too does she foresee her husband's death, which is not unlike the way Butler foresaw the death of her would-be male main character in *Kindred*. Ungendered and untimely, the relic relies on the foreseeable development and death of black males who struggle to be recognized as "men," and is thus tasked with revitalizing the dead.

In the remainder of *Autobiography*, after Joe Pittman's death, the narrative pans out from Jane Pittman's particular attachments to the milieu of Louisiana from the 1920s to the 1940s, captured through the lens of Pittman's plantation life. Thus, we have accounts of segregation and its discontents, ill-fated interracial love, enduring reverence for slain Louisiana governor Huey Long. The narrative's turn toward the life and times of the "people" leads to the final section of the novel, which returns to its focus on a singular race man. In terms of the narrative sequencing and by outright assertion, the "people" precede their leader. Unlike the first iteration of black masculine leadership that Ned represents, the narrative becomes self-reflective in its treatment of the relic's relation to who is construed as "the One." This marks one key divergence between two manifestations of the relic, Jane Pittman and Joice Heth. Heth's exhibition depended on the unimpeachable fact of George Washington's historical significance; her role was as an ancient, inhuman conduit for uncontested history to reach the masses. In contrast, the final section of *Autobiography* reverses the flow of influence, so that the people determine who will count as the exception. As Pittman narrates, "Anytime a child is born, the old people look in his face and ask him if he's the One. No, they don't say it out loud like I'm saying it to you now. Maybe they don't say it at all; maybe they just feel it—but feel it they do."[120] This silent inquiry, this collective discernment, not only destabilizes the hierarchy between the exceptional One and the insignificant many. It also undermines the object utility of the relic.

Jimmy is the One born in the plantation quarters during the 1940s, and who comes of age by the early 1960s. It is not a coincidence that the conditions of black masculine political leadership, the lives of the southern folk, and the "ancient witness to history" are situated in problematic relation to each other during the civil rights era, when, as Roderick Ferguson argues, young, black radical nationalists began to discipline the seemingly misguided black folk, which includes the elderly.[121] I return to Ferguson's argument in the next chapter. At the end of a 100-year timespan, mid-twentieth century civil rights activism is contextualized as part of a long continuum of collective struggle simply to live livable lives. Thus, the One is a public manifestation of collective desire to ease the difficulty of quotidian experience, rather than as an autonomous figure who ranks above the collective. This is how Jackie Robinson and Joe Louis are examples of the One: "When times get really hard, really tough, He always send you somebody. In the Depression it was tough on everybody, but twice as hard on the colored, and he sent us Joe. [...] Now, after the war He sent us Jackie."[122] This undercutting of the rank and autonomy of the One pertains to both the paradigmatic race leader and to the 108- or 109-year-old relic, who also bears a figurative relation to exceptionalism and autonomy. Like

Ned decades earlier, Jimmy returns to the place from whence he came, having gone to live in New Orleans and become involved in civil rights activism. He attempts to organize the community in the quarters, who reared him while deciding that he would be the One. Thus, his attempts to rally the older folks to participate in a political action—to go down to the town courthouse after a black female teenager voluntarily drinks from a "whites only" water fountain and, subsequently, is arrested. Jimmy and another activist attempt to persuade Miss Jane to join the action.

What follows is the sound of the relic who speaks on her own behalf, and on behalf of the collective rather than for the collective, having relinquished the task of carrying significant agents of history through time for the public record. In other words, the novel ultimately rejects a dominant schema of historiography, which is comprised of the actions of notable men, by illustrating the contested meaning of the moment in which both the young and the elderly, males and females, find themselves. Unlike Ned, who returns as a heroic manifestation of manhood achieved, physically larger in his soldier's uniform with a family of his own, Jimmy is represented as a young person to whom the elders of the quarters still have claim. And he, representative of the presently politicized generation, has claim to the old, since "we have no other roots."[123] Thus, the function of the relic breaks down: It does not generate proximity to "roots" without requesting something in return. The previous 100 years that the novel depicts as both "Miss Jane's story" and that of black Louisianan life generally fills the present moment and prevents any single person from occupying the center of it.

As the familiar male subject of civil rights activism, Jimmy accounts for a progressive temporality often associated with the 1960s, in which Louisiana is belated: "He had been to Alabama and Mi'sippi; he has even been to Georgia. He had met Reverend King, he has gone to his house, had gone to his church, he had even gone to jail with him. Reverend King and the Freedom Riders was winning the battle in Alabama and Mi'sippi, but us here in Luzana hadn't even started the fight."[124] "Luzana," which is both historically accounted for in Pittman's narrative and figured in her ancient persona, is behind the times. The young people are on the vanguard of national change, winning battles, while Pittman and her ilk are rooted in the past and manifest the past.

Yet, the past is here to challenge the nationalist common sense of progressive transcendence. This is what "age" means: It figures the epistemic ground for contested ways of narrating "history." This is why the strawman of this episode—a friend of Jimmy's, a fellow activist—misconstrues the elderly of the quarters as the folksy transferors of cultural realness, and Jane Pittman in particular as the relic. In an attempt to be real, this unnamed figure wears overalls and "steel-rim eye glasses like the old people wear."[125] Yet, his usurpation of the old people's lives, which includes their agedness, has limits. Only the relic can generate proximity to sacred "black history," which is a capacity that the new generation of activists hopes to exploit. Like other natural resources of the agrarian south, the relic can be exploited for the sake of leading the folk. As he attempts to persuade Pittman to participate in the planned action, the unnamed activist alludes to the object status of her ancient body: "Your mere presence will bring forth multitudes."[126] But Miss Jane knows better. Joice Heth brought forth multitudes. After she agrees to participate, Jimmy's friend repeats this bit of "retrick"—"Now there will be multitudes"[127]—for which Pittman chastises him. The rhetoric, like relic-hood, recasts a spell of Barnumesque ballyhoo that obscures, rather than reveals, who and what comprises historical time.

This is why, in the end, the plot hinges on a poignant conversation between the relic and the One. In different ways, both have the dangerous potential of being singular, exceptional, and inhuman. Miss Jane knows this. She attempts to communicate with Jimmy. She says,

> I have a scar on my back I got when I was a slave. I'll carry it to my grave. You got people out there with this scar on their brains, and they will carry that scar to their grave. The mark of fear, Jimmy, is not easily removed. Talk with them, Jimmy. Talk and talk and talk. But don't be mad if they don't listen. Some of them won't ever listen. Many won't even hear you.[128]

By attempting to situate Jimmy in the position of the talking relic, Pittman illustrates how the condition of possibility for both the relic and the One is what Spillers calls the hieroglyphics of the flesh. A formative condition of having been ungendered and unaged leaves a mark: It is the scar on Pittman's back, and relatedly, the myriad marks of violence over time, both seen and unseen, that have made fear a constitutive aspect of black life. The hieroglyphics of the flesh, which are "not easily removed" and, by the twentieth century, discernible simply as blackness itself, is a new starting place for debunking the "re-trick" of exceptionalism, and thus, for collective negotiations over various concerns, interests, and investments in the present. In other words, history is negotiated in the space between the elderly black woman and the young black man, bound together by flesh. Talk is where living occurs, where historical time is reinvented. Unlike in the Barnum-Heth exhibit, talk in *Autobiography* is a manifestation of the fullness of the present. Heth was burdened with the responsibility of enchanting inert national history; the civil rights activist uses political platitudes to represent an empty futurity. But to talk and talk and talk is to move toward emerging, unfinished, not-yet-hearable truth. For the speaker and the listener, the truth that hurts, which must be said even as it cannot be heard, is at the heart of being flesh and blood. Black humanity lies in the truth.

* * *

The transatlantic archive makes the truth—the whole truth—impossible to find. Through creatively reconstructed narrative, Hartman attempts to retrieve two dead girls who evoke the conundrum of slavery's historiography: They are immortalized in the historical record because they did not survive, and their immortality underscores their irretrievable humanity. Hartman "want[s] to tell a story about *two girls*" because "girlhood" is a figure of both non-survival and impossibility. It is the empty signifier that discloses nothing. As Hartman writes, "There is not one extant autobiographical narrative of a female captive who survived the Middle Passage,"[129] and this fact loudly resounds in *Fledgling*'s "elfin little girl" who survives by virtue of being lucky, superhuman, and in the end, a "girl" who is not a "girl." It resounds in Gilda, who survives as a "Girl" when that term is removed from the purview of liberal humanism and names an alternative humanity. Shori and the Girl who becomes Gilda illustrate how the problem of where we look for survival—the archive, the autobiography—is connected to what we look for. How do we tell a story about *two girls* when "girlhood" itself is a matter of modern fabulation?

Enter the relic, a fantasy invented for the purpose of telling an untellable story. August Wilson's 2003 play, *Gem of the Ocean*, imagines Aunt

Ester as a living relic in 1904; she carries the history of a time before the New World.[130] As she states, "I got memories go way back. I'm carrying them for a lot of folk. All the old-timey folks. I'm carrying their memories and I'm carrying my own. [. . .] I'm getting old. Going on three hundred years now. That's what Miss Tyler told me. Two hundred eighty-five by my count."[131] This is a logical, dramaturgical extension of Gaines's desire to offer a voice from the past into the present, unmediated by writing. As a staged production, Wilson's written material—the lyricism of his language, the symbolism of his characters—breathes actual breath, and lives, just as we do. When the play premiered in 2003, the relic-like Aunt Ester, born in 1619, was granted an actual, contemporary black female body. As a preternaturally aged black woman in the flesh of a present-day actor, she is both ancient and not so old. Aunt Ester fulfills a longing to return us to the ocean, which marks both an end and a beginning. She transports us to a "city made of bones"; the people who created it "were the people that didn't make it across the water."[132] *Gem of the Ocean* evokes the Oceanic lifespan that held Joice Heth in captivity and transforms it into a means of reclamation. This time, the Oceanic lifespan of black female agedness connects the historical undoing of black humanity during the transatlantic slave trade, and evidentiary fictions that dwell in the flesh, as flesh, bones, blood, and breath. Oceanic lifespans are the way we live those factual fictions that are historical, but somehow not "history."

Both vampires and relics are figurative examples of how black cultural producers imagined the liberating possibilities of living with the impossibility of humanist inclusion, through the concept of lifespans. While Toni Morrison was an editor at Random House during the 1970s, she co-edited an anthology of archival material entitled *The Black Book*.[133] This collection, which contains newspaper clippings, photographs, advertisements, and other eclectic materials spanning from the early nineteenth century into the early twentieth century, documents black existence since the "discovery of America." Bill Cosby wrote its original introduction:

> Suppose a three-hundred-year-old black man had decided, oh, say when he was about ten, to keep a scrapbook—a record of what it was like for himself and his people in the United States. He would keep newspaper

articles that interested him, old family photos, trading cards, advertisements, letters, handbills, dreambooks, and posters—all sorts of stuff. [. . .] And he would end up with a folk journey of Black America: a book just like this one—beautiful, haunting, curious, informative, and human.[134]

Given what we now know about Cosby's previously submerged past, his radical fantasy seems rife with irony. Or perhaps it replicates the duplicity with which he is now associated, which promises "the good life" on the surface, while it suppresses the violence waged against females, some of whom we may never know about. On the surface, perhaps there is no better example of an Oceanic lifespan. Suppose: Instead of delving into transatlantic slavery's only historical archive to face the violent impossibility of granting enslaved Venuses their humanity, we create our own archive. Rather than being buried underneath the inscription of modern historicism, imagine that we produce our own "sacred national history," in which we occupy the center of existence. This 300-year-old man is the proxy for the human, the version of "us" that had been foreclosed since "our" New World arrival. Thus, it reproduces familiar exclusion. This impossibly old man, a product of 1970s-era black nationalism, acts as a political corrective to Joice Heth, an actual historical subject who not only performed excessive age, but did so in a manner that emphasized a particularly gendered form of labor for the nation. We are asked to identify with "him" and the possibilities that his age promises, and thus, we are invited to accept the articulation of race, masculinity, and age as the fulfillment of collective personhood and its precondition, humanity.

But "he" is also a tacit corrective to Morrison herself. Morrison went on to imagine the (im)possibilities of being human through the analytic of age in a number of ways: Her first novel, *The Bluest Eye* (1970), was an early exploration of "the one least likely to withstand such damaging forces because of youth, gender, and race."[135] Her second novel, *Sula* (1973), invented the "deweys," three boys who never age into adulthood throughout the early twentieth century, and then mystically permeate the late 1960s, an era of new political possibility. After the publication of *The Black Book*, there is *Beloved* (1987), in which the titular character is at once an infant and woman, a ghost and an ancestor. Finally, turning back to her first novel, Morrison reimagines the abuses an "ugly" black girl suffers in *God Help the Child* (2015). Now fully grown, with eyes that are "crow-black with a blue tint,"[136] the beautiful black woman metaphysically reverts into the body of a prepubescent child. I discuss this final work of Morrison's in chapter 4.

Such returns—to the first book, to black girlhood, to the problem that resides there—indicate a key distinction between Morrison's figurations of black-gender-age and Cosby's miraculous "three-hundred-year-old black man." Cosby's figure moves forward with and within linear, historical time. We have his scrapbook to prove it. Like the five fingers that come together in the mighty fist of progress, the temporalities of American history and black masculinity are one. Yet, the fact of blackness is inescapable: ungendered and untimely, blackness signifies a denial of normative development that "manhood" requires. If not linear development, then what temporal mode leads to black male adulthood? We will consider this question in the next chapter. But first, we return to the ocean.

3

The Mass and Men

This island requires 1,000 negroes annually to keep up the original stock, which is only 80,000. So that the whole term of a negro's life may be said to be there, but sixteen years!
—Olaudah Equiano, *The Interesting Narrative of the Life of Olaudah Equiano, or Gustavus Vassa, the African*

This chapter begins with an Oceanic passage in Olaudah Equiano's 1789 narrative. His firsthand account of the Middle Passage reveals a key relation between what Hortense Spillers calls the "nowhere" of the ocean, and other spatial dimensions of black life, upon arriving in the Western Hemisphere and afterward.[1] Equiano looks upward:

> The clouds appeared to me to be land, which disappeared as they passed along. This heightened my wonder; and I was now more persuaded than ever that I was in another world, and that every thing [sic] about me was magic. At last we came in sight of the island of Barbadoes [sic], at which the whites on board gave a great shout, and made many signs of joy to us.[2]

The status of land in this passage is rife with oppositions: Clouds signify the magical impossibility of land in the sky, while an actual land mass looms ahead. Cloud-land disappears from Equiano's sight, while an actual island comes into view. While crossing the ocean, impossibility, ephemera, and disappearance on the one hand, and actuality, permanence, and emergence on the other, makes up the oppositional schema that separates how Equiano and the white crew are now related to a political abstraction called "land," and to historical temporality. The white crew's celebration of their land-sighting alludes to an overarching promise and affirmation of what modernity is for them by the eighteenth century—an epoch in which they reshape the globe to fit their new order of things. Their course toward the Caribbean island is analogous to the course of linear, progressive, predestined time. The Equiano boy, excluded from the teleological temporality of the whites aboard the ship, sees a world turned upside down, and thus, the making of a New World, of which he is now a part: For a fleeting moment, the land that hovers above the ocean is ambivalently wondrous and ominous. This is the beginning of impossible possibilities.

Such insight occurs to the Equiano boy with the vulnerability that comes from being unaged at sea.[3] It occurs as "boyhood" is undone and replaced with the calculations of size and value of cargo. In other words, such insight in the narrative occurs when an array of social categories—gender and age, but also homeland and human—are evacuated of prior meanings and replaced with others that determine how blackness becomes constituted as an amorphous, non-individuated "personality." The young Equiano cannot know that Barbados, the land on which he and other Africans are being shipped, had to be "emptied," as Jamaica Kincaid puts it, of its prior history, in order for enslaved black people to work there.[4] He cannot know Caribbean plantations "were 'planted' with people," as Sylvia Wynter puts it.[5] And yet, in the passage above, the clouds that appear to be land carry a weak, messianic power. The enslaved captives on the slave ship, once belonging to various geographical locations, tribes, and affiliations, are conflated into the mass of inhuman labor, to work on exploitable masses of land. Emptied of historical specificity, islands and Africans comprise undifferentiated wholes. The various modes of individuation and specification now collectively constitute the "one" of homogenous multitudes.

Upon arrival in the Caribbean, Equiano soon realizes that his embodiment is categorically undifferentiated from other enslaved subjects: "We were conducted immediately to the merchant's yard, where we were all pent up together like so many sheep in a fold, without regard to sex or age."[6] Perhaps more poignantly, he eventually comes to understand that this New World the Europeans invented requires the co-constitutive transformation of human time, which entails both lifespans and historical temporality, along with the land's natural development, its organic temporality. The New World would bind inhuman humans and cultivated land together. Barbados alone "requires 1,000 negroes annually to keep up the original stock, which is only 80,000. So that the whole term of a negro's life may be said to be there, but sixteen years."[7]

The land—enslavement on it, working of it—artificially determines an African's lifespan. The conflation of the natural and artificial results in modernity's epistemic shift—the rise of the natural sciences and a knowable, natural world on the one hand, the fabrication of inhuman humans and organic manufacturing units, plantations, on the other—is in part what the Oceanic names. Age carries what is chronologically, biologically natural, and what is socially constructed. Through the emptying of prior social and natural ways of being, both land and enslaved labor take on the appearance of constancy. Equiano's description of Barbados's sustainment illustrates this: Slaves can always be replenished from an endless, continental supply, productivity of the land is limitless, and the amassing of wealth is forever. Thus, constancy is the temporality of this chapter's literary figure of age, the mass.

I define the mass as the various forms of aggregation, non-differentiation, and combination that beg the question of how black individuals are entangled with each other in ostensibly in/human ways, and with the un/natural world. It begs the question of how human history is connected to the seemingly inhuman and ahistorical. Equiano's narrative provides a set of preconditions for figuring black life stages and lifespans as the mass: The eighteenth-century British slave trade led to "new modes of value production and life extraction" in the Caribbean that combined the dead, the living, and the land on which they worked.[8] As Equiano laments, "it is no wonder that the decrease should require 20,000 new negroes annually to fill up the vacant places of the dead."[9] The "decrease" of black populations do not disappear, do not get refilled without something that remains and tangles with the living. Scholarly critiques of racial capitalism and western humanism have discussed the manner in which both have alienated humans from forms of life; as Elizabeth DeLoughrey puts it, "Western capitalism turned earth into property and segregated humans from nature and thus nature from history."[10] In addition to attending to the ways in which enslaved people were alienated from the natural aspect of earth and its logical relation to history as something other than property, I am also interested in how the logics of time that comprise conquered land in the New World—as a new epoch of European modernity, as the property of self-possessive individuals, as the source of endless productivity and accumulation—buries other histories. In this chapter, the mass is a literary figure that embodies a particular relation between this buried time, histories that are aggregated in soil, and age as a dense combination of various temporalities.

Not only have African-descended bodies been emptied and refilled with the density of "blackness," tethered to the arable ground, and set in motion for mass production and consumption. From the eighteenth century to the present, this density has been constituted as essentially inert, so that fixity or movement could occur without the will or agency of the black subject. This chapter situates such inertness against the presumed psychic, biological, political, and social development of the liberal individual. More specifically, there is tension between the "mass" and liberal "manhood" that the analytic of age reveals. In the three historiographical domains with which this chapter engages—social historiographies of plantation slavery from the mid- to late-twentieth century, black feminist historical and literary interventions from the 1980s onward, and black radical nationalism of the 1960s and '70s—"gender" has been treated as the primary code for addressing how black subjects bear a relation to manhood. However, I argue that a sole focus on gender obscures what else is operative in the relation between the mass and men. The mass signifies density rather than development, of historical time that culminates in the present, the non-differentiation of subjectivity, and non-linear relations to time and space. The mass undercuts the privileged status of liberal manhood as the only adult, and thus the only receiver of liberalism's promise of freedom. By shifting the focus from "manhood" to "adulthood," this chapter makes a modest attempt at forging a new line of inquiry to explore how black liberation was imagined during the late twentieth century.

As this chapter will discuss, both the hegemonic abuses of age and black reclamation of it occur through engagement with mass-like clusters of children and elders, and share the appearance not of futurity and history, but of the constant and perpetual. Thus, as a figure of constancy, the mass expresses a dense, and liberating, conflation of past, present, and future. This chapter explores both the constancy of age and the unity of the age group in Toni Morrison's 1973 feminist novel, *Sula*, and to a briefer degree, Ernest Gaines's 1983 southern pastoral novel, *A Gathering of Old Men*. Both novels exemplify the way black subjects refuse the commonsensical linkage between the normatively developmental, gendered logic of "manhood" and national liberation. Bracketing the long 1970s, an era in which black male adulthood was saliently linked to national inclusion and individual autonomy in culture and politics, *Sula* and *A Gathering of Old Men* offer an alternative account of the era by rejecting "manhood" as a social and political telos, along with the liberal logic from whence the category's privileged relation to liberation arises. In so doing, both novels depict black boyhood and black male elderliness, two life stages that either precede or follow the only socially and politically viable version of adulthood that "manhood" names, in order to eschew liberal, possessive individualism, and temporal progression. As masses of maleness that have taken on the look of constancy under the racist, untimely term "boy," the male children and old men of this chapter harness the density of time and the non-developmental logics of constancy in order to illustrate counter-nationalist relations to historical temporality and historiography.

Sula begins with an origin story of the inauspicious founding of the black part of town colloquially known as the Bottom: A benevolent white farmer commits to giving his slave freedom and land. As a ruse designed to avoid giving up good land, the farmer convinces the former slave that hilltop land is better than the rich and fertile valley. Because of its quality and its high location, the seemingly magnanimous master refers to it as "the bottom of heaven." Heaven and earth: Consider Equiano's whimsical cloud observation at a moment of danger. The land turns out to be rocky, barren, and backbreaking, and the Bottom's inception marks an end to subjection that did not quite happen; it thus refers to the "nonevent" that was emancipation.[11] The story of how the Bottom came into existence frames the problem of emancipation as one of establishing a new, liberal relation between land and (former) hand: How can "blackness" be assimilated into the logic of liberal personhood, which would allow black subjects to be owners of land, while blackness continues to be synonymous with or derived from land owned?[12] Not only are both the hilly, rocky land and the former slave expendable surplus; both are linked together by the contingency of their utility and expendability. Thus, the problem is the impasse between the historical making of the mass—inscribing a temporality of homogenous constancy onto black bodies—and the post-emancipation conceit of making black, individuated "men."

The origin story of the Bottom is a provocation that implicitly begs the question of how to situate black subjectivity within a temporal frame other than that of progressive liberalism. As a speculative counterpoint to stymied progressivism, *Sula* makes explicit the way that age is the primary metaphor for political and social development by giving us the novel's most baffling aspect, the "deweys." The deweys, who the iconoclastic matriarch, Eva Peace, takes in during 1921, are three boys of differing ages and appearance that mysteriously become non-differentiated, everlasting children. The location of the Bottom opens the novel's overarching question: How does the incomplete transition to freedom feel during the early decades of the twentieth century? The deweys refuse "manhood"—gendered adulthood—as the only route toward freedom's completion. Unlike Topsy of Harriet Beecher Stowe's 1852 abolitionist novel, *Uncle Tom's Cabin*, who just grew from an inhuman source, and thus, from nothing at all, or the generalized version of the pickaninny who cannot grow, the deweys *refuse* to grow. By refusing, they raise questions about what growth entails and its presumed outcomes. By rejecting growth on an individuated scale, the deweys wage an implicit critique of a linear evolutionary schema, and of a western humanism that arises as the apogee of such. The deweys reveal and reclaim the latent potential hidden within black childhood as a cultural figure of black constancy overall: "Constancy" is transformed into a massive conflation and spiraling of time, which is the condition of possibility for interrupting the fallacious link between "progress" and "freedom," and of being human differently.

A Gathering of Old Men is set on a plantation in rural Louisiana in the 1970s, during a time of transformation for the agricultural industry. Those who worked the land during previous generations are represented as the novel's collective protagonist, a group of older black men in their seventies or eighties. Against the stillness of static racialization that has symbolically connected their black male bodies to the land is the recurring metaphor of the weeds. The weeds are vestiges of what once existed and obscure what continues to be. The old men, as the conveyors of historical memory, demonstrate the manner and means of redeeming that which official forms of national remembrance fail to include, and national history fails to shape. As a demonstration of historical consciousness that exceeds the bounds of official historiography, the old men form a mass that negotiates a reconstitution of the black "man" with the histories of multitudes.[13]

Taken together, both novels evoke life stages that are at polar ends of a linear, normative lifespan—childhood and seniority—in order to reimagine them as the Oceanic lifespan of the mass. The mass represents age—youth and elderliness—through the gendered register of "boyhood" and "manhood" in order to critique the presumptive maturity and masculinity of the proper liberal subject. Excluded from proper social citizenship, boys and old men represent an untimely shadow that accompanies liberalism's linear trajectory: Black maleness conspicuously circulates in culture and through time when it "takes on constancy, the look and affects of the Eternal," as Spillers puts it.[14] It is against such constancy that the white, mature, and masculine subject appears. In the shadow temporality of constancy, black male youth and old age are linked to each other through the historiographical concept of "infantilization," which young "pickaninnies" and old "uncles" equally evoke. In addition to being divergent life stages that are amassed together, each cluster of "boys" and "old men" undercuts the possessive individualism that is implicitly promised to black subjects after civil rights. As masses of youth and old age, the "deweys" in *Sula* and the "old men" of Gaines's novel are speculative wholes, oriented toward alternative futures and reconstructed pasts.

As the many-in-the-one, the deweys and the old men ask how black-male-age is situated in relation to the broad-ranging project of accounting for slavery and its afterlife in the post–civil rights era. That both *Sula* and *A Gathering of Old Men* situate the mass as mediator between historical time and the meaning of black-male-age is part and parcel of a structure of feeling during that time. The status of "manhood" is insufficient for securing the protections of liberal personhood, and the work toward freedom, beyond the promise of personhood, remains unfinished for black people as a collective, across gender and age. Yet, by the onset of the 1980s, the question of how to account for the collective is punctuated with profound unease. Spillers shares her uneasiness this way: "It would seem that certain social capabilities have been dissipated—a certain lightness of being [. . .]. In the wake of loss, we only have left, it seems, the inexorable grimness of 'competition,' of 'getting over,' of 'role-modeling,' of 'success' for the well-credentialed, and a thorough commodification of black culture."[15] In the wake of a lightness of being there occurs a new confrontation with the mass. How do we progress toward the same future as the nation—as Equiano is forced to progress toward the same goal as the white crewmen, their heaven on earth—when the social meaning of "blackness" ties us to the ground? And, viewed from another angle, what is lost when we break from the whole to "get over" one by one? During a decade in which transformations of various kinds were reshaping what was politically and socially possible, the two novels explored here suggest that the mass is a redemptive beginning, rather than a dead and deadening end.

The Mass

The "mass" possesses confluent and divergent meanings, spanning from the early modern era to the present, that pertain to what constitutes the natural and the artificial, inertness and motion, solidity and emptiness.[16] The *Oxford English Dictionary*'s primary definition of the mass, "a body of matter," has an abundant set of related meanings that describe both the natural world and people in a social world. The term's current use as "a dense aggregation of objects having the appearance of a single, continuous body" could describe the afterlife of black subjectivity, or what Hortense Spillers calls the "iconic thickness" that presumably constitutes the shared psychic life of all black subjects, having been ungendered and, as I argue, made untimely.[17] In its early modern iteration, the mass refers to a newly knowable natural world. These meanings encapsulate the epistemic transition from the spiritual to the secular, which is embedded in the sixteenth- and seventeenth-century use, "The created universe; the earth," or, from the seventeenth century, "A coherent body of pliable or malleable material, such as dough, clay, etc." Isaac Newton's seventeenth-century philosophy of the physical world defines "mass" as "the quantity of matter which a body contains, as measured by its acceleration under a given force or by the force exerted on it by a gravitational field; an entity possessing mass." From the nineteenth century onward, the mass is a geological term, referring to "an irregularly shaped deposit or layer of ore, mineral, or rock" (*OED*). In relation to meanings of the mass that come from the rise of the natural sciences in western modernity are those that bear particular weight in twentieth-century social developments: mass migration to the north, mass production and consumption of material objects. The mass also pertains to the interim-war-era circulation of black folk culture as a commodity in mass markets, and to mass action and the revolutionary potential of the masses.[18] Mass simultaneously evokes the subjection and liberating reclamation of black life that are part and parcel of Oceanic lifespans.

Overall, the figure of the mass implies an epistemological context for how the black body is situated in time: Over historical time, the body is amassed with other bodies, which are malleable enough to suit the needs of commerce and culture, even as the amassed physicality seems like a fixed part of the natural world. Like collectible memorabilia that depict undifferentiated pickaninnies, uncles, and mammies in the form of salt and pepper shakers, banks, figurines—or like the young Equiano on a slave ship—the mass requires an external force for its movement. It requires external energy for its propulsion through someone else's sense of time. Once lifted and set in motion, the mass can travel without changing, growing, maturing. In the context of New World slavery, the mass alludes to the afterlife of processes that constituted both land and slave as emptied, homogenous, and undifferentiated entities. Echoed in this literary figure is a temporality of constancy that underscores capitalism's presumed endless expansion and surplus of global resources. Such a temporality of constancy and endlessness is inscribed onto black bodies and expressed as age.

Constancy is captured in the "powerful stillness" that Spillers argues is a formative part of New World blackness. Blackness "takes on constancy, assumes the look and the affects of the Eternal."[19] In other words, blackness has been constituted as a condition that travels through linear, progressive time without moving. As a mass of unchanging sameness, blackness also names a form of forgetting: Forgotten is the effort required to remove millions of people from an originating social context and insert them into someone else's sense of time.[20] The presumed historical belatedness of blackness can find its embodied analogy in youthfulness, elderliness, or in any age at all. Yet, I argue that the instability itself, the condition that black age expresses contingency of what it means to be in time, is itself constant. "Constancy," an element of a New World fantasy, suggests that the social world we currently have has always been and will forever be.

If the clouds that begin this chapter were a flight of fancy, they underscore how fantasy has been an animating force behind other realities, such as the New World itself, and "blackness" as a signifier of subjective non-differentiation. Of this latter instance, Spillers has given us a conceptual key that unlocks a connection between the Middle Passage and various social exclusions that comprise the dehumanization of captive Africans. As I claim throughout this book, black exclusion from normative gender is contemporaneous with exclusion from normative age as a measure of chronological, biological, and psychic development. But what underpins these social exclusions—and others—is the formation of "blackness" as that which cannot contain or communicate subjective individuality or idiosyncrasy, a point Spillers forcefully makes in her 1996 essay.[21]

As she argues therein, conventional psychoanalytic paradigms cannot interpret the psychic life of any singular black person, since blackness is itself "the great Big Empty" that takes the place of psychic particularity,[22] and more pertinently: "What is missing in African-American cultural analysis is a concept of the 'one.'"[23] As a result of this missing concept, upon which the sociopolitical concepts of "property ownership" and self-possession are conceived,[24] we are hard-pressed to access the conditions of black development and maturation with the analytical tools of psychoanalysis. The site of age—the rubric under which development and maturation fall—is where Spillers's subtle critique of Freudian regression, expressed as the "oceanic" in "Mama's Baby," meets with "The individual-in-the-mass and the mass-in-the-individual [. . .] an iconic thickness" that Spillers describes in "All the Things." Regression or non-development—does the difference matter at the site of blackness?—is what the iconic thickness of the mass contains.

A formative process of emptying and non-differentiation during the Middle Passage in "Mama's Baby" leads to the commonsense of New World subjects, including Frantz Fanon, the preeminent critic of western humanism. Spillers illustrates this latter point by addressing the "abnormal" development of the black Antillean child in Fanon's 1952 work, *Black Skin, White Masks*. Fanon claims that, in the Antillean islands, "A normal Negro child, having grown up within a normal family, will become *abnormal* on the *slightest* contact with white world."[25] Spillers wonders how a "normal" black child, who is somehow hermetically sealed within the cradle of unadulterated blackness, develops within the context of colonialism, and why there are no forthcoming explanations as to why "normal" black psychic life—whatever that is—cannot happen in the "white world," of which European colonies were an extension. This problem of development is glossed over in Fanon's account of black adult psychic life, which overemphasizes racialized gendered and sexual relations. Presumably, none of these relations touch the black child of the Antilles.

Just a few years after the publication of *Black Skin, White Masks*, Stanley Elkins's 1959 work on US plantation slavery defines the condition of the enslaved black man precisely as living in a state of constancy, which he terms "infantilization."[26] More specifically, Elkins's most provocative argument was that US plantation slavery was distinguishable from sites of slavery in Latin America in that it produced a particular "slave personality," which he refers to as "Sambo."[27] Rather than being a familiar stereotype that "assumes the look and the affects of the Eternal," Elkins claims that Sambo is the actual, subjective outcome of American plantation slavery's "closed system" of domination and subordination.[28] As a result of the slave's utter dependency on his master, infantilism became his essential characteristic. Thus, the slave is "the perpetual child incapable of maturity."[29] Socially and symbolically, only the white master could be a father: "The very etiquette of plantation life removed even the honorific attributes of fatherhood from the Negro male, who was addressed as 'boy'—until, when the vigorous years of his prime were past, he was allowed to assume the title of 'uncle.'"[30] Thus, from out of the US plantation sprung a "perpetual child" of any age.[31] Under such circumstances, the transition from "boy" to "uncle" signifies a gaping chasm where the life stage of "young manhood" should be, while it simultaneously suggests that "boys" and "uncles" are developmental equals, despite an age-based transition. Recall our discussion in chapter 1, where little Harry performs the equivalence between boys and uncles in *Uncle Tom's Cabin*. Presumably, this contradiction is resolved in the plantation's closed system of power relations.

If, in Spillers's critique of Fanon, there is no way to access the psychic development of the black child or subsequent adult through the opacity of "normal" and "abnormal," then Elkins steps into this emptied-yet-opaque space of unknowing and fills it in with "infantilization." If Fanon suggests that there is a space that is closed off from whiteness in colonized societies, what Spillers refers to as "the parental cocoon" of the black family,[32] then Elkins intensifies this suggestion's underlying logic of racial enclosure by outright assertion and inverts its implication in the process: The closed system of the US plantation leads not to (adult) normalcy, but to a population of infantile grotesques. While Fanon leaves room to ask how, precisely, black communities in the modern Caribbean could have no contact with the white world, when to be colonized is to always already be touched by the hegemony of whiteness, Elkins, having inverted the outcome, offers a strident explanation: "Detachment" from African societies was so thorough, that nothing of those prior social spaces remained.[33] In a word, "detachment" is Elkins's name for an emptying process that eternally consolidates US blackness and links it to the plantation, while it strangely disavows the earlier phases of slavery on which it relies. For instance, since we cannot find Sambo in examples of Latin American slavery, the Middle Passage suddenly has little or no relevance for explaining how social subjects are unmade, "apart from what came later."[34] "What came later" are the descendants of Africans who crossed the Atlantic Ocean, who have been born on North American soil already detached from African social relations and, implicitly, from the broader sphere of global capitalism.

Taken together, Fanon and Elkins implement age as a means to close off both black and white humanisms from the historical developments from whence the concept of the human came. Fanon's attempt to write "blackness" back into the realm of the human by suggesting that the sealed-off cocoon of black life is the precondition of "normal" human development, shares the same epistemic blind spot as Elkins's easy reliance on the western humanist presumption that actual adulthood begins and ends with the white maleness of Man. Both draw from conventional psychoanalytic thought in order to install a normal human adult as a baseline of their historiographies about colonialism and slavery, which is why neither delves into the historicity of age, nor asks how age is operative in the logics of both modern racializing regimes. This is why Spillers's return to the Freudian oceanic feeling in "Mama's Baby" bears such significance: It attempts to reopen the historical closure that various modes of empiricism, from which Freudian psychoanalytic thought draws, produce.[35] And, it attempts to reanimate the stasis of historical time and temporality that such closure implies.[36] The irony is that such openness is precisely what Freud initially found to be so perverse about the oceanic feeling: The "infantile helplessness"[37] he associates with it is part of the feeling "of something limitless, unbounded—as it were, 'oceanic.'"[38] If the oceanic entails connection to an external world, then, by situating this feeling at the Atlantic Ocean, Spillers reveals a *historically constituted* external world, beyond the a priori and structural closures of institutions and families. This historical and epistemic openness is precisely where the redemptive powers of the Oceanic reside.

When Fred Moten states that "black mirror stages and/or primal scenes operate on different registers, at the level of what might be called an extended infantilization despite the fact that there are no children here," we might imagine there are no adults here, either: "Infantilization" is just another term for the mass.[39] The broad purview of black feminist thought from the 1970s onward—ranging from Spillers's poststructuralist interventions, to fiction, to revisionist historiography—circles the blind spot (or the great Big Empty) of age that concentration on normatively gendered black manhood would lead us to miss. When social historians of plantation slavery, writing during the 1960s and '70s, refuted the "Sambo" thesis, they often did so by attempting to redeem the humanity of the enslaved via their manhood.[40] In her major intervention in this field of the 1980s, Deborah Gray White claims that Elkins set the terms of the ensuing discussion by disregarding gender differences, and implicitly ignoring femaleness in particular.[41] If "infantilization" amounted to the denial of manhood and its symbolic proxy, fatherhood, Elkins and his interlocutors implicitly accepted that such an artificial construction of age had no impact on the undoing of female gender. Since female slaves could assume conventionally feminine roles as mothers and caregivers, they seemed to presume that female slaves could ontologically and socially conform to the categorical norms in a manner that their male counterparts could not. Of course, mother-work, including reproduction, and caregiving were just a part of the broader array of labor female slaves were expected to provide. As Jennifer Morgan reveals, "labor" was precisely the conditions of possibility for reinventing what "femaleness" could entail for the enslaved. Normative gender, of any social order, had to have been emptied out for a female-majority labor force in the fields to exist across the Caribbean, particularly in Barbados.[42]

Nonetheless, the blind spot of femaleness was predicated on the presumption that "femaleness" is inherently childlike. As White puts it, "If the stage Elkins set for the debate over slavery was one that reemphasized the femininity of the race, those who did most of the debating were bent on defeminizing black men, sometimes by emphasizing the masculine roles played by slave men, and sometimes by imposing the Victorian model of domesticity and maternity on the pattern of black female slave life."[43] In retrospect, White's feminist intervention in slavery studies reveals that "gender" is precisely the category that can either overshadow the empty opacity of "age," or shed some light on it. "Victorian models of domesticity and maternity" traded in the presumption that women are not quite adults; as White explains, "For centuries, women have been characterized, indeed, rewarded, for being childlike and silly."[44] Yet, as we know, both reproduction and domesticity were evacuated of their ideological relation to feminine gender for enslaved black women, and black female slaves were excluded from the social and customary meanings of femininity. Thus, black female "gender" entails a different logic of age than normative femininity. As I discussed in the previous chapter, the politicization of age during the nineteenth century potentially diverged along the axis of race: While white women struggled to attain the privileges that came with a legal age of adulthood, black women were denied the legal, social, and customary protections of girlhood. While whites of the antebellum South attributed the maternal morality of Victorian womanhood to "mammy," this attribution was predicated on their perception of this subject as elderly, even though enslaved females of various ages nursed and cared for white children.[45] Mammy is a metaphor for hegemonic non-recognition of childlike black femaleness.

Then again, if we notice that "gender" is an analytic that influences whether historians see or do not see "age" as a historical problem, then we might imagine that gender can be used as a means to deliberately avoid seeing. In other words, by strenuously focusing on the infantilization of "men" while remaining silent about the infantilization of enslaved females of any age, historians who took issue with Elkins's claims silently—unknowingly—wished to bestow normative gender onto black women and girls. Just as Fanon wished to grant the black child of the Antilles his humanity by forcefully suturing "blackness" to "normal development," conjecturally, social historians who were invested in redeeming the enslaved from the ideological narratives of the enslavers wished to endow—with silence, and unknowingness—black femaleness with the gift of femininity. Thus, if we peer into the darkness, age appears through the unstated. If the question that no one thinks or cares to ask—how is black femaleness related to the infantile?—remains unspoken, the presumed temporal normalcy of age remains intact. Thus, the Oceanic is a method for seeing in the dark: It allows us to ask how interpreters of the material past register what touches them without being seen. More specifically, the Oceanic is an approach toward analyzing modern blackness by shifting from our primary paradigm of gender to the less familiar one of age.

Still, there is the matter of the mass. The temporal constancy of infantilization is in part what determines canonical femininity: Both girlhood and womanhood are perpetually girlish. Infantilization does not necessarily feminize black "men," since "femininity" is not a category that stably encompasses black subjects of any gender. Rather, the potentially feminizing aspect of infantilization is its static temporality, and not the particular customs, labor, and social roles that have been normatively attributed to canonical femininity. Viewed from this lens, "emphasizing the masculine roles played by slave men" is not enough to rescue them from the massive, static temporality of blackness. Instead, the constancy of infantilization grants black femaleness an illusory place in a social order that attributes different temporalities to gender categories, while simultaneously denying a place to black maleness. Thus, the problem of black males being "men" lies with an intractable contradiction between the progressive temporality of white-male-adult masculinity and the static temporality of ungendered blackness. After emancipation, with the logic of liberalism in the spotlight, this contradiction gave shape to the outlines of a distinctly gendered "black manhood," while emphasizing a massive problem at the center of it.

In other words, the "gender" of manhood simply indicates a version of blackness that had to conform most conspicuously to a socially and politically hegemonic logic of "adulthood," which entailed conformity to national time. While discussing how Reconstruction legislation transformed the law in order to push racial subjection deeply into the folds of equality, Saidiya Hartman points our attention toward the senate debates concerning the equality of "man." All sides of the debate silently conspired to separate a white, standard version of manhood from a derivative and substandard black version of manhood. Such a division, which was essential to maintaining "the constancy of black subjection,"[46] predictably relied on the language of development. She writes:

> Noteworthy is the discursive tenor of these statements—that is, the masculinist and paternalist lens through which the condition of the freed was refracted, with terms like "infantile race" and "mature manhood" framing issues of freedom, equality, and citizenship. Beyond the obvious masculinism of such language and the paternalist articulation of race [. . .] was the danger that inhered in the translation of degradation—the wretched material and social conditions of the freed transposed into an ontology of black difference [. . .] that established the innate inferiority of blacks by reference to the laws and social conditions that situated blacks as inferior.[47]

I want to underscore the connection between how the very question of black social readiness is situated in terms of development, and the (subsequent) danger of transforming the meaning of inferior material conditions into inborn inferiority of blackness. As Hartman characterizes it, the congressional debate did not unvaryingly cover the freed population with the heavy shroud of infantilization. Rather, for some the question was whether black "men" would mature into manhood—if so, then the prospect of their "emergent manhood" was worrisome; for others, the question was whether they could ever outgrow their infantilism at all.[48] This debate about development, which turned on a question of whether black men could mature, was resonant of how Europeans discussed the possibility or potential of "Native" and African self-governance since the Enlightenment and the rise of colonialization. Whereas David Theo Goldberg identifies concomitant developments in these discussions over time, in which a philosophical tradition holding that racialized "others" were always-already prehistorical—and thus, frozen outside of historical time—occurs alongside of a paradigm of racialized historical development that placed an emphasis on the possible emergence of the racial other's maturation, Hartman introduces the possibility for yet another iteration: Implicit questions about black maturity—or, the very uncertainty about it—were transposed onto the ontology of black difference.⁴⁹ In other words, it is the unresolvable uncertainty of maturation, and not any fixed notion about the concept itself, that contributes to what blackness means after the achievement of nominal equality.

This racial "childhood" needed to be invented in order to place colonized subjects into the European order of things; it was an approach to fitting other genres of humans into European schemas of historical time. "Immaturity" is a concept of belated historical time that is nested within the dominant history of western hegemony. This nesting, this imminence of racial maturity, as Goldberg explains, was "more nuanced and easily hidden, harder to pin down and tougher to dismiss" than deeming the racial other as permanently prehistorical in precisely the manner that Hartman describes.⁵⁰ Simply put, artificial maturity was a weaponized concept, much like other knowledge-based weapons in the arsenals of both colonialism and slavery. As such, it could accomplish various things at once. Just as the question of maturity becomes the pivot that allows Reconstruction-era senators to maneuver between rhetorical strategies that perpetuate the myth of black inferiority, it could do something at the level of the body: It could transform adults into children and children into adults; it could render adults and children as interchangeable; it could evacuate the meaning of these categories altogether. Transposed onto race, "immaturity," or the possible arrival at "maturity," were both part of the mass's temporality that could be manipulated to tuck racialized subjects into the folds of a hegemonic historicism in endless ways—and thus, the unending labor of infants, the social adolescence of liberal men. As a result of this manipulation, race incoherently communicates the existence of age. Black subjectivity encompasses the experience of such incoherent communication.

Two years after the publication of White's *Arn't I a Woman*, Toni Morrison delivers us directly to this territory of experience when she offers us the Sweet Home Men. During the Reconstruction era in 1873, Paul D experiences slavery's immediate afterlife as an ongoing contradiction embedded in black male adulthood: He was "The last of the Sweet Home men."⁵¹ Or he was the last surviving male to have been enslaved on Mr. Garner's farm. Of his five male slaves, Mr. Garner claims to have made men: "Y'all got boys [. . .] Young boys, old boys, picky boys, stroppin boys. Now at Sweet Home, my niggers is men every one of em. Bought em thataway, raised em thataway. Men every one."⁵² Of course, the irony is that much like the homogeneity of enslaved "boys"—the differences among them meld into the mass—Paul D, Paul A, Paul F, Halle, and Sixo are homogenous. The repetition of "Paul" harkens back to the "deweys" of Morrison's 1973 novel: It is a proper noun that underscores the absence of a proper liberal individual at the center of it, and thus spotlights the problem that male adulthood has historically presented for black males.

As Paul D comes to realize, the spatial and conceptual enclosure, the patriarchal cocoon of the farm, determines what his manhood means: "They were only Sweet Home men at Sweet Home."[53] This realization is like a crystallized particle of forgotten history breaking the seamless surface of our dominant historical narrative: What black gender becomes relies on its relation to conquered, settled, cultivated land, and by extension, on structural, conceptual, epistemic closures. Both the ostensibly benevolent Mr. Garner and the tyrannical schoolteacher—who imposes overtly violent forms of subjection in the wake of Mr. Garner's death—reproduce the epistemic closure of developmental stasis. Like a microcosm of how the modern "racial state" is borne out of concomitant philosophies that, despite their differences, nonetheless situate the racial other in belated relation to European historical time, Mr. Garner's logic is related to schoolteacher's. Like two sides of the same coin, one benevolently confers his slaves with artificial manhood while the other violently deprives them of official manhood. By deeming his slaves to be always-already "men," borne out of non-development, Mr. Garner anticipates the second-tier "maturity" that will perpetuate the myth of black inferiority after emancipation. The "manhood" of Sweet Home men is but one of many technological uses of age to relocate the enslaved within a dominant schema of historical time. Sweet Home "manhood" can simultaneously, paradoxically, be purchased and raised, since it does not belong to a human lifespan.

Paul D's nascent realization of the stasis that is foundational to both the conferral and denial of his manhood leads to what he experiences as a crisis of gender. This gender crisis is a vestibule that leads to the problem of historical time and temporality that is incoherently expressed as age. Beloved moves Paul D. Imperceptibly, she controls his movements as if he were "a rag doll—picked up and put back down anywhere any time by a girl young enough to be his daughter."[54] Like what Robin Bernstein refers to as a "scriptive thing"—a thing that indiscernibly scripts behaviors a social subject loosely performs, as a black rubber doll with a permanent smile cues a white girl of the mid-nineteenth century to beat it viciously—Paul D the rag doll cues Beloved, the agential embodiment of the dead, to respond. As a manifestation of the awakened 60 million and more, she denaturalizes the common sense about black being that Mr. Garner and schoolteacher share. She calls attention to the artificial substance they created. She moves Paul D because "black manhood" has been constituted as hollow in the middle and inert on its own, available to be "picked up" from a social world beyond Man's meanings and "put back down" into the time of western modernity, now the only history there is. In the words of Fanon, "The Negro is a toy in the white man's hands."[55] "Black manhood" signals the mass that makes it possible for one to be uprooted and re-rooted: it cues an engagement with a racialized version of humanity that is physically (biologically, evolutionarily) unable to determine its own destiny. Imagine the Equiano boy being moved toward the destiny of someone else's history. In order to be a man, and not a boy or a plaything for a girl that "was not a girl,"[56] Paul D instinctively asks Sethe to have his baby, which is a way to "document his manhood." As the patriarch of his own black family, he attempts to establish and situate himself within the linear temporality of generations, a paradigm of human development.

Yet, nested within this scene in which Paul D reclaims a manhood—a self, a gender, a meaningful adulthood—from the grip of modernity's awakened dead, is an alternative version of freedom. During their walk from Sethe's job to 124 Bluestone Road, Paul D and Sethe covertly, irrepressibly, express their affection for each other in public. They playfully negotiate the gray area between owning and stealing their own bodies, by "snatching each other's fingers, stealing quick pats on the behind."[57] In the midst of this negotiation that their affection produces is an awareness of something that is neither movement nor stasis: they were, "joyfully embarrassed to be that grown-up and that young at the same time."[58] This simultaneity of life stages not only eschews linear development. It marks a tacit acknowledgment that age is a site of subjection. If intractable doubt about maturation, development, evolution—all concepts of temporal progression—have been transposed onto the ontology of blackness and have seeped into the meaning of age, then Sethe and Paul D stage a reclamation of that doubt. To be grown-up and young at the same time is suddenly transformed into their own kind of happy. It is a happiness in stillness, their own kind of constancy. They have reached a pause point in their walk; with Sethe's head on Paul D's chest, "they stopped and stood that way—not breathing, not even caring if a passerby passed them by."[59] To be grown-up and young at once—neither progressive nor belated within a dominant schema of time—to pause in a caesura between racialized timelines, and to await the discovery of another temporality, even as others pass them by, is something akin to human.

In sum, by the 1980s and '90s, black feminist historiography and historical fiction had opened epistemic closures that various spatial arrangements—the black family in the Antilles, the plantation in the United States—have gestured toward and reproduced by elaborating on the relation between human temporalities and inhuman history. Gender, as a socially constitutive part of the human, has been a key starting place: Genders have temporalities, and blackness troubles conventional relations between the two. Thus, age, as a social category that trades in the inextricability between gender and temporality, communicates that the terms of this inextricability are incoherent at the site of blackness. In order to expand the epistemic grounds upon which black life exists, one needs to enter the vestibule of gender and approach the meaning of age.

Age is the terrain upon which the temporalities of the natural world, social invention, and fantasy converge. The outcome of this convergence is that black subjects seem to embody temporality in contradictory ways. Yet, contradictory modes of temporality have been readily interpretable as the historical problem of gender. Thus, the status of black "manhood" has arisen as a preeminent example of the racial contradiction nested within the gendered, human terms of Man. "Black manhood" does the particular work of raising an unresolvable question: How does the ungendered subject assume the linear, sequential timeline of liberal personhood? Our consideration of this unanswerable question need not be limited to the terms of normatively linear timelines, as "infantilization" and "maturation" suggest. As contradictory and incoherent, age reveals broader logics of how blackness has been endowed with super/natural temporality.

One example of how "black manhood" bypasses the normative logic of human time unexpectedly came to light in 1972. Between 1932 and 1972, the US Public Health Service ran and oversaw the now infamous "Tuskegee Study of Untreated Syphilis in the Negro Male."[60] The study solicited participation from syphilitic black men in and around Macon County in Alabama to examine the effects of the disease as it ran its "natural course." The men, primarily sharecroppers, were unaware that they were subjects in a study, and not actually being treated for what they were told was "bad blood." On September 29, 1932, in a written correspondence, Dr. O. C. Wenger, chief of the government-run Venereal Disease clinic in Arkansas, shared the following assessment with Dr. Taliaferro Clark, chief of the US Public Health Service's Venereal Disease Division: "We must remember we are dealing with a group of people who are illiterate, have no conception of time, and whose personal history is always indefinite."[61] Both health professionals were in agreement about the value of observing a disease progress in black male bodies. Racial capitalism, the transformation of people into commodities into labor, the sharecroppers' attachment to the same land that their ancestors worked, and their ultimate disposability converge to reveal what Dr. Wenger did not say: The racial formation of blackness was an embodying process that presupposed the dispossession of "conceptions of time" and "personal history," such as the chronology of a lifespan. Once dispossessed of time, black bodies can be the vessels for all kinds of temporal needs, which includes ungendered gestation of an inhuman disease.[62]

Dr. Wenger made his claims in 1932, but the question of blackness and temporal movement would bear heightened relevance with the exposure of the Tuskegee Syphilis Study to the general public 40 years later. The 40 years between the study's inception and reportage of it on the front page of the *New York Times* highlights the temporality of the mass: Within a linear schema of progressive time that includes the legislative advances of the civil rights era, black subjects, yoked together from the Great Depression to the time of Black Power, travel without moving, taking "the look and affects of the Eternal." Neither the racial temporality of infantilism, detached from everything other than the immediate context of the plantation, nor maturity, the normative time of manhood, describes the way the black men enlisted in the study were entangled with time. Still, the logic of lifespans-as-development is applicable, insofar as scientific discourses that transfigure the political temporality of civilization into the seemingly natural temporality of biological development were the conditions of possibility for the study. The study was predicated on the scientific racism of the early twentieth century, which provided an epistemic framework for analyzing the post-emancipation "race problem." Social Darwinists of the era presumed that the natural, temporal trajectory of blackness was deterioration, in opposition to the progressive evolutionary trajectory of white civilization.[63] In other words, the precondition for the syphilis study arose from the Oceanic: The temporality of black embodiment is made untimely, and then reconstituted as abnormal against the logic of normative, human development. As a result, the lifespan of syphilis is deemed more worthy of preservation than the human bodies that are ravaged by it, which are circumscribed by the timeline of such ravaging.

By looking at how the convergence of the natural sciences, national racism, and flights of imagination literally imposed a temporality onto black bodies, we can begin to consider how such an imposition was possible. Those bodies, the meaning inscribed into their blackness, must have communicated an emptied terrain in which any notion about temporality could be implanted, and any temporal use could be extracted. In the novels discussed below, the stakes of this concern lay in an imagined future in which blackness moves through time differently. In order to point us in the direction of this future, both novels unearth the past in order to discover new modes of living. Even as they appear to be in stasis, the deweys evoke the question of what future lies ahead, which is reminiscent of a young Equiano doing the same. The old men engage the past from the crisis of the present. Between a future, toward which the deweys are oriented, in which the human is differently imagined, and the power of the past, with which the old men are preoccupied, there is the density of the present. The present is thick with numerous temporalities, with hegemonic, alternative, competing, speculative conceptions of time.

The Bottom

Set between 1919, in the aftermath of World War I, and 1965, at the apex of the civil rights era, *Sula* is a coming-of-age novel that follows the close friendship of and eventual rift between Sula Peace and Nel Wright. Sula and Nel's evolving relationship occurs in the context of black life nestled among the clouds, in a hilltop neighborhood called the Bottom.[64] Shadrack, the first character that the reader encounters, returns to Medallion after his deployment in Europe. Shell-shocked, alienated, and out of sync with the rhythm of social life, Shadrack establishes National Suicide Day in 1920. He remakes calendrical time to fit the emergence of a new temporality of the early twentieth century, of which the global reaches of World War I at home, post-Reconstruction marginalization, and overall, the will to survive amidst the subtle and overt violence in the aftermath of emancipation are a part. Reserving one day on the calendar for sanctioned, mass self-destruction formalizes the relation between survival and death. Thus, the inception of Suicide Day, an emergent, modern feeling of time, is describable as a response to the profound ambivalence of black freedom in the afterlife of slavery.

By addressing one overarching question—how did black people experience the incomplete transition to "freedom" during the modern era, the early 1920s to the early 1940s?—*Sula* connects the town's origin story about a former slave being swindled out of arable land to the contemporary circumstances of postwar (and post-enslavement) trauma, the linear coming-of-age of two black girls, and the endurance of black community. Survival, growth, and the will to carry on—in a word, the persistence of black being—comprise the novel's thematic response to ubiquitous disregard for the future of black existence. Thus, the novel begins with a future that sprouts from barren land; "it was lovely up in the Bottom [. . .]. Those heavy trees that sheltered the shacks up in the Bottom were wonderful to see."[65] There are strategies, both quotidian and extraordinary, for sheltering each other from the specter of death that arises from slavery and haunts modern life. Shadrack makes a future out of the temporality of trauma when he remakes the calendar. Girls irrepressibly grow into women. A public works project to build a tunnel for facilitating commerce between towns holds the promise of dignified labor and normative manhood for young black men.

Eva Peace is the novel's key figure of resilience. She is among the first generation of black people born after slavery, survives the bleak years at the end of the nineteenth century while caring for three children alone when, "Things was bad. Niggers was dying like flies."[66] She is rumored to have caused the "accidental" loss of her own leg in order to collect insurance, and allows her well-worn, M. C. Escherian home to be a waystation for itinerants. As an emblem of resilience that makes black life possible into the twentieth century, Eva is the bridge between two, divergent versions of futurity, which will guide my discussion. These divergent versions are manifested as her granddaughter Sula and her adopted children, the deweys. In different ways, Sula and the deweys create a vision of black freedom that denaturalizes gender's relation to age. In both cases, Eva's resilience, the constancy of black survival, spins out in one direction as the "one" of the autonomous (female) subject, and in the other direction as the undifferentiated (male) "mass." The gendering of this divergence is significant, but not for affirming the integrity of binary gender categories. Rather, it does the opposite: It highlights the question of how "oneness," the singular psychic life and maturation of the socially normative subject, leads to a political conception of liberal individualism, which combines white maleness with adulthood and is only provisionally granted to black subjects of any gender or age. Both Sula and the deweys play with various refusals: no to the *white maleness* of the self-possessive adult, no to the *white adulthood* of maleness. Just as "womanist," Alice Walker's maturation-based term for an inclusive black gender politics suggests, black feminist thought of the long 1970s covered terrain that the era's social historians gestured toward: Discerning what constitutes an emancipatory politics of social life requires an account of how blackness and gender have been articulated to the social meaning of age.

As scholars have frequently noted, the intimate relationship between Sula and Nel is at once subtly erotic and overtly intersubjective, as the two seem to complete each other, like two halves of a whole. Both are sibling-less children who find "in each other's eyes the intimacy they were looking for,"[67] which is a familiarity of the self that extends to the other. As two intersubjective selves that extend into the other, I think of Sula and Nel as girls that, together, comprise a mass. Although their friendship is idiosyncratic in relation to others, together, the two become something more than separate individuals. Their recognition of a self in the other is predicated on a nascent realization that, as black females, they are inherently excluded from social categories of the human, which include canonically feminine gender and liberal personhood: "Because each had discovered years before that they were neither white nor male, and that all freedom and triumph was forbidden to them, they had set about creating something else to be."[68] In a word, "something else to be" is an alternative way of being human.

Creating a new way of being human defines what "girlhood" is in *Sula*: It is a developmental process that moves toward a new horizon of humanity rather than toward canonical or rights-bearing "adulthood." Thus, Sula and Nel participate in a mass-like childhood that eschews the logic of liberal individualism, and the logic of adulthood as a social, natural, and teleological end of a developmental process. Mass-like girlhood evokes undifferentiated relations to land, not as a barren, backbreaking sign of freedom's failed arrival, but of something fecund and open. The girls, "unshaped, formless things,"[69] are mass-like, malleable material. At the dawn of their adolescence, they lay on the grassy ground, and as they shape each other by being "girls together,"[70] they shape the malleable earth: "Nel began a more strenuous digging and, rising to her knee, was careful to scoop out the dirt as she made her hole deeper. Together they worked until the two holes were one and the same."[71] In a scene that most vividly illustrates emerging maturity for black girls, Nel and Sula signify on the problem of black maturation overall: Intuitively, silently, they empty the land. Unlike the former slave who attempts to express his newly granted freedom (or manhood) by merging ownership of his land with ownership of his labor, the girls focus on their mass-like relation to the (w)hole in the ground. They transform the empty space into an epistemological opening, a site for creating something else to be. They fill the shared, empty space with refuse like bottle caps and cigarette butts, and then "replace the soil and [cover] the entire grave with uprooted grass."[72] Instead of making a space in which to plant a seed that will grow according to the governing laws of natural development and linear time, the resulting mass of discarded objects is covered over like a grave for lost genres of the human, or like a secret that awaits discovery in the future, beyond Miranda's meanings.[73]

"Always." Like the improvised mass grave, it captures the past and future of alternative humanity. Shadrack speaks the word after the girls' earth-play, after Sula accidentally flings the little boy called Chicken Little into the river and causes his drowning death, after Nel watched. Upon discovering a shaken Sula standing in the middle of his cottage, in the aftermath of sending a boy flying through the air to his death, Shadrack offers a cryptic reminder that we are not inert, inhuman objects propelled through someone's sense of time. There is a life to be made in the deadening condition of the Eternal. Thus, "he had said 'always,' so she would not have to be afraid of the change—the falling away of skin, the drip and slide of blood, and the exposure of bone underneath. He had said 'always' to convince her, assure her, of permanency."[74] He could have said, just as easily, "constancy." Yet, instead of comforting, Sula understands this word as proscriptive and threatening: Shadrack "had answered a question she had not asked, and its promise licked at her feet."[75] This is the beginning of what will characterize the second part of the novel, which is Sula's break from her girlhood intimacy with Nel in order to become a self-made, liberated woman like no other. While Nel discovers her own "me" as a 10-year-old, her "me-ness" is what "gave her the strength to cultivate a friend."[76] "Cultivation," as an analogy for development between black girls who, together, grow with the grain of human time despite their exclusion for normative humanity, signifies a radical reconceptualization of what constitutes "growth," beyond the liberal logic that equates the self-possessive (white, male) adult with private property and autonomy. In contrast, the adult Sula becomes an iconoclast, a consummate individualist who succeeds in her quest "to make myself,"[77] which is both a beginning and an end.

If, as the title of a groundbreaking work in black feminist studies of the long 1970s claims, all the *women* are white, and all the blacks are *men*, then tucked inside of the problem about racialized gender for black females is a question about adulthood.[78] To acknowledge that black females of any age, including children, have been dispossessed of the legal, social, and customary protections of "youth" gets us only part of the way through. Both Sula and the novel point to a historical problem, which is the indefinability of what "adulthood" means for black femaleness, aside from the dispossession of "youth." What does it mean to be all grown up, and yet neither canonically female nor canonically adult? To the degree that the novel explores "the risks of individualism in a determinedly individualistic, yet racially uniform and socially static, community," and more broadly, the nature of "Female freedom,"[79] it raises the question of what political rubric, if not liberalism and the possessive individual at the heart of it, instantiates "freedom" for the black female adult. The opening that the novel creates for imagining a social schema that encompasses the concept of "black female adulthood" is manifested in the incongruous appearances of black female adults.

As a social pariah who is separated from other black women, "Sula did not look her age. She was near thirty and, unlike them, had lost no teeth, suffered no bruises, developed no ring of fat at the waist or pocket at the back of her neck. [. . .] she was free of any normal signs of vulnerability."[80] Is "aging" just an accumulation of vulnerability—the heavy by-product that results from years of sparse economic options, abusive husbands, compulsory reproduction, political and social exclusions? Is "adulthood" just an amount of vulnerability endured over time? If so, Sula refuses. By doing so, by fashioning "adulthood" as an individualism so self-possessive that it exists strictly for its own sake, Sula sustains the gender-age logic that has rendered "black female adulthood" unthinkable in the first place: She claims, "You say I'm a woman and colored. Ain't that the same as being a man?"[81] While Sula claims "manhood" as the only route to black liberation, she neglects to ask whether there is something else to be, or another way of linking the condition of being grown to the condition of being free. Sula's liberated life is short-lived; she dies an early death in Eva's bed. Always. While dying, she thinks about Shadrack: "Who was it that had promised her sleep in water always?"[82] This promise is an Oceanic answer to a question she did not ask.

While Sula chooses to be the consummate individual that we associate with manhood, the deweys play with the infantile. In other words, if "growth"—normal development, as both Freud and Fanon alike would have it—is directly related to "individuation," then the deweys instantiate a dual refusal: They refuse growth as the route to individuated manhood, which is presumed to be the only horizon of liberation, and they refuse to inhabit their "boyhood" as a life stage that has been emptied of human meaning and subsequently filled with the malleable, homogenous clay of infantilized "blackness." This refusal to become either "men" or what Elkins describes as all-aged "boys" corresponds to a cultural genealogy that is separate from the one that determines Sula's strivings. If Sula implicitly asks, "can black women be adults?" then the deweys engage the assumption that black children "just grow."

The deweys evoke the figure of enslavement on which they signify Topsy of Harriet Beecher Stowe's *Uncle Tom's Cabin*, and Topsy's pre- and post-emancipation progeny, the pickaninny. A garish composite of black genders and ages, the pickaninny is frequently grouped with others like it, making a mass of black inhumanity.[83] Further, the pickaninny signifies an imperviousness to change and cultivation that characterizes the unworkable land that establishes the Bottom: The pickaninny, the former slave, and the land all function within the spatially and temporally closed-off logic of constancy. In this logic of closed-off constancy, black children are presumed just to grow, which is not an indicator of human development, but rather, a supposition of endless production and replication. This mode of engagement is precisely why the deweys signify on Stowe's paragon of black childhood, Topsy, and her unscrupulous brood, commonly referred to as "pickaninnies."

Topsy, that sullen, irascible child borne out of the wretchedness of slavery's brutality, undergoes a conversion of the spirit when the angelic white child, little Eva, quite actually touches her.[84] Benevolent slave owner Augustine St. Clare places Topsy under the tutelage of his austere cousin, Miss Ophelia, for proper rearing. Approximately eight or nine years old, Topsy is the consummate brutish child, a conflation of terms that signifies a concentration of blackness, since "She was one of the blackest of her race."[85] In addition to being one of many "little plagues" with which St. Clare has apparently filled his home,[86] Topsy is notable for her insistence that she "Never was born."[87] She claims not to know her age, which another slave explains by stating that "low negroes [. . .] don't know anything about time."[88] This supposedly absent knowledge about time is joined with the uses of this absence. When Topsy claims, "I spect I grow'd. Don't think nobody never made me,"[89] she becomes analogous with emptied, homogenous land: As St. Clare tells a reluctant Miss Ophelia about her new ward, "You find virgin soil there, cousin; put in your own ideas,—you won't find many to pull up."[90] Just as the presumption that black southern sharecroppers had "no conception of time" made it possible to study syphilis that "just grew" for decades, the fact that Topsy just "grow'd" by her own admission situates her not within the human time of development, but rather within a schema of endless fecundity that is associated with the plantation.

If Topsy inexplicably grows from an unknown, asocial, and inhuman source, then her progeny, the stereotypical pickaninny, cannot grow.[91] Instead, the feral, ungendered, and unaged figure of abject black childhood is developmentally stunted but, strikingly, able to travel through historical time without moving. If Topsy first reveals how black "childhood" signifies an economic calculus that conflates the reproduction of enslaved women with the production of plantations, and then erases these conflated conditions of (re)production as a child-commodity that "never was born" and "just grew," then the later stereotype of the pickaninny actualizes this latent condition of being a metaphysically produced, movable thing—an image, a figurine, a character that appears in various stage productions that were loosely based on Stowe's novel across the country. As a figure of the Eternal, the pickaninny's movement through time gained velocity through the mass production and consumption of material culture from the 1880s to the 1930s, which included the collectible items that depicted caricatures of the "Old South"—pickaninnies, mammies, and uncles.[92] As Patricia A. Turner explains, the pickaninny, who was often underdressed, unsupervised, closely associated with animals who might consume them, prone to eating or stealing watermelons, placed in dangerous situations but generally impervious to injury, was dominant "until the mid-1960s": "For at least one hundred years, the public—black and white—was presented with platoons of plucky pickaninnies as its only image of black children."[93] Thus, in addition to permanent unsuitability for citizenship, the pickaninny's lack of growth evokes an obsolete, yet mourned for, political-economic ideal of the future, which includes the lucrative potential of black children as "increase," as an ever-abundant resource that imminently increases in monetary value for white slave owners but not black families.[94] The years of the Civil War and after slavery's formal end had been a time of flux with regard to the transforming role of black subjects, and I conjecture that the meaning of black age—no longer calculated according to the general market values of life stages—was caught in this flux. When black women's reproduction was no longer profitable, when a captive black labor force could be imprisoned rather than raised, the figure of the errant black child evokes nostalgia for an envisioned future in which "blackness" continues to emerge on its own, naturally or metaphysically, ready to be manipulated like virgin soil.[95]

Little Eva touches Topsy with Christian love and changes the black heathen's heart. Eva Peace, in contrast, gives her adopted boys a name that is up to them to define. And as Eva asks in another context, "Ain't that love?"[96] The deweys—having been granted the opportunity to become such a mass—decide that the meaning of their name is a refusal to grow. Consider this decision in relation to Topsy and the pickaninny: Topsy's black childhood is defined by the inevitability of her inhuman growth, while the stereotypical pickaninny remains developmentally inert in order to circulate endlessly through time and culture. The deweys, however, instantiate a critique of the shifting economic calculus of black childhood—as that which either existed for someone else's future gain or as that which stokes nostalgia for this future gain, which has been lost—and become an indecipherable mass of black boyhood. As a mass, they are full of potential to define their own version of human development, and thus, their own version of freedom.

On the day of Nel's wedding, it is clear to all at the Bottom that the deweys would remain perpetual children.[97] Their childhood is a densely concentrated, stand-alone life stage that has been cut off from the expectations of adulthood. As such, it evokes the artificial or metaphysical childhood of Topsy and the pickaninny, and references strange details associated with those figures, such as wiliness, prominent teeth, and unchildlike independence. On Nel's wedding day, "everyone realized for the first time that except for their magnificent teeth, the deweys would never grow. [. . .] The realization was based on the fact that they remained boys in mind. Mischievous, cunning, private and completely unhousebroken, their games and interests had not changed since [Sula's mother] Hannah had them all put into first grade together."[98] This description of the deweys echoes that of the female Topsy: "Her mouth half open with astonishment [. . .] displayed a white and brilliant set of teeth. [. . .] The expression of her face was an odd mixture of shrewdness and cunning, over which was oddly drawn, like a veil, an expression of the most doleful gravity and solemnity."[99] "Infantilization," that term for being excluded from human time, is also like a veil; it closes these figures of childhood off from our ability to know them. All of their privacy and shrewdness that hides the psychic life of black children are epistemic closures, which the deweys illuminate through reflection. At times, the deweys are less reflective of Topsy's wretched guile and more evocative of the pickaninny's generalized and exaggerated mischief and abjection. At one point, they claim to be sick in order to get soda money; Sula hangs one over an upstairs banister until he urinates, which is a reaction of no consequence; and since no one can tell the boys apart, their collective name, "dewey," seems like as much of a denial of proper personhood as "pickaninny."[100]

Yet, if the deweys choose to remain "boys in mind," it is a refusal of liberal personhood as the only foreseeable horizon, and of "manhood," which always already bears an unstable relation to racial blackness. Further, if black males of any age have been presumed to be "boys in mind" if not of body, as Elkins's mid-twentieth century historiography reveals, then the deweys reflect the gendered dimension of this metaphysical condition of age. The racial infantilization for which "boys" is just one name—Sweet Home "men" is another—does not require a firm allegiance to the categorical norms of gender. This is why infantilization has often been taken as a matter of non-normative gender. As Michael Awkward has claimed, the deweys illustrate "black males' relationship to the female within," because their non-differentiation strongly evokes Spillers's theory of black subjective non-differentiation during the Middle Passage, and thus the oceanic ungendering of blackness.[101] If the "female" within the deweys is Topsy, if the gender of the stereotypical pickaninny is often irrelevant, if during slavery young black children had been of equal monetary value, irrespective of gender, then being black "boys in mind" is a reclamation of something that has been deemed unknowable in our current social world.[102] We have seen the afterlife of unknowable black "boyhood" in the fates of Emmett Till, Trayvon Martin, Tamir Rice: In a heavy contradiction, all black males can be "boys" even as black males are perceived to be menacing and adult-like, regardless of age.[103]

Overall, the collapse of the historical past—evoked through Topsy, pickaninnies, slavery, plantations—into the present-day stasis of "dewey boyhood" is key to the communal rejection of linear schemas of time in the novel's climax. On Suicide Day, the residents of the Bottom participate in a spontaneous mass action: They march down from their neighborhood to the white section of Medallion, where an unfinished public works project, the building of a tunnel, serves as the latest reminder of incomplete freedom. "Most folks said it was the deweys" who were first to lead the charge,[104] but everyone follows behind Shadrack in this mass refusal. Refused is the promise of a liberated adulthood toward which there is no black gendered route. They reject the structural constitution of blackness as socially inert, and thus their mass movement was "from gravity, from the weight of that very adult pain that had undergirded them all those years before," and from everything that kept them tied to the ground, "picking beans for other farmers; kept them from finally leaving as they talked of doing; kept them knee-deep in other people's dirt."[105] In a manner that is circular rather than linear, the mass encounter with the unfinished tunnel returns to the "promised freedom and a piece of bottom land"[106] that ostensibly begins the liberal dream of full inclusion after slavery. Yet, this time, "There was the promise: leaf-dead."¹⁰⁷ Whereas the land itself had been unyielding in the beginning, in this return, the seemingly natural non-fulfillment of freedom ("leaf-dead") is overshadowed by deliberate and structural denials, manifested as white refusal to hire black laborers. While for the former slave, "manhood" is a burden meant to be suffered alone, in this revised instance, the Bottom community becomes a massive force that reengages the land as both a site of ongoing violence and a source of identification. In so doing, the community rejects the categorical distinctions that are intended to separate persons from non-persons, masses from men: "Old and young, women and children, lame and hearty, they killed, as best they could, the tunnel they were forbidden to build."¹⁰⁸ As a result of this response to the actual and epistemic opening in the earth, they fall in. Many of them die when "[t]he earth, now warm, shifted," and they are swept away in a combination of earth and water.¹⁰⁹ They merge with the mass of the land in a final, fatal, Oceanic rejection of leading a singular, linear life with no promise of freedom—as manhood, adulthood—to be achieved at the end.

Although the deweys apparently are among those who meet their demise, the novel offers reason for skepticism: "The deweys (at least it was supposed; their bodies were never found)—all died there."¹¹⁰ This doubt is confirmed 24 years later, in 1965, when Nel looks around and notices how times had changed. Signs of progress appear to be everywhere, with black people hired in positions of authority, as teachers and store cashiers. Yet, Nel is now old enough to be wary of progress. She sees something familiar in this new era: "The young people had a look about them that everybody said was new but which reminded Nel of the deweys, whom nobody had ever found."¹¹¹ If the deweys are the Oceanic mass that comprised both the historical denial of black youth as a human condition—as illustrated by Topsy, the pickaninny—and the creation of a new mode of human existence, then they offer an alternative to national, linear temporality. The deweys are neither compelled to follow nor pushed through someone else's progressive schema of time because their massiveness marks the compression of time, of pasts and futures that exist in the present, of time that winds rather than extends in a straight line. Thus, in 1965, the deweys continue to exist alongside the time of civil rights. The reminder of the deweys in the looks of the young is where their undifferentiated boyishness evokes the potentials of girlhood that both Sula and Nel squander for a mess of pottage. Sula wanted an equivalent manhood. Remorsefully, Nel finally realizes that she too had been misled. She had mistaken her pleasure at seeing a black child flung through the air for "maturity."[112] In the end, the developmental narrative that makes *Sula* seem like a coming-of-age novel gives way to a circle of time, the "girl, girl, girlgirlgirl" that extends from "the tops of trees" down to the "mud [that] shifted,"[113] and in relation to the "circles and circles of sorrow" for something lost—girlhood—and the deweys, who are the something that remains.

The Weeds and the Ocean

When Hortense Spillers writes of the post–civil rights era, "In the wake of loss, we only have left, it seems, the inexorable grimness of 'competition,' of 'getting over,' of 'role-modeling,' of 'success' for the well-credentialed, and a thorough commodification of black culture," she is referring to the cost of a certain logic that has permeated black communities by this time, a certain logic that involves keeping pace with the movement of normative time. In the wake of loss, we have what Roderick Ferguson describes as the rationalities of western institutions, along with hegemonic affirmations of liberal nationalism and personhood that underwrite them.[114] I suggest that tucked inside of these rationalities is a temporal logic, the same that has given rise to "age" as the West's key metaphor for its advancement, in relation to its under-developed, non-western other. Thus, in the wake of loss is an acceptance of how to appear to be human in the context of liberal institutions. There is also an acceptance of how to be "men" in the context of western civilization, rather than latter-day "savages" or "Sambos" that take on the look of juvenile belatedness or stasis. As I have discussed in this chapter, African-descended people and New World land had undergone an emptying process: Dispossession of their prior social and natural ontology made it possible to fill both people and land with an inhuman and unnatural temporality that I have referred to as "constancy." But dwelling on the emptying, the "loss," potentially reveals something about the making of historical time. If we keep focusing on the fact that something has been lost, then does it become possible to see something (aside from the success of the singular social subject) of what remains?

In Ernest Gaines's 1983 novel, *A Gathering of Old Men*, the answer is in the weeds.[115] Set on what was, at one time, a thriving plantation in Southern Louisiana during the late 1970s, the body of a white Cajun farmer named Beau Boutan has been shot to death near the home of Mathu, an elderly black man. Candy Marshall, who is the partial proprietor of the plantation and fiercely protective of Mathu as the man who raised her, believes he is responsible for the murder. In the interest of protecting him, she takes full responsibility, although no one believes her. For further reinforcement, she sends for other elderly black men in the parish, all of whom are upward of 70 years old. The group of old men gathers in Mathu's yard; each man fires a single shot from a shotgun that resembles Mathu's, and each man claims responsibility for the murder. Eventually, the white Sheriff Mapes arrives on the scene, and his expectation of making a quick arrest is thwarted by the group of geriatric men who refuse to cower under the force of his intimidation and leave. The threat of Beau's white supremacist father, William "Fix" Boutan, mobilizing a lynch mob in order to seek retribution looms large over the afternoon's events, yet the men refuse to leave. In effect, this collective act of resistance is a belated response to decades of intimidation and brutality. Their mode of action is to be collectively immovable among the weeds.

Seldom do historiographies of the 1960s and 1970s focus on the thoughts and actions of the elderly. The era's most enduring iconography of black manhood arise from the Black Panther Party; an organized collective of young, rifle-bearing, leather-clad men are the backdrop to charismatic young, male leaders, Huey Newton, Bobby Seale, Eldridge Cleaver. To infer from iconography and the historiography it supports, the locus of black liberation and revolutionary action is the reclamation of "manhood." Conversely, to view the 1970s from the "quarters" of what had been a plantation in the Deep South, rather than from Oakland or Los Angeles, and from the perspective of armed and yet ostensibly feckless old men, is to turn the iconography inside out. Just as Spillers conceptualizes "flesh" as "the marks of a cultural text whose inside has been turned outside," so too does the aberrant place, time, and age of the novel's gathered group reveal the insides of a nationalist narrative that takes "men" as its ideal subject and becomes saliently tied to black liberation by the 1970s.[116]

Ferguson's reading of Toni Cade Bambara's 1971 short story, "My Man Bovanne," is a useful point of entry to what, precisely, in the name of "manhood," is actually being retrieved in Gaines's novel.[117] Taking Jacques Rancière's notion of "stultification," or "the presupposition of a radical break between two forms of intelligence,"[118] as his own point of departure, Ferguson argues that western liberalism's institutional logics and exclusionary, constraining practices have been reproduced within black radical nationalism, which then are carried out within black communities. While the older generation "represent the unbroken pace of tradition and history, they are—to the children—just as much the broken-down inheritors of a grave miseducation."[119] This "break" between the ill-informed, apolitical old folks and the militant youth who know better is schematic of radical nationalism's adaptation of hegemonic liberal nationalism's regulatory norms. In this case, the young, militant agents of black nationalist narration exalt the elderly as the "love objects" of black national liberation movements,[120] so the elders could be buried, just like the revered past they manifest. Once buried and memorialized, the young are free to regulate the apolitical black "masses," who expressly include the elderly in this story. Significantly, Ferguson argues that this process in "My Man Bovanne" is allegorical of western historiography, since this and black nationalist historiography are "both forms of history writing [that] represent the people on condition that they remain silent."[121]

I situate *A Gathering of Old Men* as a companion piece to Ferguson's interpretation of "My Man Bovanne." Imagine that the old men, with their rickety shotguns, their country ways, their inconspicuously lived long lives, refused to be buried. This refusal is treated with light irony. When two of the old men, Robert Louis Stevenson Banks, "aka Chimley," and Matthew Lincoln Brown, "aka Mat," realize with trepidation that they must participate in this collective action, they acknowledge that they are both past their prime. Mat declares that "This can be my last chance."[122] Chimley, reading the expression in Mat's eyes, sees the unasked questions, "We wait till now? Now, when we're old men, we get to be brave?"[123] Since the problem of having waited too long is what old age summons with regard to the temporal logic of liberalism, Sheriff Mapes hints at how western nationalism and black radical nationalism share this logic: "'Isn't it a little bit late for you to be getting militant around here?' Mapes asked Clatoo. 'I always been militant,' Clatoo said. 'My intrance gone sour, keeping my militance down.'"[124] That old men choose something akin to militancy now suggests that their actions are in response to two forms of historical violence—the ostensible form of white supremacist violence of the Deep South that has carried on for decades, and its shadow, the black radical nationalism of the 1970s that renders the old men incapable of exerting any power in the production of history. Both forms of political regulation operate through a tacit logic of age: The first trades in a dense, artificial lifespan in which "boys" and "uncles" are essentially the same in a schema of non-development, with "uncles" playing the role of conveying "nothing but pleasant memories of the discipline of slavery," as the fictional Uncle Remus does in Joel Chandler Harris's late nineteenth-century children's stories.[125] The second trades in the black radical youth—like Sula, in her own way—standing in as the only adults, since older generations are revered, buried, and made to seem just as fictional as Uncle Remus.

One marvel that western humanism has achieved is the fascinating ability for western liberal "men" to be the only adults and innocently boyish at the same time. Recall the 2014 grand jury testimony of Darren Wilson, the white police officer who shot and killed Michael Brown, an unarmed black teenager: "When I grabbed him, the only way I can describe it is I felt like a five-year-old holding onto Hulk Hogan. [. . .] Hulk Hogan, that's just how big he felt and how small I felt just from grasping his arm."[126] Ferguson credits black feminism of the 1960s and '70s with "illuminating and analyzing how the ghosts of western institutionality gave breath to black nationalist organizations,"[127] and I would add that by doing so, we are indebted to black feminism for enabling us to identify "adulthood" as one of these ghosts. Haunting the projects of western and black radical nationalism is the presumed adulthood of the western colonizer, in relation to the permanent childhood of the colonized. Thus, in *A Gathering of Old Men*, Candy Marshall's sentimentality for the elderly black man who raised her is a vestige of racist paternalism. Similarly, black radical youth are the only adults in relation to the masses, the "grassroots." Placed in the broader national context of the 1970s, the standoff that the old men effect in the weeds of Mathu's yard is a reclamation of a temporality that haunts the progressive historical time of western and black nationalisms from which the old men are excluded. Their ostensibly newfound expression of "manhood" occurs in this space between being stuck in the past by white social norms of the South on the one end and moving forward as revered manifestations of the dead on the other. In this space between the pull of the violent past and the silencing within a (black) nationalist future, the grassroots give way to the weeds, which is a temporal refiguring of the mass.

Yet, even as the elderly are caught in a regulatory squeeze between the white supremacy of the South and an imaginary community of young, black radical nationalists, they must claim canonical manhood in order to install elderliness within the realm of agential personhood. Having been summoned by a young boy who runs from house to house at Candy's behest, the old men coordinate among themselves. One of the old men, referred to as Clatoo, makes two trips to pick up the others in his truck; the first group waits at the Marshall graveyard so that the whole group of 16 could walk up through the plantation entrance, toward Mathu's house, together. The first group of men evoke familiar images of canonical masculinity: One referred to as Yank "was in his early seventies, but he still thought he was a cowboy";[128] another named Jacob "had his gun over his shoulder, carrying it like a solider," while Mat carried his "like a hunter."[129] The most obvious connection between this belated collective action and soldiering appears: "Old Coot was in his World War I uniform. Even had on the cap, and the belt 'cross his shoulder. He carried his gun 'cross the other shoulder in a soldier's manner."[130] After everyone has been rounded up, Clatoo shores up the group: "We going in like soldiers, not like tramps. All right?"[131] Soldiering evokes a discursive route that led newly freedmen to citizenship, with "manhood" as a constitutive part of citizenship. As Saidiya Hartman explains, "This conception of the citizen-soldier, according to Nancy Fraser, imagines the citizen as 'the defender of the polity and protector of those—women, children, and elderly—who allegedly cannot protect themselves.'"[132]

This scene in which the two groups of men meet up at the graveyard underscores that, while they conform to soldiering logics of defense, the men serve more aptly as protectors of the dead than the polity. Thus, their elder-soldiering has a counter-nationalist goal. The World War I uniform highlights military service as a promise of citizenship; yet Shadrack has illustrated the fallacy of this promise with madness and ingenuity. From an intertextual perspective of the era, *Sula*'s Shadrack is the repressed outcome of black participation in the Great War; the uniform that Old Coot wears on the way to the graveyard communicates both national inclusion and the return of nationalist injury.[133]

The dead and the land with which they have merged need defense from the threat of being reburied by nationalist historiographical forces and detached from the realm of the thinkable. While walking to the graveyard, an old man known as Cherry ruminates on the impetus for their actions, Candy's paternalist beckoning notwithstanding: "Beau and his family had been leasing all the [Marshall family] land the past twenty-five, thirty years. The very same land we had worked, our people had worked, our people's people has worked since the time of slavery. Now Beau had it all. Or, I should say, had it all up to about twelve o'clock that day."[134] This is a potential moment of redemption: Beau, who once had it all, now "was laying [. . .] in the weeds all bloody,"[135] while the land and the people, brought together well into the past, rise to inspire the day's action. Beau's body is hard to see in all the weeds; as the white elderly Miss Merle observes, "The weeds were so high I could hardly see anything more than just the tip of his cowboy boots."[136] The graveyard, which had been "the burial ground for black folks ever since the time of slavery,"[137] is where the old men pause in symbolic acts of redemption. In this novel, such an act is pulling up the weeds: One of the old men, Jacob, was "pulling up weeds from Tessie's grave. Tessie was his sister," and white men killed her in 1947.[138] Another old man, Dirty Red, does not pull up weeds, but sees what remains through them. Although he sees "My mon, Jude; my pa, François, right there [. . .]. Uncle Ned right in there—somewhere," none of this is obvious to his friend, Cherry: "The whole place was all sunken in, and you had weeds everywhere, so I couldn't tell for sure where Dirty Red was looking."[139] That Cherry follows Dirty Red's line of vision is less significant than his being made aware that there are people who had lived where it seemed there was nothing but weeds.

Thus, weeds in this novel are often the source of visual obscurity, and concomitantly, redemptive insight. The obscurity comes first: At the beginning, the young boy, Snookum, observes that, "You had too much weeds and bushes even to see the houses sometime."[140] Informed of the shooting, the black housekeeper, Janey, sees her oblivious old mistress in the back pasture, poking around for pecans: "now just s'posing, just s'posing, now, a snake or something come up there and bite that old woman in all them weeds."[141] The weeds, what develops over time by virtue of indifference, potentially contains "something [that could] come up" and bite back at any time. This is emblematic of how Gaines describes his philosophy of history during the 1990s:

> I feel that anything can happen at any time. Since I wrote [*A Gathering of Old Men*], you know what has happened in lots of places: you see what happened in Los Angeles recently, the same thing is happening in New York. A lynch mob is a lynch mob—you can be in police blues, or you can be a gang of kids and have someone accidentally go into the wrong neighborhood at the wrong time.[142]

By subverting the logic of nationalist manhood with their elder-soldiering, which is militant only insofar as they engage in a battle of historical memory, the old men are figures of redemption. They are a massive analogue to Walter Benjamin's angel of history, who wishes to pause and explore the catastrophic rubble of all of human time amassing at his feet, if only he did not have to contend with the force of progress that would push him along with his back facing a vacant future.[143] As S. D. Chrostowska describes the body of Paul Klee's strangely rendered angel in "Angelus Novus," the painting that inspired Benjamin's figure, "its ears are overfleshed with age, its lips with youth. [. . .] This is how time marks the likes of angels."[144] With its age-related contradiction—old ears, young lips—the angel symbolizes an in-between of agedness and youth that figuratively resembles the old men's squeeze between revered elderliness of the "grassroots" and the perpetual boy-uncle status of the Deep South. Both versions emphasize a kind of temporal suspension between the past and the present: If Benjamin's angel is tormented by the dehumanizing toll of being pushed into a future it has no power to produce, then the old men constitute a mass that can remain unmoved. Against the empty forces of progress, in Mathu's yard they make something like a wall, "a wall of old black men with shotguns."[145] They remain unmoved in defense of the vanquished and in defense of themselves.

The weeds contain the potential to reconstruct lost human lives, and the men constitute an immovable mass to reckon with the historical wreckage. Thus, the task of historical retrieval is expressed through a visual economy of what is seen and unseen. As a representation of the law, which is temporarily stalled because of the old men's standoff, the sheriff, Mapes, maintains a positivist stance between knowing and being. In a key exchange, Mapes responds to one old man's claims that he killed Beau because of "What they did to my sister's little girl"[146] with an offhanded figure of speech, "I see." Another old man openly rejects this:

> Johnny Paul grunted out loud. "No, you don't see."
> He wasn't looking at Mapes, he was looking toward the tractor and the trailers of cane out there in the road. But I could tell he wasn't seeing any of that. I couldn't tell what he was thinking until I saw his eyes shifting up the quarters where his mama and papa used to stay. But the old house wasn't there now. It had gone like all the others had gone. Now weeds covered the place where the house used to be. "Y'all look," he said. "Look now. Y'all see anything? What y'all see?"
> "I see nothing but weeds, Johnny Paul," Mapes said.[147]
> Not comprehending Johnny Paul's point and impatient with what he views as a ploy to stall the investigation, Mapes once again glibly claims to see:
> "Yes, sir," Johnny Paul said. "But you still don't see. Yes, sir, what you see is the weeds, but you don't see what we don't see."
> [...]
> "I see," Mapes said.
> "No, you don't," Johnny Paul said. "No, you don't. You had to be here to don't see it now. You just can't come down here every now and then. You had to live here seventy-seven years to don't see it now. No, Sherriff, you don't see. You don't even know what I don't see."[148]

Unlike Mapes, who sees "nothing but weeds," what the old men "don't see" is "the people, the history, the soul, and spirit and everything [that] is there."[149] In other words, the weeds is hermeneutical of historiography that recognizes its own absences. Just as there are two key flashpoints that are the impetus for the events in *Sula*—the swindling of a former slave out of arable land and World War I—so are there two flashpoints that influence conceptions of historical time in *A Gathering of Old Man*—the swindling of black sharecroppers out of arable land and the growth of an agricultural commercial industry during the 1960s and '70s.[150] In both cases, the present is shaped by its dynamic interaction with the past. While there is no explicit mention of the commercial industrialization that was moving into the Sunbelt during the 1970s, when the novel is set, this development is nonetheless epitomized in the novel's primary moment of crisis, which is the dead body of a Cajun farmer in the yard of a black man.[151] Whereas *Sula* retrospectively casts emancipation as a moment of continued subjection that depends upon what Hartman terms the "burdened individualism" of manhood, *A Gathering of Old Men* evokes the same moment through the voice of the living collective: "All you old people know this already. After the plantation was dying out, the Marshalls dosed out the land for sharecropping, giving the best land to the Cajuns, and giving us the worst—that bottomland near the swamps."[152] Unlike in *Sula*, where the tragedy of "bottom" land is its failure to distinguish a break between enslavement and liberal personhood, here the historical grievance is the failed recognition of how the land evokes continuity: "Our own black people had been working this land a hundred years for the Marshall plantation, but when it come to sharecropping, now they give the best land to the Cajuns, who had never set foot on the land before."[153] Relegation to the bottomland is an attempt to break historical continuity, and yet, continuity persists, the past remains.

The weeds: In the present of the 1970s, a dead Cajun farmer takes his place among the weeds as dehumanizing accumulation intensifies. As Jodi Melamed claims, in the wake of capitalist accumulation, which has been the source of "the disjoining or deactivating of relations between human beings (and humans and nature)," we need a means to achieve "interconnections, [. . .] viable relations, and performances of collectivity."[154] The silenced history of the 1940s that the old men "don't see" portends what is emerging in the present, producing an alternative historiography of collectivity and an anti-capitalist version of constancy. To see the weeds only as weeds—as either the inevitable endurance of the order of things, or as the inconsequential and disposable—excludes an epistemology of the "don't seen," which leads to a failure to connect both black and Cajun communities that are under the threat of a state-subsidized commercial industry by the 1970s. Thus, the mass of old men, forged out of the exclusions of liberalism's progressive logics, figures a model of collectivity—comprised of the forgotten dead, the conquered, the enslaved and nominally free, themselves, newly displaceable populations, the Cajuns and many more—that forgoes the presumption of linear and developmental temporality contained in the concept of adulthood.

Near the end of the novel, we learn that the 82-year-old Mathu did not kill Beau Boutan. It was Charlie Biggs, a 50-year-old black field hand who worked for Beau, and Mathu's godson. Charlie had fled before the action of the novel, but returned in the end because, as he states repeatedly, he "is a man": "I ain't Big Charlie, nigger boy, no more, I'm a man."[155] The measure of his manhood becomes evident at age 50, "half a hundred."[156] It was not a boy or an uncle who retaliated when a white man thought he could beat him with a stick of cane during the 1970s. A black man on the verge of old age returned from the bottom of the swamps in defense of his own story—"I want you to write in your paper I'm a man."[157]—which is also a defense of Mathu, the other old men, the history, the soul, and spirit and everything (not) there.

* * *

Meanwhile, back in the eighteenth century, Olaudah Equiano would cross the ocean several times, over the course of several years. He would grow from enslaved boyhood to liberated manhood. His autobiography is a testament to his successful development. Yet, as Lisa Lowe argues, even while Equiano wrote in a genre that most exemplifies liberal individualism, his narrative leaves room in which to dwell on freedom's incompletion. The haunting failure of freedom is manifested in Equiano's remembrance of his sister, the little girl from whom he is separated before his wondrous-ominous first crossing of the Atlantic. The little girl is part of *The Interesting Narrative*'s shadow text. Imagine: the liberated man who is haunted by—meshed with, connected to—a little girl. It is in this register of shadows and haunting that we turn to the final chapter, which explores the Oceanic lifespans of ghosts.

4

Ghosts

There is not one extant autobiographical narrative of a female captive who survived the Middle Passage.
—Saidiya Hartman, "Venus in Two Acts"

Old age or youth—one no longer counts in that way. The world has more than one age.
—Jacques Derrida, *Specters of Marx*

Before young Olaudah looks up at portentously shaped clouds from the deck of a slave ship that crossed the Atlantic Ocean in the 1789 *Interesting Narrative*, he had made other passages. And he was not alone. Eleven-year-old Olaudah and his sister were abducted from their home in remote Essaka, a province of Benin, captured into slavery. The siblings were separated from each other shortly thereafter. Once, during the long trek from the interior of Guinea to the seacoast, the two had an unexpected and too-brief reunion. This was the last time Olaudah saw his sister. Historian Wilma King notes that, "There is no extant account of how the Equiano girl, whose name and age remain unknown, responded to the shock of abduction and detachment from her brother and other loved ones."[1] This missing account might be bound up with the indeterminate status of the text, resulting from literary critic Vincent Carretta's archival findings. Carretta has influentially called the historical veracity of Equiano's African origins into question.[2] As part of what might be historical fiction, the "Equiano Girl" is figured as Equiano's shadowy and ultimately absent counterpart within the action of the narrative. And as a ghost of what was and might be, the Equiano Girl is never far from the historical person, the erstwhile Olaudah Equiano, better known in his time as Gustavas Vassa.[3]

This final chapter turns to the figure of ghosts. Of all the figures discussed throughout this book, the ghost may be most analogous to Oceanic lifespans as a cultural analytic: Both have a way of troubling our sense of time, complicating the conditions of visibility, and drawing our attention to the vicissitudes of embodiment. Just as age is a framework for reading black embodiment and subjectivity as that which is constituted by virtue of a counter-normative experience of western modernity, the ghost is never a straightforward representation of the way the past "really was." Nor is it fully available to be seen or comprehended all at once in the present. Rather, the ghost prompts an ongoing practice of assessing how we know what we think we know, and of continuously recognizing what or who troubles the foundations of knowledge and being. As Avery Gordon notes, the haunting of ghosts "is a very particular way of knowing what has happened or is happening."[4] Further, this particular mode of perception, which defies the impermeable boundaries of conventional facticity, is impressed upon someone, either an individual or a collective: Haunted subjects are entangled in some way with the ghost who haunts.

Each text that I discuss in this chapter illustrates a specific characteristic of haunting, and a particular relation between haunting and the untimeliness of black age. Generally, the entanglement between the haunting and the haunted is interpreted as encounters between simultaneous, yet disjoined, versions of age. One version exists in and as a manifestation of hegemonic time—linear, progressive, developmental, conventionally factual time. It is an embodied temporality that finds formal expression in the autobiography and romance, and historical-political expression in the nation. Another version shares the untimely character of ghosts, and its untimeliness disturbs the singular, factual reality of hegemonic time. Both the ghost and its haunting induce someone into an alternative register of reality, which reveals what has occurred or is occurring.[5] This chapter focuses on the way the conspicuously untimely age of ghosts is the key inducement that leads the normatively liberal and neoliberal subject to the haunting recognition that one is caught up in an ongoing, formative process that is both historical and personal. While each of the preceding chapters focuses on two complementary cultural figures, this chapter unfolds through exemplary pairings of a ghost who haunts and the one who is haunted. Yet, the relation between the two does not comprise a tidy or enclosed sphere of influence. Ghosts are never only one-dimensional; they are the re-enchantment of spirits that are multiple, unto themselves.⁶ The past's multiple spirits may be reenchanted in the present at any time. Only some of these, such as the spirit of western liberalism and its progressive temporality, have become knowable as "history."

Lisa Lowe's method for investigating the relations between liberalism and its dehumanizing underbelly in the political economy of oceans influences my approach to thinking of how historical time appears as a "history." Lowe refers to the "past conditional temporality," also known as "what could have been," a ghostly space of differently knowing: It "symbolizes aptly the space of a different kind of thinking, a space of productive attention to the scene of loss, a thinking with twofold attention that seeks to encompass at once the positive objects and methods of history and social science, and also the absent, entangled, and unavailable by its methods."⁷ For Lowe, to think with such twofold attention reveals how our efforts to recognize and protect human life are continually limited to the historically narrow terms of liberal humanism. We need a means to imagine what could have been, which relies not only on positively knowable objects and methods, but also on responsiveness to routinized forgetting and disavowal. In this chapter, and indeed throughout this book, black age figures such possibility.

We begin with a speculative consideration of the one I refer to as the "Equiano Girl," as an early model for the haunting and untimely presence that emerges in the black literary imagination. Rather than think of her only as either an absence in the historical record or a vague indication of the historical record's inauthenticity, I consider how suspended, ghostly girlhood presses on a text that focuses on Equiano's developmental manhood. Equiano's sister—whose proper name we never learn—indexes an unthought-of, non-developmental, and alternatively gendered dimension of what survives the first phases of the slave trade, and expressly, what is not reducible to liberal subjectivity. Imagine that Equiano, who makes the progressive transition from African child, to slave, to liberated man, is entangled with a ghostly counterpart—a silent, unnamed, Equiano Girl, a perennial female child. To keep such an entanglement in mind is to remember that, in the beginning, there were *two* Equiano children. In her brother's narrative, the Equiano Girl's female childhood signifies the end of one historical trajectory and the beginning of another, which the Middle Passage divides. It signifies both the end of progressive maturation and a historiographic spirit of what never really ends, what can always return. I briefly discuss how two ghostly appearances of the Equiano Girl in *The Interesting Narrative* illustrate two divergent spirits of historical time with which Equiano is entangled: One is the spirit of liberal humanism that bolsters Equiano's singular course toward proper manhood, at the exclusion of his female, statically juvenile, counterpart. Yet, she also conjures up a mode of melancholic affect that troubles Equiano's self-fashioning as a knowable, progressively moving subject. In both forms of entanglement, the Equiano Girl is cast beyond what is thought of or represented within "history." She is emblematic of how ghosts function in this chapter: They are an aberrance of age—both temporal and embodied—that reveals, in another plane of knowing, how the black liberal subject makes a claim to history.

In two ghost stories that bracket the emancipatory promises of liberalism's expansion in the twentieth century, Charles Chesnutt's 1898 short story, "The Wife of His Youth," and Toni Morrison's final novel, *God Help the Child* (2015), time becomes conspicuously peculiar. In both, haunting troubles the aspirations of black subjects who strive to make progress in liberal humanist terms—as citizens, entrepreneurs, husbands, wives. In addition, haunting is an embodying process, thus, to be haunted is to be transformed by and into the untimely alternatives to proper liberal and neoliberal subjectivity. In Chesnutt's story, 'Liza Jane, the wife that the bourgeois and upwardly mobile Ryder had forgotten about since their separation before the Civil War, suddenly reappears. Due to her agedness, the elderly 'Liza Jane resembles the relic, a figure of black untimeliness that we have seen in chapter 2. Like the relic, the ghost is immortal, forever bound to appear. Yet, Ryder's entanglement with the ghost ironically conjures a past that undermines his manhood—his masculine adulthood—upon which romance is conventionally predicated. As we learn, during slavery, Ryder was a free-born juvenile whose freedom became most precarious on the verge of his becoming an adult. Just as Equiano's proper liberal subjectivity depends on his developmental maturation, so too does Ryder's. The elderly ghost, the wife of his "youth," returns to reveal that the modern age is comprised of multiple registers of racial time. Lovingly, she releases Ryder from the binds of aspirational manhood.

But at the start of the twenty-first century, the ghost critiques the progress narrative that still typifies our time and shapes our sense of the world's age. Morrison's final novel, *God Help the Child*, is set in the present, and its protagonist, Bride, is born in the 1990s. Bride is a shallow-yet-successful dark-skinned black woman who magically regresses into the body of a pre-pubescent girl. Bride's mother, Sweetness, who would have been about 40 years old when Bride was born, seems much older than her current 63 years. Her narrating voice, which evokes the Jim Crow era and is most critical of Bride, makes the textual absence of the 1960s and 1970s conspicuous. Given when the novel is set, Sweetness should have come of age during that era. The absence—which is indicative of a spirit of black feminism we have lost—is from whence her ghostly voice emerges. Sweetness conjures the ghost of feminism, and the ghost's influence manifests in the disappearance of Bride's bodily maturity.

There is no extant autobiography or coming-of-age narrative written by a black female of any age who survived the Middle Passage, as Hartman reminds us. As a result, "girlhood" represents historical loss that draws scholars into the archives in search of missing subjects at the phase of enslavement called the Middle Passage. But in Morrison's final novel, black "girlhood" appears as a warning from history, an indication that we bear some responsibility for what we lose. Thus, Bride's artificial, conjured, "neoliberal girlhood" stands in stark contrast to the black girlhood of actual historical subjects and the black girlhood of Pecola, the under-loved child of Morrison's first novel, *The Bluest Eye* (1970). As I have argued in the introduction and elsewhere in this book, black feminists of the 1970s have drawn from their girlhood experiences to fashion a critical framework for analyzing the interlocking oppressions that impacted their social lives. In a word, black girlhood was a key subjective standpoint of black feminist critique. By bringing forth the absence of the 1970s, Sweetness—and Morrison's final novel overall—beseeches us to reexamine the substance of what we had decided counts as maturity, where we have arrived, and who we aspire to be. What possibilities for liberating relationality—with girls and women and adults and boys and children—can we make for ourselves, now?

The Equiano Girl and Equiano: *The Interesting Narrative*

To be haunted, as Avery Gordon helps us to realize, runs against liberalism's promises of freedom and transcendence, since one never chooses with whom or with what one has become entangled: "Haunting is exactly what causes declarative repudiations and voluntaristic identifications eventually to fail."[8] This is no less true for the formerly enslaved person who writes himself into liberal subjectivity than for the contemporary white subject who denies identifications with the slave-owning past. Up until the time of their capture, the Equiano siblings share the same social world. The Equiano boy was destined to inherit the "mark of grandeur" conferred upon his father, a brother, and other respected statesmen.[9] The Equiano girl was "the only daughter" in their large family of high standing.[10] Had they remained in Essaka, both boy and girl would have matured along a socially normative, chronological timeline in which gender norms inform how each inhabits the status of adulthood.[11] Yet, the story of their capture introduces another temporality that breaks into the previous one and effectively splits the siblings apart. This splitting off occurs during what Walter Johnson has called the First Passage, the several months of transport from the continental interior to the coast, where Africans were sold into the European trade. Equiano remarks that he had never seen as much water as the ocean before reaching the coast of Guinea.

Although this book has situated *the Oceanic* as a key analytical concept for attending to such divergence from hegemonic experiences of time that the transatlantic slave trade had wrought, we can acknowledge that the Atlantic Ocean is far from the only site at which the untimely effects of modern black formation are discernable. Indeed, we noticed such effects through the domestic slave trade of the nineteenth century, discussed in chapter 1, and on the plantation, as we saw in the previous chapter. To restate, *the Oceanic* is my term; it combines the subjective non-differentiation that defines Sigmund Freud's concept of the "oceanic feeling," a state in which the fully mature, individuated subject gives over to a regressive sense of wholeness, of being attached to a presence outside of itself, with Hortense Spillers's reading of the Middle Passage as the site at which human cargo is undifferentiated by virtue of being violently ungendered. The Oceanic, then, frames modern black racial formation as a process that renders black subjects socially non-conforming to normative age and life stage distinctions. Thus, the Oceanic names non-normative modes of social belonging that conspicuously appear as untimely black age.

Yet, the Equiano Girl is a textual occasion for asking how to account for such modes when the effects are unseen, or when they challenge what we know about transatlantic slavery's formative geographies. The First Passage usefully draws our attention to the overrepresentation of the Middle Passage as the presumptive origin of modern blackness and emphasizes transatlantic slavery's multidimensional temporality.[12] Between Essaka and the Middle Passage, the Equiano siblings split off in divergent directions—one that leads to historical prominence and another that leads to historical obscurity. We do not know whether the Equiano Girl ever reached or crossed the Atlantic Ocean; as King suggests, she could have been "integrated into domestic slavery elsewhere in Africa," among other possible fates.[13] She defies what Michelle Wright calls "the simple linear progress narrative of the Middle Passage epistemology," since we lose her before the Middle Passage.[14] She joins the many unnamed women and girls for whom we have no experiential details about the crossing.[15] Further, as a subject without an extant autobiographical account of crossing and surviving the Middle Passage, the Girl widens the geographical purview of where modern black subject formation occurs. It occurs across the Middle Passage and through the cultural exchanges of what Paul Gilroy has referred to as the Black Atlantic. But it also occurs before captives reached the shores, on land, perhaps before or without direct contact with European traders. Thus, the split between the siblings is metaphorical of which timelines and geographies emerge as the epistemological basis for history, and which ones dissipate like dust on a road.

As others have noted, Equiano's ethnographic sketch of Igbo social life in the opening chapter lacks the subjective details presented in the rest of the narrative and may have drawn as much from secondary source material as from his own recollection.[16] As a result, the Equiano Girl, like the other members of Equiano's family, is vaguely rendered, devoid of identifying details. But this representational opacity regarding Equiano's sister is particularly curious, since she is the only sibling who shares Equiano's experience of abduction, the only relative included in the narrative's pertinent captivity plot. She is the only other Equiano to be snatched out of the idyllic tableau of Essaka and dropped into the transatlantic political economy of the slave trade. Thus, like her brother, she is pulled from the chapter in which Africa and Africans are treated as objects of European knowledge, into a market from which Equiano will progress from enslaved boy to self-possessive, individuated man.

But if the moment of abrupt and catastrophic seizure from one condition and placement into another functions as the impetus for Equiano's self-actualizing journey, it does the opposite for the Equiano Girl. She becomes an ephemeral bridge between the undisturbed, Igboland past and the diasporic present. Bridges that are temporal as well as geographic enable others to move while they remain static: having been seized from her home and yet disappeared before reaching the sea coast, she is situated in neither the distant African past nor Equiano's modern, oceanic travel narrative. As the frequently overlooked subject of literary criticism, and as either the outcome of historical fiction or historical fact, the Equiano Girl is in this liminal position of representation. The girlhood of the Equiano Girl indexes what remains unthought-of in the archives of transatlantic slavery and in the liberal imagination, and because of its own lack of both conceptual and fleshy substance, girlhood appears as an ephemeral, perhaps hovering, non-progressive presence that contrasts with the properly historical subject who moves with developmental time. In the pace of history, there is no time to say her name or to bury the dead.

But the dead, unburied, remain. They are the "ghosts of slavery," as Jenny Sharpe terms the elusive and partial appearance of evidence of how enslaved women understood their own lives and actions in the historical record.[17] Black girlhood, through historical absence and partial—ghostly—presence has been constituted as a historical category of anonymity, against which the singular, positivist reality of other subjects and objects appear. To this point, Christina Sharpe refers to an anonymous black girl of our own time. She is captured in a photo with the word "Ship" taped to her forehead "in the wake" of ecological disaster and an anti-black episteme. Sharpe writes, "In that 2010 photo the meager child is not Phillis [the slave ship after which Phillis Wheatley was named], but *Ship*; that is, she is not a *particular* ship/girl named Phillis but *any* ship/child/girl; the part for the whole."[18] Yet, while Equiano does not write of his sister in specifying terms, he does confer particularity to ships. As William Boelhower points out, Equiano is diligent about naming the more than two dozen ships on which he sails: "The ships' names seem like so many unopened documents waiting to be studied—visible signs of a connecting practice which can best be traced on transatlantic mappemondes."[19] Like the evolving maps that represented transatlantic space, the ships index histories that await our discovery—presumably, unlike the Girl.

Yet, the Equiano Girl survives in her brother's autobiography as an index of evidence that has yet to be unfurled. More important, she survives as a provocation that troubles the very conditions of historical survival and discovery, conditions that give form and substance to the past in the present and vice versa. As Hartman writes of the "Venus" who survives the archives of slavery as evidence of the unknowable, her value "is in illuminating the way in which our age is tethered to hers. A relation which others might describe as a kind of melancholia, but which I prefer to describe in terms of the afterlife of property, by which I mean the detritus of lives with which we have yet to attend, a past that has yet to be done."[20] A kind of melancholia and the afterlife of property name two different relational frameworks for the historical, and both are applicable to the reading of Equiano's narrative. In the first, we might consider ourselves suspended by and with historical loss. The archive's dehumanizing absences and neologisms, and the array of social losses that produced them, constitute our own sense of loss with which we cannot come to terms.[21] As the lost object that is not entirely knowable to the one who assimilates the loss, the Equiano Girl haunts as ghosts do: She is beckoned, she (partially) appears, and she arises at various times and places while seeming not to move across time and space. As a figure of temporal, geographic, and epistemic suspension, she gestures toward Equiano's representational choices, and his own unlikely suspension. He is aware of his losses, and yet in ways that are subtle and inexplicit, Equiano's textual persona is produced in a constitutive relation to loss that is emotionally fraught, but such an affective state cannot be fully recognized in the narrative's governing terms of liberal self-possession and progress.

As a figure of the afterlife of property, the Equiano Girl gestures toward what has happened and is happening in terms of the opacity of black girlhood subjectivity in dominant culture. She gestures toward an under-examined link between the property relations of the slave trade, a process in which black girlhood subjectivity has been constituted as historically and culturally un-representable through those relations, and the manner in which the remainders of this history live with us now, as in the routine invisibility and "adultification" of black girlhood.[22] She draws a connection between "now" and "then": *Now*, in our time, she haunts as silence that shrouds the subjectivities of enslaved girls and women in the historical record of slavery; *then*, in the eighteenth century, she haunts her brother with the precariousness of his survival, freedom, and manhood. In effect, Equiano's narrative subtly expresses and shares social concerns that are currently recognizable to us as the evidentiary absence of black girlhood.

As I am arguing, the text both conceals and reveals the fact that Equiano is tethered to the Equiano Girl, and melancholia and the afterlife of property are concomitant temporal structures of this entanglement. Since the narrative ostensibly disavows the haunting condition of entanglement, social loss appears as a constitutive aspect of political progress's social gains. The disappearance of the Equiano Girl seems to be an inevitable part of the proper Equiano's development, in all senses of that word. But the narrative begins with two Equianos, and I suggest that we consider both as Janus-faced sides of avowed and disavowed pasts. As such, the inevitability with which one singular, textual Equiano survives into our present gives way to conditionality: Which gendered Equiano survives as an individuated, singular subject? Which one disappears?

In what follows, I read two moments in Equiano's narrative that illustrate how the Equiano Girl haunts her brother's narrative by giving rise to two distinct historiographic spirits. The occasion for the first is Equiano's recounting of how the two siblings were separated before his transport as chattel across the Atlantic Ocean. The first historiographic spirit is liberalism's political ideology of propertied manhood: Equiano is the consummate self-made man, the slave who became the autonomous, propertied subject. To enchant this historiographic account in his autobiography, Equiano marks a clear separation between himself and the Equiano Girl. Instead of emphasizing a lateral, shared kinship of condition with his sibling, Equiano uses the conventions of sentimentalism to install a hierarchy between himself, the properly masculine adult, and a sister who is the object of his humanizing care and concern. Through this hierarchical schema, the subjectivity and ontology of black girlhood are hidden in the enchantment of proper liberal personhood. By burying and then sentimentally memorializing the Equiano Girl, Equiano speaks as the only reasonable subject of history.

Yet, as Lowe argues, although Equiano wrote in a genre that most exemplifies liberal individualism, his autobiography is haunted by other subjects who are susceptible to a process of historical forgetting.[23] The autobiographical genre contributes to the disavowal of enslaved masses that constitute the backdrop of Equiano's adventures, and his own enslaved status after manumission. In Lowe's reading, Equiano's freedom is complicated by the failure of forgetting, by the way freedom is entangled with the ghostly remains of transcontinental social relations, through which Equiano was constituted as a slave.[24] Aligned with the failure of forgetting, the second historiographic spirit enchants a version of the past that has been disavowed, of which the Equiano Girl is emblematic. Equiano evokes her as the object of humanizing sentimentality in the first instance. In the second, she reemerges as an illustration of unfinished grief, which cannot be adequately or fully expressed in his autobiography. Taken together, both moments demonstrate how the Equiano Girl conjures historiographic conditions that cast Equiano either as a properly knowable subject who develops in progressive time, or as a not-quite-representable subject who is ambivalently entangled with the missing sibling. In both cases, the Equiano Girl appears to us as a historical problem: as a figure who conjures the conditions of possibility for what counts as history and who counts as a historical agent, her own subjectivity is beyond the pale of representation, and deemed as insufficiently historical. In other words, the Equiano Girl, like the slave across ideological discourses, occupied what Hartman has called "the position of the unthought."[25]

Here is what that looks like in a sentimental mode:

> Sharer of my joys and sorrows; happy should I have ever esteemed myself to encounter every misery for you, and to procure your freedom by the sacrifice of my own! Though you were early forced from my arms, your image has been always rivetted [sic] in my heart, from which time nor fortune has been able to remove it [. . .]. To that Heaven, which

protects the weak from the strong, I commit the care of your innocence and virtues, if they have not already received their full reward, and your youth and delicacy have not long since fallen victims to the violence of the African trader, the pestilential stench of a Guinea ship, the seasoning in the European colonies, or the lash and lust of a brutal and unrelenting overseer.[26]

Nazera Wright observes that this moment in *The Interesting Narrative* is paradigmatic of a function that black girls play in black male-authored protest literature, particularly of the nineteenth century: They are the objects of black men's protection. As Wright reads the moment quoted above, "Equiano emphasized the connection between his sister's suffering and his budding masculinity."[27] In a word, Equiano achieves his political subjectivity in relation to his sister, who is cast as a suffering object that stands in as an exemplary effect of slavery's depravity. The residual logic in nineteenth-century cultural politics that Wright describes corresponds to routinized objectification of black girlhood in the archive of transatlantic slavery. Black girls routinely appear in the archival record as anonymous figures against whom myriad forms of violence are waged, and of whom we know little else.[28]

By evoking the Equiano Girl as his abject counterpart with whom he is riveted, Equiano summons western humanism's social grammar of gender pairs, which the "Native" and the "savage" are denied during an early modern epistemic shift.[29] In the process of constructing the Equiano Girl as a sentimental object, for whom a white reading audience has sympathy, the narrative confers proper female gender to her, so that she becomes intelligible to the reader as innocent, virtuous, delicate, young, and thus worthy of the paternalist protection that Equiano rhetorically bestows. With a gendered subject and object of protection installed in the reader's imagination, the inevitable brutalities of transatlantic slavery also become gendered, and implicitly take on a temporal dimension: the one who transcends the trader, the slave ship's pestilential stench, plantation labor, and lash is also the fully mature man who might very well be "seated by [his] own table, in the enjoyment of freedom and the happiness of home, writing this Narrative," as Frederick Douglass wrote more than 50 years later.[30] As Henry Louis Gates, Jr., has claimed, Equiano's narrative is comfortably situated in the African American literary canon as Douglass's "silent second text," which is to say, as the model for the nineteenth-century slave narrative that constructs a writerly persona that is, most famously, a man.[31] Equiano enchants manhood in the register of the human, and in the process, he shores up the patriarchal logic of chivalry, by which he offers the rhetorical sacrifice of his own freedom for hers.

But just as Equiano's rhetoric in this moment conjures up some spirits, it also "conjures away," as Derrida has put it, other interpretations of the past, ones that would reenchant slavery's constitution of western blackness as both ungendered and untimely.[32] This other, dismissed spirit would enchant the ongoing implications of what is described later, when the slave ship on which Equiano is transported arrives in Barbados. When describing what happens next, it becomes impossible to avoid thinking of slavery's endless technologies for manipulating bodies while unmaking humanity: "We were conducted immediately to the merchant's yard, where we were all pent up together like so many sheep in a fold, without regard to sex or age."[33] In a narrative genre that affirms individuation, Equiano attains his humanity by rhetorically distinguishing himself from an array of undifferentiated others, starting with those left behind in Essaka. Equiano distinguishes himself from the Equiano Girl. Somewhere along the under-thought-of journey that leads to the ocean, Equiano is severed from the "Girl," which is like an appendage that undercuts his future claims to being human. As a carryover of something not properly civil, "Girl," past tense, is like the dehumanizing marks of facial scars that the anonymous masses of "African nations" etch into flesh, marks that Equiano is thankful he did not get.[34]

In this process of differentiation, the "Girl" is distinguishable from the "child," which Equiano once was. It is significant that Equiano the *slave* was once a *boy*, because boyhood, like manhood, is a social condition that separates the male subject from female subjection, and therefore from the femaleness that characterizes enslavement. Since Gates and others have regarded *The Interesting Narrative* as the urtext of Douglass's *Narrative*, the critical and textual negation of Equiano's sister can be interpreted as the "silent second text" upon which Aunt Hester's spectacularly brutalized flesh is written, whose subsequent scream echoes throughout the sounds of subsequent black culture.[35]

Through her brother's sentimental rhetoric, the Equiano Girl can only "appear," albeit as an abstracted figure, in the context of subjugation and, thus, as the natural bearer of the slave trade's brutality. Yet, in contrast to his sister's narrow representational capacity, Equiano recalls his own boyhood as a subjective stage of nuanced and complicated perspective. Amidst the horrors of the slave ship—with undifferentiated human cargo in the stifling, pestilent hold—Equiano, as a boy too young for fetters, manages to marvel at the leaping fish and solid-looking clouds, as we observed in the previous chapter. Even as he endures the fear and uncertainty of his passage to the sea coast, the boy finds something akin to comfort and belonging in the homes of two African families during his servitude.[36] Equiano's boyhood appreciation of a wondrous world and domestic order invokes emergent ideologies of middle-class childhood of late-eighteenth century Britain, in which the child, lacking the morality, rationality, and productive acumen of the properly male, adult subject, could be correctly managed in the domestic home to become such, with suitable religious training and rational education.[37] Such discipline is demonstrable in Equiano's time in London, when relatives of his master, the Guerin sisters, oversee his education and baptism, to developmentally beneficial effect. Moreover, during his entire adolescence at sea, Equiano receives practical training from paternalist masters. If Equiano fashions himself as having been the proper child, the subject of adult management and knowledge production, then he narrates his past to illustrate this, so that we may see how the boy becomes a self-regulating man of business and industry.

By contrast, the Equiano Girl anticipates the limits of representing enslaved girlhood and female development in socially hegemonic terms. Thus, just as Douglass recaptures the spirit of Equiano's properly developmental masculinity, so too does Aunt Hester enchant the Equiano Girl's untimeliness. Aunt Hester's subjection amounts to her degeneration into carnality, which is the opposite of young Frederick's developmental trajectory into manhood. She makes the horrifying, developmental reversion from the "woman of noble form" to bleeding, screaming flesh.[38] While Equiano rhetorically figures his sister's fate in the debasing terms of slavery, thereby implying that female childhood has no projected future as meaningful adulthood, Douglass illustrates that enslaved female adulthood can be brutally unmade. As a boy, Frederick sees Aunt Hester being beaten and expects that "it would be my turn next."[39] Yet, the prolepsis of this boyhood experience ensures that Frederick will refuse his turn, as his battle with Covey dramatizes. Unlike Aunt Hester, whose feminine adulthood serves as a conduit to her subjection, Frederick will one day be a man, an actual adult, rather than a slave.

But as abject, vague, and ephemeral as she is, and as much as the narrative does to mark rhetorical and subjective separations between the two along the lines of gender and age, the Equiano Girl is riveted to her brother. She haunts him; it is, as Gordon puts it, "haunting as memory."[40] She comes closest to appearing, being seen, returning—in a word, to haunting—in the fourth chapter, when Equiano believes himself to be close to freedom, but is ultimately abducted anew, and captured into a more brutal form of slavery. The Equiano Girl's reemergence anticipates what becomes clear at the end of the chapter, which is that her brother's proximity to freedom is illusory.

After a period of being treated well in London, Equiano and his master, Michael Henry Pascal, sail to the Mediterranean. There, a fleeting reminder of the past arises. It is of so little ostensible consequence that we, like Equiano, are inclined to let it disappear without reckoning with what happened, is happening:

> I had frequently told several people, in my excursions on shore, the story of my being kidnapped with my sister, and of our being separated, as before related; and I had as often expressed my anxiety for her fate, and my sorrow at having never met her again. One day, when I was on shore, and mentioning these circumstances to some persons, one of them told me he knew where my sister was, and if I would accompany him, he would conduct me to her. Improbable as the story was, I believed it immediately, and agreed to go with him, which my heart leaped with joy; and, indeed, he conducted me to a black young woman, who was so like my sister that, at first sight, I really thought it was she; but I was quickly undeceived; and, on talking to her, I found her to be of another nation.[41]

Without a doubt, Equiano remembers his sister. He frequently talks about losing her. He repeats what he has already dramatically described in the narrative, but this time without sentimentality or any clearly identifiable mode of emotional expressiveness. Equiano's straightforward description of his encounter with the young female stranger has led critics either to undermine the significance of Equiano's family of origin in the narrative, or to dismiss the sentimentalism of Equiano's previous rhetoric.[42] According to Carretta, since Equiano successfully developed other kinship relations after losing his African family of origin, "he was not overwhelmed by grief when his hopes of being reunited with his sister were disappointed in 1759."[43] As evidence of how little Equiano grieved his sister, Carretta directs us to the following paragraph, where we notice that he "reacted far less dispassionately" to the death of his friend, Dick. Regardless of whether she is evoked as the object of sentimentalism or dispassion, the Equiano Girl eludes serious consideration as historical evidence of things not seen. Yet, she is figurative of an aspect of Equiano's subjectivity that the conventions of the autobiography cannot capture.

Just as sentimentalism is the conventional affective mode for conferring humanity to improperly gendered and aged objects, dispassion conceals an alternative mode of affect, along with other ways of seeing how Equiano's subjectivity has been constituted in relation to the Girl. We have seen the dominant version of his relation to her: Equiano rhetorically conjures and affirms the spirit of liberal humanism in the first excerpt, burying and honoring his enslaved sister in the process. They are riveted together in a "you-or-me" schema that is double voiced: Equiano gallantly speaks of manly sacrifice for her, while at the same time, he affirms his own survival in the face of her intensified obscurity. The double voice of this schema underscores how beyond the realm of representability the enslaved Equiano Girl is. In contrast, the second excerpt illustrates how the "inevitable failure" of writing a historiographical account of the profoundly dispossessed, such as all the anonymous Venuses in the archives of transatlantic slavery, touches Equiano.[44] Through seeming dispassion over the renewed loss of his sister, Equiano casts himself as one who, like his sister, defies representation. This failure of representation, the opacity of subjectivity, indicates that Equiano has a melancholic relation to the Equiano Girl, "the other-made-ghostly," as Anne Cheng describes the haunting of melancholia. The one who is lost—the one who could not survive the passages of slavery by being either a child or a masculine subject deemed suitable for social development—constitutes the other.

Haunted by the lost object that he assimilates into himself, Equiano expresses emotional responses that are discernable in various registers. We know that he was conscious of the loss, and that he continued to mourn it, as he repeatedly told strangers. It is possible for the melancholic subject to mourn. Anxiety and sorrow are on the surface. To mourn is not only to maintain a separation between oneself and the object that is lost; it is to allow the separation to function as a condition of possibility for the object to return. Between letting go and holding on, Equiano leaps at the improbable possibility of reuniting with his sister, perhaps because this very same improbable possibility has already occurred roughly three years prior, along the First Passage. The numerous repetitions in this scene—the evocation of the two earlier separations with his sister in the narrative's second chapter, the frequent retelling of these separations to strangers, and a potential repeat of an improbable reunion—are illustrative of a wound that has not been adequately attended to and incorporated as memory. The reality of traumatic loss flashes up in the unlikeliest of narrative spaces, between two unrelated events, that would have a more disruptive effect on narrative causality, were it not for its seeming lack of consequence. In this haunted moment, Equiano cannot fully repudiate the way the past claims him. In between mourning and melancholia, between a conscious recognition of loss and an unconscious loss of self, the scene provides, on a lower frequency, what Jermaine Singleton calls a disavowed, "hidden affect."[45] Equiano affirms his love for his sister, *and* he harbors hidden resentment of the Equiano Girl who refuses to survive. Resentment toward the sister he loves is not representable in the narrative for being disavowed. Equiano's ambivalence, which lends itself to the scene's emotionally muted tone, can only appear as "progress," which is to say, as the evidence that Equiano has successfully acclimated to a worldly life at sea.

But the young black woman on the shores of Gibraltar is a ghost. At first, Equiano believes that his sister has returned—has decided to return, to be retrieved. And yet, unlike the earlier moment when the Equiano children were briefly reunited, this ghostly moment reveals that ghosts never move through just one temporal direction: The figure of a person who seems to return is simultaneously appearing for the first time as something, someone new.[46] This newness, figured as a black woman, signifies social loss as a formative condition of modern black subjectivity. Equiano's renewed sense of losing is unspeakable. It is what Equiano likely experiences when he encounters yet another stranger from another nation, and what comes to dramatic fruition at the end of chapter 4, when Pascal betrays Equiano's expectations of being manumitted by selling him into a more brutal mode of slavery. Pascal's betrayal is preceded by the Equiano Girl's deception—her false newness, her false survival—which Equiano perceives as self-deception. With a flesh-and-blood body that seems to have matured with virtue intact, undisturbed, over the years of their separation, the Equiano Girl deceives her brother by appearing in the world as if she could have grown as he has. She deceives him; growth is for the living. Her grown, fleshy-specter body is an impossibility, not to be believed. The ghost manifests a moment of non-recognition that Equiano must rationally dismiss, in order to move on with his narrative of development. But by doing so, he leaves an unreconciled remainder, a trace of unfinished, unattended-to grief-as-history, behind. This trace is the Girl.

'Liza Jane and Mr. Ryder: "The Wife of His Youth"

Thus, conjuring ghosts is not an entirely conscious act, nor does one have total control over what will be. Melancholia is just one structure of ghostly relations: As we have seen, the ghost can be a constitutive part of the person who is haunted, and in this melancholic relation, the course of naturalized development is troubled and held in suspension. Equiano rejects the Equiano Girl for deceptively appearing in the form of a familiar stranger, as if her development is possible. And through this rejection, Equiano tacitly and unknowingly confronts his own stymied route to mature personhood—baptism, proper education, and maritime training notwithstanding. In that moment, Equiano is suspended in the non-developmental status of the slave. But before this melancholic haunting appears in the text, Equiano engages in another mode of Derridean conjuration: He calls on the past he needs. The spirit of the recent past—the ongoing legacy of liberal humanism—is reenchanted, and it influences what could be now and in the future. As the heroic liberal subject, Equiano speaks in memory of the defeated Equiano Girl, and thereby conjures liberalism as the spirit of survival over historical defeat. Before his melancholic haunting, Equiano speaks as the only surviving Equiano, the only living adult.

Conjuration figures history as indeterminate, as that which defies progressive determinism. Charles Chesnutt is a literary master of conjuration—the bewitchment and superstitions that live on in the folkloric tradition of black elderly folk in the South—and uses it to make the arrival of the twentieth century feel less inevitable.[47] The post-emancipated present is shot through with traces of what is both no longer and still here. It is shaped by the paradoxical ontology of haunting that Derrida referred to as hauntology. In what follows, the relation between the liberal subject and the ghost shifts from the two modes we have just considered—historical triumph and melancholic suspension—to one of romance.

For the purposes of this discussion about black subjective life at a moment of historical transition, "romance" maintains its conventional connotations, which are associated with medieval chivalry and knightly comportment, but it also serves as a metaphor for other, under-recognized types of attachments, love, and commitment. In this second, metaphorical register, romance reimagines an exchange that we saw in chapter 2, between the elderly, female relic and "the One," the exceptional, masculine race leader. Under the metaphorical veil of romance, the properly liberal, free-willed, and self-possessive masculine subject does not simply desire the ancient black woman's capacity to act as a mediator between a sacred, longed-for past and the present moment of progress. In Chesnutt's story, such desire is precisely what is missing. Rather, through his intimate entanglement with the relic—who is reimagined in this chapter as a ghost—the liberal subject transforms into another, improper mode of being. Instead of thinking of this transformation as a form of regression, I suggest that the liberal subject in this case willingly embraces his own non-adulthood, which is a mode of alternative humanity that does not entail the normative aspiration toward possessive manhood. In this relation, "romance" is a metaphor for a queer heroism that levels out the gender and age hierarchies between subjects and objects in western humanist genres, which includes the autobiography discussed above. Sometimes we summon our ghosts; sometimes our ghosts are a constitutive part of ourselves. At other times, our ghosts lovingly pursue us, and lovingly unmake us.

In Chesnutt's 1898 short story, "The Wife of His Youth," Mr. Ryder is a dashing and respectable man of middle age—no one knows how old he is, exactly—who works as a railroad company clerk in a fictional version of Cleveland, Ohio.[48] He is the head of a social organization that is colloquially referred to as the "Blue Vein Society," since its members are "more white than black," fair-skinned enough for their blue veins to show.[49] The members refute the common perception that nearly white skin is an actual requirement for membership. Significantly, they also reject another misconception, which is that all members must be free born. As we will see, this second rumor hints at the reason why Ryder in particular is haunted. Ryder has decided to host a ball as the occasion to propose marriage to Mrs. Molly Dixon, a widow who is much younger, whiter-skinned, and better educated than he. But just as Ryder is deciding on which poem to read in Dixon's honor, an elderly, homely, very dark-skinned stranger arrives. 'Liza Jane has been inquiring throughout the town about the husband from whom she was separated during slavery, a man named Sam Taylor. She shows Ryder a daguerreotype of Taylor that she wears around her neck. In what is ultimately revealed to be an amnesic moment, Ryder claims never to have seen her husband. Eventually, at the ball, just when Ryder seems primed to toast Dixon, he instead asks his guests whether a man who had been parted from his devoted wife during slavery should reclaim her after their 25-year separation, despite how harshly time has treated her. Should he reclaim her, or profess his love to another? The guests, including Dixon, are touched by the story and overwhelmingly agree that such a man should reclaim his wife. And with that, Ryder brings 'Liza Jane into the room, and introduces her as the wife of his youth.

From the outset, it seems as if Ryder is the least likely person to call on the influence of specters. To the contrary, he is the paragon of timeliness. As the "dean of the Blue Veins," he is the untroubled standard-bearer for the organization's elitism. As he sees it, the Blue Vein Society, with him at the helm of it, bears the unique responsibility of shepherding the black masses through the challenges of the post-liberated present. They are "a lifeboat, an anchor, a bulwark and shield [. . .] to guide their people through the social wilderness."[50] If it turns out that the Blue Vein Society is a de facto mixed-racial organization, this just underscores its unique role in effecting social progress, which ironically entails maintaining a black-white color line by seeing to the upward immersion of racial mixed people into white society. The "fate" of mixed racial subjects "lies between absorption by the white race and extinction in the black. [. . .] we must do the best we can for ourselves and those who are to follow us. Self-preservation is the first law of nature."[51] As Ryder sees it, "marriage with Mrs. Dixon would help to further the upward process of absorption he had been wishing and waiting for."[52]

It is significant that Ryder yokes his own deeply desired social ascension to marriage, an institution that reproduces patriarchal gender norms. Self-preservation—the will to survive as a matter of historical posterity—relies on this gendering process. Ryder's aspiration to achieve patriarchal manhood sparks his wishing and waiting. This may seem unlikely, since Ryder appears to have already achieved manhood: He is a leader of the black bourgeoisie. He is self-possessive enough to own his own home and leisure time. From the very beginning of the story, Ryder is in possessive control of time, tout court: We are told that, "There were several reasons why this was an opportune time" for Ryder to host a ball, and these reasons are entirely self-serving.[53] Still, while Chesnutt's story forefronts race as the primary category of analysis, so that all of the major plot points, from the racial mixedness of the Blue Veins to Dixon's near-whiteness to the eventual arrival of the very dark-skinned 'Liza Jane are already framed with that singular lens, I suggest that Ryder's desire for both upward absorption *and* marriage directs our attention to a tacit problem that lies in the heart of both gender and age. Thus, Dixon is an emblem of ascendance into whiteness, but less obviously, she is a supplement for a lack of "manhood." It is this lack that engenders Ryder's desires.

Lack further pertains to the adulthood connoted through manhood. As Catherine Keyser notes, Ryder's racial theory recapitulates dominant views of the time: "Ryder blends the modern myths of historical progress, uneven development, and social Darwinism and condemns himself to liminality and competition."[54] Timely racialist discourse has the remarkable, unwitting effect of condemning Ryder to his own disavowed untimeliness. As I have been arguing throughout this book, all of these myths contribute to what constitutes human time, which is socially expressed as age. Ryder's own profound sense of liminality is attributed to the ostensible problem of his "mixed blood," but I read this as a deflection from an underlying problem of development, for which mixed race is merely a metaphor. "Development" encompasses the vast array of historical, social, and scientific discourses about who has a useable past, mastery of the present, and claim to the future. And at stake in relation to all of these temporalities is the achievement of a western humanist version of adulthood. An example of how a liberated relation to time has been envisioned for black subjects dispossessed of precisely that is in post–civil rights era historiographical treatments of plantation slavery, which have sought the retrieval of enslaved subjectivity through the liberal humanist terms of "resistance" and "agency."[55] If we can retrieve a free-willed subject from under the layers of enslavement, we might rescue the person—who is frequently the male adult—from the slave. Thus, the story's affirmation of Ryder's timeliness, as a matter of his own will and the hegemonic views he holds, is a red herring that tacitly indicates a problem, which eventually leads to the haunting of history. At first, we see a free-willed, self-possessive, properly liberal subject who is not only aligned with the times, but in control of it, who moves apace with it toward a progressively upward ascent. But to look past the dominant dilemma of Ryder's milieu, which is the fate of racial mixed people during a time of intensifying Jim Crow segregation, is to notice how the second curiosity associated with the Blue Veins—the question of "free birth"— speaks directly to the conditions that engender the present.

Before 'Liza Jane's arrival, Ryder peruses the poems of Alfred Tennyson, "his favorite poet,"[56] looking for an excerpt to include in his toast to Dixon. The first few lines that he considers are from Tennyson's "A Dream of Fair Women" and "Margaret" (1832), each of which describes idealized white feminine beauty. But neither is quite right for Molly Dixon. Ryder marks a verse from the first poem, which describes a statuesque lady who is "most divinely fair," but then moves on to the next, which reads in part, "O sweet pale Margaret, / O rare pale Margaret."[57] Even as Dixon is the idealized object of Ryder's affection and desire for social ascent, she is nonetheless too "ruddy," "lively," and "buxom" to conform to the fantasy of Tennyson's neo-romantic heroines.[58] The ill-fitting comparisons between Dixon and the canonical female figures of chivalric romance draw our attention to Ryder's oblique failure as the masculine hero, an appropriate counterpart to the idealized woman. Which is to say, his trouble with settling on appropriately gendered representation in Tennyson's Victorian-era medieval fantasies is symptomatic of his own untimeliness, his own unachieved arrival at the age-gender status of manhood.

Discontent with the suitability of the first two poems, Mr. Ryder's gaze eventually "rested on" lines from Tennyson's "Sir Launcelot and Queen Guinevere" (1842). I quote the lines at length in order to illustrate how they enchant the past in unexpected ways.

> She seem'd a part of joyous Spring;
> A gown of grass-green silk she wore,
> Buckled with golden clasps before;
> A light-green tuft of plumes she bore
> Closed in a golden ring.
> [. . .]
> She look'd so lovely, as she sway'd
> The rein with dainty finger-tips,
> *A man had given all other bliss,*
> *And all his worldly worth for this,*
> *To waste his whole heart in one kiss*
> *Upon her perfect lips.*[59]

Just as Equiano's intersubjective existence troubles the autobiographical function of capturing a singular subject, so too does the afterlife of being constituted outside of the laws of western humanism weigh on the genre of chivalric romance. Ryder is not consciously aware of this. Yet, unlike with the first two poems that focus only on the feminine ideal, Ryder is entangled with this last poem, which not only represents a canonical gender pairing, but also makes a sudden shift from its description of Guinevere, the feminine object, to the perspective of Lancelot, the masculine, romantic hero. Significantly, this shift conjures 'Liza Jane: "As Mr. Ryder murmured these words audibly [. . .] he heard the latch of his gate click, and a light footfall sounding on the steps."[60] Chesnutt's story cuts sharp distinctions between the fair Molly Dixon, the lovely Queen Guinevere, and the dark 'Liza Jane. The queen's sunlit goldenness, the nature-inspired greens of her plumage and silken form, sharply contrast with 'Liza Jane's lesser "blue calico gown of ancient cut" and the "little red shawl fastened around her shoulders with an old-fashioned brass brooch, and a large bonnet profusely ornamented with faded red and yellow artificial flowers."[61] One imagines that it takes artificial flowers—just one indication of a merely mimetic relation to orthodox femininity—a very long time to fade. By every standard, 'Liza Jane fails to manifest humanized femininity, and the most outstanding measures of this failure are her extreme agedness and blackness, which are inextricable from the fact of her ghostly arrival:

> [S]he seemed quite old; for her face was crossed and recrossed with a hundred wrinkles, and around the edges of her bonnet could be seen protruding here and there a tuft of short gray wool. [. . .] And she was very black,—so black that her toothless gums [. . .] were not red, but blue. She looked like a bit of the old plantation life, summoned up from the past by the wave of a magician's wand, as the poet's fancy had called into being the gracious shapes of which Mr. Ryder had just been reading.[62]

Having incanted a spell that shifts the feminized object to the masculine subject, Ryder conjures 'Liza Jane, who is now the masculine-like, chivalrous, romantic hero. As Keyser observes, "Tennyson dreams of Chaucer, while Ryder dreams of Tennyson dreaming of Chaucer," but rather this evidencing Ryder's trans-historicism in this moment, such dreaming brings forth the historical untimeliness of black life, excluded from humanist sociality on the old plantation.[63] Clearly, 'Liza Jane's failure to be conventionally female is signified through her blackness and the plainness of her garb, but the failure of femaleness is more poignantly evidenced in the crisscrossing of her one hundred wrinkles. In order to decipher how this spell works, we are obligated to follow the crisscrossing of signification. Just as "manhood" signifies the full social, political, historical, and evolutionary maturation of the human, 'Liza Jane's extreme agedness—in a word, her extreme maturation— signifies that she is the masculine part of an untimely gender pairing. Gallivanting in the world, having virtuously sacrificed "all other bliss" to find her husband, she approaches Ryder, who has been ostensibly "swaying the rein" of a black civic agenda, at the threshold of the domestic sphere of his home. 'Liza Jane's agedness codes her heroic adventures and sacrifices as masculine. Ryder conjures this ghost, but his present-day existence relies on not knowing what he wants by wanting "her."

The story represents this unknowing as amnesia, and the ghost gallantly helps Ryder to remember.

Remembering requires 'Liza Jane to regale Ryder with the story of what transpired in the previous decades, which is a slave narrative that stands in for the hero's quest. Sam Taylor, 'Liza Jane's "merlatter" husband, was free-born. After his parents died, white people of unspecified relation to Sam sent him to work as an apprenticed field hand on the plantation where 'Liza Jane was enslaved. Sam was to work there until he came of age. One day, 'Liza Jane discovered her master's plans to kidnap and sell her husband. She tipped Sam off, and he fled. Of this decision, 'Liza Jane notes, "His time wuz mos' up, an' he swo' dat w'en he wuz twenty-one he would come back an' he'p me run erway, er else save up de money ter buy my freedom."[64] In other words, Sam was on the verge of full adulthood when his nominal freedom was most imperiled. For prompting Sam's escape, 'Liza Jane was whipped and sold "down the river." After the Civil War, she spent years on her own, moving across the South and then up North in search of her husband. Her search has led her to Ryder's home, whom she does not seem to immediately recognize as Sam. She concludes by asserting that one day she and Sam will be reunited, and both will be "as happy in freedom as we wuz in de ole days befo' de wah."[65]

Just as the ghost on the shores of Gibraltar reminds Equiano that he is entangled with the non-developmental temporality of property, so too does 'Liza Jane deliver a similar reminder: Ryder is still Sam Taylor, the juvenile whose freedom was precarious. This is why the ghost is summoned. As we have seen, although it is not summarily true that a condition of Blue Vein Society membership is being free born, it is nonetheless supposed that "very few of the members would have been unable to meet it."[66] And while there might be exceptions, "one or two of the older members who had come up from the South and from slavery," if this is the case, then, "their history presented enough romantic circumstances to rob their servile origin of its grosser aspects," which in effect would erase their enslaved origin altogether.[67] Ryder is in fact free-born. Yet, 'Liza Jane's story reveals an enduring form of liminality that can neither be resolved through upward absorption into whiteness nor eliminated through disappearance into blackness: Ryder/Sam Taylor is caught in between being a free person and being a slave.

The "free slave," an unthought-of category that combines full liberal personhood with the unfree body—a different sort of mixedness—exists in between juvenility and adulthood. Both age statuses have oppositional relations to social and historical progress, a topic that preoccupies Ryder at the beginning of the story. At the dawn of the twentieth century, what is the temporality of the slave who is free? What does the freedom of full personhood mean when one is embodied with the sign of racial juvenility, which undercuts the condition of manhood, the only gendered adulthood there is? The ideological viewpoints of social Darwinism, liberalism, and black capitalism fail to produce adequate responses to these questions, which will continue to haunt black people in the new century. After hearing 'Liza Jane's story, the grosser aspects of not being a full person face Ryder as he looks in the mirror, as it begins to dawn on him that he is the one the ghost has been looking for. But the fact that this is a romantic fantasy places limits on what is openly expressible. Thus, the story itself robs the topic of slavery—and the devastating years that followed—of its grosser aspects. It suffices that Ryder/Taylor, having been ungendered and unmade, and left bereft of a ready social trajectory to follow, decides to give his fancy full "rein" to imagine his entanglement with 'Liza Jane. He embraces the devotion of his erstwhile wife, who continues to be the wife of his youth.

'Liza Jane is older than Ryder/Taylor in both appearance and fact. As he mentions to his guests at the ball, "he was young, and she much older than he."[68] 'Liza Jane alludes to her advanced maturity as a type of non-possessive—which is to say, non-patriarchal—adult responsibility when she muses that, "I 'spec's ter haf ter suppo't 'im w'en I fin' 'im, fer he nebber would work 'less'n he had ter."[69] An ancient black woman with a direct connection to the past, 'Liza Jane is evocative of the relic. As I argue in chapter 2, black women are often figured as preternaturally elderly when it is time to do the endless work of preserving and conveying valuable, seemingly unmediated history for other people. And just as the very elderly Jane Pittman asks Jimmy to "talk and talk and talk"—to share with her an ungendered and untimely kinship of condition—so too does Ryder/Taylor take on 'Liza Jane's ostensible role as the relic when he recounts her story, and speaks to his guests in her "same soft dialect" of the Southern past.[70] As evidence of the relic's power, Ryder/Taylor transports his future-oriented guests to another time: "The story had awakened a responsive thrill in many hearts. There were some present who had seen, and others who had heard their fathers and grandfathers tell, the wrongs and sufferings of this past generation, and all of them still felt, in their darker moments, the shadow hanging over them."[71] This recognition is transformative, insofar as it enables a mode of knowing that occurs in another register, on a lower frequency. Collective awareness of the looming shadow of historical wrongs and sufferings is only one part of the enchantment that occurs. Additionally, and more poignantly, I suggest that an awareness that is closer to the beating heart of black life is awakened. It is the subtle and everyday means by which those who had "seen" survived, which involves the touch, the voice, the look, the humanity of the others who saw. It is the affective attachments to fathers and grandfathers—and mothers and grandmothers, since Ryder/Taylor is telling a story we have already heard 'Liza Jane tell—and the ephemeral details of those moments of hearing have nothing to do with the wrongs and sufferings themselves, but rather, with the language used to tell those stories, and the humanness of those who were doing the telling. Collectively, "their fathers and grandfathers" become less singly possessive, and more like "*the* fathers and grandfathers" and uncles and mothers and everyone else.[72] Ultimately, this is the gift that the ghost gives to the moment: In the space of Ryder's forgetting, the ghost enchants an alternative historicity of the present, which enchants a spirit of the collective. For Ryder, it is a form of rescue. With 'Liza Jane, he can live as an improper subject because she reveals conditions of possibility to survive as such.

And yet, because she is figured as a ghost rather than as a relic, 'Liza Jane appears only *after* history has already been forgotten, which means that the haunted subject does not consciously decide on which past is awakened. "The Wife of His Youth" illustrates that as a condition of enchanting an alternative historicity of the present, the ghost must remain silent about—must disenchant—other historical possibilities. Thus, a curious Ryder asks 'Liza Jane questions about the 25-year period of separation, without receiving anything but inadequate responses. The most significant question is, "How have you lived all these years?"[73] Embedded in the question is an awareness of the material obstacles to black survival in the years after the war. Newly emancipated women, children, elderly, and men were routinely denied basic protections from and treatments for rampant illness and hunger; further, sexual violence and terror were inextricable from the reconstitution of white supremacy in the South.[74] According to historian Hannah Rosen, white Southern rhetoric about race created a climate of terror by reproducing a black gender binary, which contributed to the gendering of violent acts such as rape. Thus, in an act that momentarily suspends this black romantic fantasy, Ryder asks an ethical, grown-up question: What happened to *you*, 'Liza Jane, and how did you survive? But this ghost won't allow all of that to weigh on Ryder's mind. Rather than speak in nuanced terms about what is being asked, 'Liza Jane responds with, "Cookin', suh. I's a good cook."[75] Lovingly, the ghost closes off vectors to the past, and enchants only the history you did not know you needed.

But what happens when the liberal subject's transformation into a state of untimely juvenility is not the result of a ghost's benign desire to set the subject free from the aspirations of liberal humanist maturity? In the intergenerational entanglement between the ghost and the neoliberal subject, what becomes of maturity, and why does it matter?

Sweetness and Bride: *God Help the Child*

Morrison's 2015 novel, *God Help the Child*, begins with an unwavering denial: "It's not my fault. So you can't blame me. I didn't do it and have no idea how it happened."[76] This is how Sweetness, a 63-year-old woman who lives in the present day but outside of a clearly specified milieu, speaks of the fact that her daughter, Lula Ann Bridewell, was born with dark skin. As Sweetness explains, she and her husband were light-skinned, and the birth of a mystifyingly dark-skinned baby ultimately ended their marriage. Thus, Sweetness is refusing responsibility for *some aspect* of Lula Ann's being, and we are told that it is skin color. But just as Ryder's dilemma was not actually about the fate of mixed-race people, in this case skin color is a metaphor for another mark of difference that separates Sweetness from her daughter. I suggest that "colorism" stands in for "feminism," which has been rendered unspeakable in the contemporary moment of the text. Sweetness's denial points to a rift between a black feminist ethos of the 1970s, when Sweetness should have come of age, and the aspirations of the neoliberal subject at the start of the twenty-first century, which a few individual black women of considerable wealth and prominence—Michelle Obama, Oprah Winfrey, Beyoncé—embody. Colorism is thinkable as a metaphor for the difference and divide between one era's feminism and another's when we briefly consider how it appears in Morrison's first and last novels. In *The Bluest Eye* (1970), colorism was the *effect* of an ongoing historical process of dispossession, and a means by which to explore that process.[77] The process, although difficult to explain, nonetheless pressed upon the everyday lives of black people. Claudia cannot say *why* her dark-skinned, 11-year-old friend Pecola was so devalued as to become her father's "plot of black dirt" in which he drops his seed, so instead she took "refuge in *how*."[78] Similarly, Sweetness's colorism is the impetus for her explanations about how a bygone social world worked, and how one maneuvered around public, institutional, and legal oppression in order to survive. And at the same time, it is a means of distancing herself from a person—an emblem of what I call "neoliberal girlhood"—that she somehow gave birth to but does not fully claim. Thus, the repeated denial—"It's not my fault"—announces a view of intergenerational failure that is simultaneously retrospective and anticipatory. And through the surface route of colorism, the ghost of the repressed enters the scene, and haunts.

Although Sweetness is a character in the narrative, she functions more profoundly as the voice of the novel. She justifies her alternatingly aloof and abusive parenting style to an obligation to prepare Lula Ann for a world that is brutal to dark-skinned girls and women. An only child of a single mother, Lula Ann grows up starved for affection and validation. She receives both at the age of eight when she falsely accuses an innocent schoolteacher of sexual abuse and, in effect, sends the woman to prison. In the present, Lula Ann, now known as Bride, is a beautiful, successful, 23-year-old entrepreneur who has established her own cosmetics line called, "YOU, GIRL: Cosmetics for Your Personal Millennium."[79] In order to thrive in the cosmetics industry, Bride brands herself, and wears nothing but white to capitalize on the aesthetic appeal of her blue-black skin. Bride's boyfriend, Booker, suddenly breaks up with her, and sends her spiraling down a path of misfortune. She is badly beaten after an ill-advised attempt to apologize to the erstwhile teacher with a gift of cosmetics; she gets into a car accident while trying to find Booker. All the while, Bride feels the incremental loss of her bodily maturity:

She loses the pierced holes in her ears, then her body hair and breasts, and her body shrinks. Yet only Bride seems to notice that she is slowly transforming into a little girl. Bride eventually finds Booker living near his aunt, Queen, and after a candid confrontation that entails owning up to their mistakes, the two reconcile. Being forthright with Booker is a sign of maturity, and as a result, Bride's womanly body is miraculously restored. In the wake of Queen's tragic death, Bride happily discovers that she is pregnant with Booker's child. Having heard the news, Sweetness has the final word.

I turn to two aspects of the novel that reveal significant thematic differences between Bride and Sweetness: Bride's neoliberal girlhood, and Sweetness's untimely voice. I argue that the ghost of feminism haunts through these differences, of which only Sweetness seems to be aware. Although Sweetness never explicitly speaks the word "feminism," her untimeliness, like her daughter's neoliberal girlhood (which I describe below), connects a temporality to a feminist ethos. Sweetness lives in historically conflated time: All the twentieth century has been fused with the present into a single frame of reference. From her own ghostly perspective of then-and-now, Sweetness enchants the spirit of radical black feminism by explicitly speaking of conditions that engender it, which come from black life. Sweetness speaks of second-class citizenship and the contradictions of having freedom without being free. Instilled with a core black feminist commitment to achieving bodily autonomy for the least possessive among us, Sweetness's account of black life draws our attention to the contradictions of self-possession. Although Bride is unaware of it—even as she notices that her body is regressing—the ghost of feminism haunts her in the historically shallow present. In the present, feminism nominally exists as a mode of neoliberal self-regulation. Sweetness, who inhabits a temporality of historical fullness, conjures a ghost that enters the historical void of neoliberal feminism. Haunting is a particular way of knowing beyond the limits of convention and facticity, but Bride is oblivious. Thus, as gauzy and spare as the novel seems, *God Help the Child* sounds a sharp warning. Something that we currently need—but cannot see or speak of—is disappearing. Sweetness re-enchants it for the sake of our bodily autonomy, our freedom, and our future.

Notice how Bride views the world: "The road looks like a kindergarten drawing of light-blue, white or yellow houses with pine-green or beet-red doors sitting smugly on wide lawns. All that is missing is a pancake sun with ray sticks all around it."[80] The description is no more facile than the context in which it belongs, which is Bride's plan for making amends with the woman who went to prison because she lied as a child. Upon seeing Sofia Huxley after her release from a 15-year prison sentence, Bride imagines cosmetic fixes for the woman's pallor, her "trembly" mouth, her diminished appearance. Rather than consider the measure of her own blameworthiness, or what a person who was wrongly imprisoned might feel, think, or need, Bride imagines how "A little Botox and some Tango-Matte, not glitter, would have softened her lips and maybe influenced the jury in her favor except there was no YOU, GIRL back then."[81] In other words, Sophia would have taken responsibility for keeping herself out of prison, except there was no cosmetic product that interpellated one into taking such personal action. To the adult Bride, the problem that led to Sofia's imprisonment was not about anything external to the individual. It was not about causal events, such as the rising commoditization of self-help expertise during the 1970s and 1980s, therapeutic trends of the 1990s, subsequent controversies over children's false memories of sexual abuse (although Lula Ann knowingly made a false accusation), an overly punitive judicial system, or sexism. Which is to say, Bride does not comprehend the problem as historical, social, or structural. Rather, the problem then and the solution now depend on whether one achieves an idealized femininity that is ageless. The eight-year-old who was not responsible for telling the lie about the woman the adults called "the lady monster"[82] converges with the 23-year-old who is not responsible for furthering the offense in the present day. As a kindergartener, Lula Ann might have drawn pictures of colorful houses under a pancake sun. As a 23-year-old entrepreneur, Bride gives names to colors meant for spreading over the surfaces of women's faces.

In a word, Bride is a 23-year-old child. Through her, Morrison formulates a fictional and non-developmental subjectivity, "neoliberal girlhood." The term names an artificial infantilism that is constituted through a knowing or unknowing refusal to accept modes of responsibility that exist outside of the purview of neoliberal governmentality. Developmental psychologist Erica Burman uses the term "neoliberal childhood" to explain how developmental discourse shores up the abstracted neoliberal subject, saliently figured as the child whose play is work and the mother whose housework is play.[83] As Burman asserts, developmental psychology cannot account for how the "child" is figural of neoliberal ideologies, and Morrison imagines such as figure. But more precisely, the concept combines "neoliberal feminism," an ethos of women's empowerment that conforms to the demands of neoliberal market values, and what James Baldwin has referred to as American "innocence," the disavowal of historical racial violence.[84] Bride is black, but her historicity reveals how neoliberal feminism and white liberal innocence converge in the making of a subject who is individualist and wholly responsible for her own success, while, paradoxically, innocent and wholly devoid of responsibility, despite her own participation in a rationality that deepens social inequities. This subject can mobilize a version of "identity politics" that has been completely emptied of historical, political, and social critique, while innocently believing that this is the only version there is. "Innocence" is a matter of comportment, a manner of moving through a world that is supposedly without depth. The neoliberal girl of any age confidently enters the social world as if she is the first one to do so. And such illusory novelty casts the ghostly aura of feminism onto this otherwise simply female subject. In a world that has no history, she does not attempt to achieve the liberal feminist goal of gender equality—which is to say, the fully mature citizenship of men. Rather, her infantilization is constituted by turning away from the domain of social, political maturity, where thought and ideologies are publicly contested, toward the entirely self-absorbed concerns with personal achievement, self-improvement, self-commodification, wholly individuated injuries, needs, and desires. There is no subjective development here because the markets do not require it. Neither do romantic partners, for a time. Bride's "innocent, oblivious sense of humor delighted" her boyfriend, for a time.[85]

But Booker eventually leaves, and his break-up incantation seems to catalyze Bride's physical regression. His words, "You not the woman I want," and her spontaneous response, "Neither am I,"[86] indicate that Bride is not *the* woman since, in some way, she is not *a* woman, a feminine adult. After a brief consideration of what, exactly, she lacks ("I'm not exciting enough? Or pretty enough? I can't have thoughts of my own? Do things he doesn't approve of?"), Bride faults the relationship: "It was nothing like those double-page spreads in fashion magazines, you know, couples standing half naked in surf, looking so fierce and downright mean, their sexuality like lightning and the sky going dark to show off the shine of their skin. I love those ads."[87] Even at her most introspective, Bride is conspicuously unknowing, since she is subjectively constituted through ideologies the ads express. She cannot explain why "I kept comparing us to magazine spreads and music," but as someone who lacks developmental depth, Bride is drawn to the surfaces of glossy spreads, half-naked flesh, and shiny skin.

Bride's own dark skin signifies as surface, as an attribute that belongs in a depthless world in which everything and everyone has been transmuted into commodities. This view is evident in Bride's relationship to her own dark skin—a key aspect of her commercial image. Bride's dark skin had signified a devalued form of human existence for much of her young life (and modern western history), so she is triumphant when she realizes how to profit from its exchange value: "I sold my elegant blackness to all those childhood ghosts and now they pay me for it."[88] "Colorism," the ghost against which Bride wages her retribution, signifies the historical formation of intersecting social categories that are non-possessive. Bride first experiences her skin color as a mark of dispossession. Because she is dark, even her own mother denies her the entitlement of using the word "Mother." But even though Bride manages to profit from a historical mark of dehumanization, and although she sells her "elegant blackness" as if there are no other routes to full humanity, the novel's condemnation of Bride indicates that these responses are not inevitable.[89] There was another, now repressed possibility: Bride's formative experience as a dark-skinned black girl could have enchanted spirits of a radically feminist past. It could have been the catalyst for a mature analysis about social dispossession, rather than the springboard for an innocent leap into a vacuous, endless, neoliberal girlhood. Exemplary of the former possibility and spirit of black feminist enchantment, the Combahee River Collective cite their childhood experiences as the "undeniably [. . .] personal genesis for Black feminism" in their foundational Statement.[90] The point is that "colorism" signposts the presence of numerous spirits of the past and the contingency of the present.

Further, the formative link between colorism and dispossession denaturalizes the condition of "having" a body. On the surface, Bride seems to have it all. Her body is an asset. She possesses the blue-tinted eyes that

Pecola could not have without losing her mind. Yet, Bride's neoliberal-girlish response to being dark-skinned—she sells herself—signifies the problem, rather than the achievement, of self-possessiveness. Bride's *skin* has value, but Bride herself is bewitched out of the ability to control her own body. It may seem as if Booker conjures something when he leaves—something that interrupts the present, a spirit that entangles with Bride's body and reveals her own historicity to her, to horrifying effect. Yet, the ghost of the repressed that haunts is the ghost of feminism, and Sweetness speaks it into existence.

Sweetness's incantation is of the "really wrong" nature of her daughter's dark skin, and the problem of owning one's own body is germane to both colorism and feminism. But one term substitutes for the other because colorism, unlike feminism, is still recognizably historical. Indeed, one cannot think of it without being firmly rooted to the ground of modern western history. Even Bride confronts the historical when she describes the abuse she received from other children: "curses—with mysterious definitions but clear meanings—were hissed or shouted at me. Coon. Topsy. Clinkertop. Sambo. Ooga booga."[91] Less innocent than Bride, actual children routinely and knowingly reproduce historical meanings that reproduce a social order. Conversely, feminism, like the woman on the shores of Gibraltar, appears both as a repetition of the past and as something entirely new. It is everywhere, in evocations and repetitions that re-enchant feminist pasts in the present, as well as in the spurious hailing of every "YOU, GIRL" of commodity culture. Feminism is both surface and depth, ephemeral and material. Without certain recourse to a feminist ethos that entangles one generation with another, without certainty that radical feminist critique is still intelligible in an age of "Botox" and "Tango-Matte," Sweetness speaks of colorism in order to speak obliquely of feminist concerns as history.

Because she speaks, albeit obliquely, of what has been repressed, Sweetness's voice is untimely. As Kara Walker claims, "It's [...] difficult to pin down when the book takes place: Bride sounds contemporary, but Sweetness's voice seems to belong to another era entirely."[92] It belongs to a composite of eras: pre-civil rights, the 1990s, and the present. In Sweetness's voice the world is neither old nor young—it has more than one age. Such untimeliness explains Sweetness's simultaneously anticipatory and retrospective vision. At once, she sees the surprisingly dark baby to whom she had just given birth and anticipates a neoliberal subject with whom she cannot identify, *and* she looks back at the events that engendered that subject. Sweetness does not belong to any single time, which is why we should not take her 63 years literally. But to do so is to realize that a formative era for Sweetness is missing. Just as feminism is repressed in the text, so too is the era of second-wave black feminism, and the 1970s in general. The only cultural references that possibly evoke that moment are "Michael Jackson's soprano or James Brown's shouts,"[93] which are for Bride and Booker to enjoy in the heat of their romance.

Rather than explicitly speak of an era in which many of her generation developed their political consciousness, Sweetness describes how black liberation movements were engendered in terms of the quotidian aspects of black life and subjection. If Ryder apparently thought of mixed-racial absorption into whiteness as a means of self-preservation—of survival as something akin to human—then so too does Sweetness see the lightness of skin color as a means of holding on to one's humanity at a time when whites denied it at every turn. Both of Sweetness's parents were very light-skinned and thus were afforded some privileges, but they consciously bore the mark of darkness that routinely resulted in being spat at, overcharged, name-called, elbowed, and forced off the sidewalk and into the gutter.[94] Such subjection is the prologue for Sweetness's pride when Lula Ann testifies at Sofia's trial: "Young as she was, she behaved like a grown-up on the witness stand—so calm and sure of herself."[95] Lula Ann's maturity was not real, but Sweetness believed that her daughter took adult responsibility. She publicly accused an entire racist social order of being guilty: "It's not often you see a little black girl take down some evil whites."[96] To Sweetness, Lula Ann took responsibility on behalf of every black person who bore the weight of social subjection. And in so doing, she became the picture of maturity.

To Sweetness, maturity is a constitutive part of black life: Across the twentieth century, you exercised your best judgment and did what needed to be done. You disappeared into whiteness if you could pass, as Sweetness's grandmother had, never to be heard from again; when someone else passed, you "let her be"; you took bits of privilege here and there, and you understood when others did the same. And even though you were a child, you were mature enough to condemn the status quo when it was your turn to testify. This is precisely the sort of maturity that Michele Elam argues is operative in James Baldwin's conception of boyhood: "'maturity'—the undoing of innocence—is not a function of age [...] but [...] an opportunity for perpetual return to the world."[97] Sweetness, who sounds at times like she shares generational kinship with Baldwin, understands childhood maturity in these terms: It is a capacity to comprehend the real world and the people who negotiate with it while supporting each other.

And yet, mature responsibility is a lot to expect of a little black girl. Ultimately, as the voice and spirit of *God Help the Child*, Sweetness is at a crossroads between the previous generations' perspective on preparing black children for the world and the risks of compulsory black maturity, of which we are keenly aware at the start of the twenty-first century. We know that black children are more likely to be denied the social and customary protections of childhood to punitive and deadly effect. Black children must be prepared for a world that "adultifies" them and shields them with loving attention at the same time. Sweetness could not do both and has regrets: She should have been more forgiving when Lula Ann "stumbled or dropped something."[98] She should not have shouted or screamed or "slammed the lid and warned [Lula Ann] of the names she'd be called."[99] Sweetness regrets how she treated a child that felt like a nuisance. Thus, at the crossroads between preparing and loving the black child is regret.

But regret is not Sweetness's alone. Rather, it is baked into the tenuous structure of relations between numerous people throughout the text. Letters to Sweetness's grandmother were "sent right back, unopened"; Sweetness's husband "started sending [...] money once a month," an inadequate act of support after he had left his family for good; phone calls from Bride's best friend become "fewer and fewer"; and Sweetness receives news of Bride's pregnancy but, "There is no return address on the envelope." Regret is a social by-product, an outcome of conditions that divide us according to our categorical differences and individuated obligations. These conditions result in regret because they limit the terms by which we think of our responsibility to one another. An episteme of social division impacts us at the most intimate levels, and thus it influences how a mother feels about her own child. Without a support system, Sweetness carries the burden of raising a child by herself. This is one more thing that her untimely perspective captures in retrospect: Lula Ann's dark skin signifies the entirety of forces that weigh on a single black mother, and the awesome responsibility of keeping an unvalued black girl safe in a white, capitalist, hetero-patriarchal world. The burden includes everything from finding and keeping a decent apartment, to negotiating with the clerks at the welfare office, to earning a living. Thus, as a constitutive aspect of black life, "maturity" connotes the distribution of responsibility for ensuring each other's survival, and it entails a feminist critique of the ways such distribution is structurally inequitable. Yet, at some point, all of this becomes lost on Sweetness's supposedly grown-up daughter.

Sweetness does not know why it happened, but at some point, Lula Ann became Bride. Bride cannot see how maturity has worked as a technology for keeping black people of all ages alive, or that maturity is entangled with regret. Looking back, Sweetness eventually acknowledges that, "When my husband ran out on us, Lula Ann was a burden."[100] This insight from the past is usable for the future, which will be Bride's responsibility. The end of *God Help the Child* is a reckoning with what it means to survive or succeed when the trace of something unfinished—like mourning, like the precarity of freedom, like regret—remains.

Bride is a "rich career girl,"[101] which is a strong measure of both Sweetness's and Bride's success. But the advent of Bride marked the suspension of a developmental process that never reached the point of maturity. And as a result, the next generation is at stake:

> Now she's pregnant. Good move, Lula Ann. If you think mothering is all cooing, booties and diapers you're in for a big shock. Big. You and your nameless boyfriend, husband, pickup—whoever—imagine OOOH! A baby! Kitchee kitchee koo!
>
> Listen to me. You are about to find out what it takes, how the world is, how it works and how it changes when you are a parent.
>
> Good luck and God help the child.[102]

These are the novel's final words. They come at a time when aspirational images of motherhood crowd social media and celebrity culture. Like Bride's California condo and Jaguar with the vanity license plates, a baby is a status symbol, another thing you can have.

But it is not too late. Radical black feminists of the 1970s mobilized around the issue of reproductive rights because they knew that when limits are imposed on what the least possessive subjects of a white, capitalist, hetero-patriarchal social world can do or not do with their own bodies, then nobody is truly free. Morrison's final novel about a dark-skinned black woman who loses control over her body by supernatural means and yet believes herself to be utterly free alludes to the disappearance of such an analysis. For most of the novel, Bride has no control over her diminishing body, nor over the conditions of its diminishment; she has no idea why or how it is happening. It is the not knowing, not the bodily immaturity itself, that is the actual problem. It takes maturity to tell the truth about oneself, and doing so does restore Bride's adult body in the end. Still, Bride misses the point entirely.

While she is focused on the pickup, boyfriend, lover, there is something among us being re-enchanted, *now*. Listen: It is the only time that Sweetness speaks directly to Bride, as her own body fades away from a "creeping bone disease," and as Morrison herself has passed on. Like the ghost that haunts to remind us that no mode of knowing ever completely dies, Sweetness shocks us into focusing on the future for *the* child, the one that belongs to all of us.[103] At the very least, knowing the "how" of the world and its workings, how each of us bears a tremendous burden without robust relations between women, girls, children, boys, adults, and men, is the condition of possibility for making another world, another humanity.

Epilogue

And with Black Children

If I had a son, he'd look like Trayvon.
—Barack Obama, "Obama Speaks Out on Trayvon Martin"

In this book, I have foregrounded age as a historicizing tool for the purpose of challenging our assumptions about which social categories are worthy of thoroughgoing analysis in black literary studies. Age is a constitutive aspect of black embodiment, subjectivity, and experiences of time. Yet, black literary studies have seldom treated it as a key analytic for the study of black social life, tout court. The concomitant rise of black feminist criticism and black literary studies overall during the 1970s and 1980s, and methodological transformations in the field of the late 1980s, which enabled a decisive turn to the ongoing effects of transatlantic slavery, threaded history through gender, a primary category of black literary and historical analysis. Rather than stake out new archival ground, I have focused on familiar cultural objects that either expound on the condition of enslavement or attend to the afterlife of slavery, to demonstrate a different way of reading. By turning to gender categories of liberal personhood through which conventional historicization has been threaded—manhood, womanhood, girlhood, boyhood—I have rethreaded the historical through the framework of age. Reading texts of enslavement and slavery's afterlives that span from the eighteenth to the twenty-first centuries in this way shows us that both the abuses of and emancipatory responses to liberal humanist exclusion have been expressed in terms of age, development, and life stages. I have referred to the outcome of these contradictory responses as Oceanic lifespans. Thus, the texts show us a rich history of how freedom has been imagined and contested through age.

The spirit of this book draws from black feminist critiques of proper liberal subjectivity that were generated from outside and inside of the academy from the 1970s onward. This spirit enchants the outcomes of seeing history through age, which are renewed potentials for emancipatory modes of relationality. To imagine a version of liberation that is capacious enough to include those of us who are farthest from the hegemonic center entails a rethinking of our relations to each other, which in turn entails a rethinking of power. Power operates in relations between patriarchal gender categories, which are themselves social classifications that divide timely subjects from untimely subjects. And this dimension of time is hidden in the buried assumptions we make about gender. I have envisioned alternatives for black social existence that challenge underlying assumptions about the unevenness of gender temporalities by rerouting those temporalities through the rubric of age. In the outcome, we find the potential to refuse exclusionary modalities of timeliness that have been baked into the social grammar of gender. To refuse patriarchal adulthood, to imagine maturity and responsibility differently, is to open the possibility of another horizon of freedom toward which we can all move.

I started to write this book in the aftermath of an era-shifting tragedy: the shooting death of Trayvon Martin in 2012. The event ruptured the appearance of our timeliness, which had no better representative than the first black president of the United States, Barack Obama. Suddenly, the "post-racial" era that is associated with Obama's presidency broke into another moment. As it had been widely observed after Trayvon's murder, black children are not seen as children. But this observation prompted my wondering: When and how is *any* age of black embodiment accurately seen? An answer, in part, had infused the Obama era with the air of progress: The proper appearance of black age—the heroic version—is when black men are the representative adults. Black age is properly aligned with social convention when black patriarchal manhood exerts leadership over the black masses, the wayward children of the world. Over the years of his presidency, Obama was notably comfortable with rebuking black people for everyday behavior, the supposed root of black social disadvantage.[1]

But Trayvon's death shifted the era-defining focus from black masculine adulthood—and the historical achievement associated with it—to black childhood. Time was not moving backward. Rather, it was transforming into something else, and the discourse about black age was one way to track the changes. George Zimmerman took it upon himself to murder an unarmed teenager because, on that fateful night, he did not see a human being of any age. He saw an intruder, a "black male" drug dealer, a figment of his imagination, a "walking personification of the Negative."[2] The menacing figure he thought he saw was not a young person, but an old ideation. In Zimmerman's mind, there was no difference between the two. Details of the murder seeped into the public. In 2012, while a black man held the highest office in the land, a black boy had been lynched in the street, and no one was held accountable.[3] During the days and weeks in which no local, state, or federal authorities charged Zimmerman with a crime, the public response was right on time. In mass protests across the country, the public demanded that the time for justice was now. The timeliness of the protests paradoxically relied on the rupture of time. Suddenly, 1955 blasted into 2012. The initial impact of Mamie Till-Mobley's demand that we look at her son's missing face / destroyed flesh had been reawakened. Without the protection of law, without governmental action, without the power of the first black president, the public decided that it was time to take responsibility for preserving and loving each other's flesh—because we are bound together. If local, state, and federal authorities will not take responsibility for the prevention and adjudication of murderous violence against boys, girls, the elderly, transgender and genderqueer adults and children, women and men of all ages, then it is up to us to invent new ways of relating to each other, of protecting each other, of evolving into a new way of being human.

After weeks of mass protests and demands for justice, President Obama, the timely vision of national progress, provided the press with a belated response. "If I had a son, he'd look like Trayvon." The comment expressed a respectful recognition of Trayvon's parents, and other parents who feared for the lives of their children in this moment. And it evoked Obama's paternal relation to a boy like Trayvon. But, in addition to a paternalistic relation to a child who is a victim, there were other modes of relation that had inspired timely action. Next to Obama's speculative son was Alicia Garza's brother, who bore a bodily resemblance to Trayvon, of whom she thought in the wake of the murder.[4] And next to them was a social media network of people who reeled and reached out to each other in the aftermath of the not-guilty verdict of Zimmerman's 2013 trial, and next to that are the relations between activists of the Black Lives Matter movement that Garza, Patrisse Cullors, and Opal Tometi founded shortly after. At a time of national inaction, black and queer women took the lead with many others. Horizontal modes of biological and non-biological kinship enabled timely actions at a moment of crisis. The lesson was that the authority and responsibility to care for our communities need not—and sometimes cannot—be structured from the top down.

Lateral maturity as a social paradigm for meeting human needs, coupled with a new iteration of black feminist activism, reenchanted the black feminist 1970s. Imagine Nel Wright, the properly bourgeois black lady of Toni Morrison's 1973 novel, *Sula*, in 1965. Speaking to a girlhood companion who is long dead and gone while, at the same time, speaking to the newness of a moment when full citizenship has ostensibly arrived, the most coherent statement Nel can make is, "We was girls together." In the context of the impasse of 1965, when loss and progress are intertwined, I imagine that "girlhood" names a different kind of social subject. Being "girls together" marks a refusal of the hierarchies and exclusionary priorities that are baked into a binary gender schema and the teleology of a lifespan.

"Girls together," I imagine, is re-envisioned in a 2015 policy report that Kimberlé Crenshaw co-authored, entitled, "Say Her Name: Resisting Police Brutality against Black Women."[5] The report was a corrective to the deafening silence around black female victims of police brutality within the Black Lives Matter movement, which initially focused on the black male subject. The report calls attention to several brutality cases against black girls as young as seven years old (Aiyana Stanley-Jones), and black women as old as 93 (Pearlie Golden). Such a reframing of violence reveals how perceptions of black gender underlie anti-black violence. But at the same time, it reveals that policies often associated with masculinity, such as racial profiling of black drivers, are non–gender specific. Thus, "Say Her Name" reframes the problem of anti-black brutality, which is so frequently seen though the categorical differences of age and gender, in order to reveal where shared and overlapping vulnerabilities lie. In such a reframing, black grandmothers and schoolgirls, young, old, and middle-aged women—along with black boys and teenagers and men—appear together on a shared plane of sociality. Saying *her* name, along with those of black boys and men, is a means to remind us of how wide our circle of relations continues to be and has historically been. As I think of it, being "girls together" is an allurement, like saying her name: Start from the subjective standpoint of those who are most likely to be forgotten, the most likely to disappear from the frame, and build social affinities from there.

As I have imagined them, the shape-shifter, vampire, relic, mass, and ghost are all figures of intersubjective connection, like water in the ocean, and of certain modes of social and historical reclamation. They sustain Kevin Quashie's formulation of the "preposition *with* as [an] ideological compass" that leads the way.[6] As I conclude this book, I think of where the building of a new social world happens with the names that we give to each other to describe our relatedness. In his 2018 memoir, *Heavy*, Kiese Laymon explores the complex interconnections between the Deep South, the single black mother who raised him, the grandmother who raised them, his personal and shared experiences as a "boy man" who comes of age, his body, black poverty, black brilliance, the nation's moral depravity, the words he reads and writes and revises. Each site of connection is a site of memory, which is the basis for the truth, lies, shame, harm, responsibility, and love that constitute bonds between kin. Shaping a new relation to memory, Laymon specifically writes to his mother. In differing ways, they made each other. To her he writes, "I am your child. And, really, you are mine. And we are Grandmama's. And Grandmama is ours."[7] Beginning with the figural flexibility of the child—the subject to whom we are responsible and to whom we have claim—Laymon extends this horizontal relatedness outward to include a wide network of kin, all working together to bring forth a new age of freedom:

> The work of bending, breaking, and building the nation we deserve will not start or end with you or me; but that work will necessitate loving black family, however oddly shaped, however many queer, trans, cis, and gender-nonconforming mamas, daddies, aunties, comrades, nieces, nephews, granddaddies, and grandmamas—learning how to talk, listen, organize, imagine, strategize, and fight fight fight for and with black children.[8]

By including black children in the frame of social action, it becomes increasingly possible to bend and break our presumptions about who gets to lead us all, and who stands at the vanguard of national time. In 1955, Mamie Till-Mobley put her son's flesh on display for the world to see, and in the process, she allowed Emmett to play a crucial role in sharing the nation-bending truth. She revealed the truth for *and with Emmett*. I imagine that she had the foresight to let her son participate in their shared demand for justice because, at one point, they were like siblings together. As Till-Mobley describes, "As [Emmett] grew up, it was more like we were sisters and brothers almost. Because my mother raised him while I went to work. So it was like he was hers, and I knew I was hers, and we had fun together, we laughed together."[9] Being girls, and sisters and brothers together, with black children, all speak to potentially emancipatory social relations, and a new kind of maturity. Obama's paternalist sympathies—"If I had a son . . ."—marked the end of an era. What we make of our humanity in a new era is up to us.

ACKNOWLEDGMENTS

I completed this book at a nadir like no other in my lifetime; it expresses a will to imagine alternative ways of being. I am grateful for the support of The Helen Riaboff Whiteley Center; I especially thank Kathy Cowell for the friendly welcome, time, space, and quiet. Completing this book would not have been possible without all the support of the University of Washington, which includes a sabbatical leave, a Royalty Research Fund award, and a Society of Scholars fellowship from The Walter Chapin Simpson Center for the Humanities for a Society. My thanks to Kathleen Woodward for her stewardship of the humanities at the University and her pioneering work in aging studies. Thanks to former Chair of the English Department, Gary Handwerk, and to former Chair and Dean Brian Reed for their help. Thanks to the current Chair, Anis Bawarshi, for his leadership and unwavering support.

I am grateful for the numerous occasions I had to discuss and share portions of this project from its earliest stages of development. Thanks to Corinne Field for her work at the intersection of gender and age, and for inviting me to participate in the first Global History of Black Girlhood conference at the University of Virginia. Thanks to Allison Curseen, Melanie Dawson, Sari Edelstein, and Marah Gubar for their insights and reading suggestions across the gamut of age studies. I thank Michele Elam for her work on black boyhood and ongoing support. Thank you to Michelle H. Martin, for her valuable insights on blackness in children's and young adult literature. Thank you to Badia Ahad for being a trusted reader at a crucial time. Thank you to Roderick Ferguson for his support, and for double-voiced writing that speaks to the frequently unspoken to.

It has been my good fortune to collaborate, converse, write, read, and spend leisure time with esteemed colleagues and scholars at the University of Washington. I'm fortunate to have had such rewarding involvement with the Washington Institute for the Study of Inequality & Race

(WISIR), the year-long Capitalism and Comparative Racialization: Mellon Sawyer Seminar, and everyone who took part in those generative conversations, which left an imprint on my thinking as I worked on this book. I am grateful to Eva Cherniavsky for her leadership and generosity. Thank you to Alys Weinbaum and Chandan Reddy for key observations, to Dian Million for our amicable conversations that bring Indigenous and African American critical theories together, and to Kemi Adeyemi, Raquel Albarran, Michelle Habell-Pallán, Ralina Joseph, Bettina Judd, Sonal Khullar, Linh Thủy Nguyễn, LaShawnDa Pittman, Sonnet Retman, Stephanie Smallwood, and Sasha Su-Ling Welland for invigorating discussions about the work-in-progress. A warm thank you to LeiLani Nishime, Ileana Rodriguez-Silva, Manka Varghese, Rae Paris, and Suhanthie Motha for their kindness and company. While I was writing a book that imagines black age as the key to black life, those who made such imagining possible slipped away from us. I honor the lives of Ernest J. Gaines (1933–2019), Toni Morrison (1931–2019), and Paule Marshall (1929–2019), whose 1959 novel *Brown Girl, Brownstones* was a needed addition to public library bookshelves, to go along with the fairytales and Faulkner. I'm grateful that they had lived long lives and for the work they left behind.

Thanks to all the graduate students who have taken my seminars over the last few years. Our collective thinking about black life and alternative humanisms was a pleasure. Thanks to Laura De Vos, Thaomi Michelle Dinh, Brittney Frantece, Safi Karmy-Jones, Matthew Howard, C. R. Grimmer, Kym Littlefield, Rachel Schlotfeldt, and Meshell Sturgis. It's your world; take it apart, find what you need, reassemble, and create something new.

I extend my gratitude to the editorial and production staff at New York University Press. Special thanks to editorial assistant Furqan Sayeed for the critical assistance and to editorial director Eric Zinner for his insight and commitment to this book. Thank you to the anonymous readers who offered careful and substantive comments. It was a privilege to have such attentive readers consider my manuscript.

Thanks to where it all began, with my family and my mother, Amina Ibrahim. Thank you to Michael Swailes for the constant support, and for making life sweeter when the work is done.

NOTES

INTRODUCTION

1 Sheldon specifically refers to the masturbating child, the Foucauldian figure of biopolitical management. See Rebekah Sheldon, *The Child to Come: Life after the Human Catastrophe* (Minneapolis: University of Minnesota Press, 2016).

2 Karen Sánchez-Eppler, *Dependent States: The Child's Part in Nineteenth-Century Culture* (Chicago: University of Chicago Press, 2005), 114–119.

3 I am reminded of Fred Moten's observation that the violence done to Emmett's face warps the sequence of before and after, since the public circulation of the photograph of his facial destruction is most salient in our collective memory, rather than the image of him prior to his lynching. See Fred Moten, "Black Mo'nin.'" In *Loss: The Politics of Mourning*, edited by David L. Eng and David Kazanjian, 63 (Berkeley: University of California Press, 2003).

4 For a fuller definition of racial capitalism as "a technology of antirelationality," see Jodi Melamed, "Racial Capitalism," *Critical Ethnic Studies* 1.1 (Spring 2015): 76–85. Significantly, Melamed turns to the Indigenous principle of relationality to address the limits of classical Marxist analysis.

5 I gesture toward past and future work that brings black and Indigenous epistemologies together. For but one expression of relationality as an indigenous worldview, see Leanne Betasamosake Simpson, *As We Have Always Done: Indigenous Freedom through Radical Resistance* (Minneapolis: University of Minnesota Press, 2017); also Tiffany Lethabo King, Jenelle Narvarro, and Andrea Smith, eds., *Otherwise Worlds: Against Settler Colonialism and Anti-Blackness* (Durham, NC: Duke University Press, 2020).

6 Gilmore succinctly argues: "The fiction of race projects a peculiar animation of the human body, and people take to the streets in opposition to its real and deadly effects. And in the end, as the relations of racial capitalism take it out of people's hides, the contradiction of skin becomes clearer. Skin, our largest organ, vulnerable to all ambient toxins, at the end, is all we have to hold us together, no matter how much it seems to keep us apart" (240). See Ruth Wilson Gilmore, "Abolition Geography and the Problem of Innocence," in *Futures of Black Radicalism*, edited by Theresa Gaye Johnson and Alex Lubin (New York: Verso, 2017).

7 Walter Johnson, "Time and Revolution in African America: Temporality and the History of Atlantic Slavery," in *Rethinking American History in a Global*

Age, edited by Thomas Bender, 153 (Berkeley: University of California Press, 2002).

8   For one discussion on the "adultification" of black children, see Rebecca Epstein, Jamilia J. Blake, and Thalia González, "Girlhood Interrupted: The Erasure of Black Girls' Childhood," Georgetown Law's Center on Poverty and Inequality, 2017, www.endadultificationbias.org.

9   Sánchez-Eppler, *Dependent States*; Kathleen Woodward, *Aging and Its Discontents: Freud and Other Fictions* (Bloomington: Indiana University Press, 1991); J. Halberstam, *In a Queer Time and Place: Transgender Bodies, Subcultural Lives* (New York: New York University Press, 2005); Elizabeth Freeman, *Time Binds: Queer Temporalities, Queer Histories* (Durham, NC: Duke University Press, 2010).

10 Grace Kyungwon Hong, *The Ruptures of American Capital: Women of Color, Feminism and the Culture of Immigrant Labor* (Minneapolis: University of Minnesota Press, 2006).

11 Lisa Lowe, "Autobiography Out of Empire," *Small Axe* 28, 13.1 (March 2009): 98–111, and *The Intimacy of Four Continents* (Durham, NC: Duke University Press, 2015).

12 Roderick A. Ferguson, *The Reorder of Things: The University and Its Pedagogies of Minority Difference* (Minneapolis: University of Minnesota Press, 2012).

13 See David Lloyd, *Under Representation: The Racial Regime of Aesthetics* (New York: Fordham University Press, 2018). Lloyd refers to this measure of humanity in terms of aesthetic philosophy and its presuppositions about who does and does not have the capacity for representation. Only humans, who are the only adults, have this capacity: "representation regulates the distribution of racial identification along a developmental trajectory: The Savage or Primitive and the Negro or Black remain on the threshold of an unrealized humanity" (7).

14 Audre Lorde, "Age, Race, Class, and Sex: Women Redefining Difference," in *Out There: Marginalization and Contemporary Cultures*, edited by Russell Ferguson et al., 281 (New York: New Museum of Contemporary Art, 1990).

15 Of particular influence are Halberstam, *In a Queer Time and Place*; Freeman, *Time Binds*; and C. Riley Snorton, *Black on Both Sides: A Racial History of Trans Identity* (Minneapolis: University of Minnesota Press, 2017).

16 Kai M. Green, "Troubling the Waters: Mobilizing a Trans* Analytic," in *No Tea, No Shade: New Writings in Black Queer Studies*, edited by E. Patrick Johnson, 67 (Durham, NC: Duke University Press, 2016). Christina Sharpe develops a Trans* analytic to generative effect, particularly as the "Trans*Atlantic." See Sharpe, *In the Wake: On Blackness and Being* (Durham, NC: Duke University Press, 2016).

17 Saidiya Hartman, *Scenes of Subjection: Terror, Slavery, and Self-Making in Nineteenth-Century America* (New York: Oxford University Press, 1997), 75. The means by which Hartman arrives at this term provides its definition: "The notion of 'subterranean history' is informed by [Michel] Foucault's notion of repressed and subjugated knowledges and [Edouard] Glissant's notion of the submarine roots of the African diaspora" (223 n.107).

18 See Paul Gilroy, *The Black Atlantic: Modernity and Double Consciousness* (Cambridge, MA: Harvard University Press, 1993); Dionne Brand, *A Map to the Door of No Return: Notes to Belonging* (Toronto: Vintage Canada, 2001); Sharpe, *In the Wake*; and Omise'eke Natasha Tinsley, "Black Atlantic, Queer Atlantic: Queer Imaginings of the Middle Passage," *GLQ* 14.2–3 (2008): 191–215, and *Ezili's Mirrors: Imagining Black Queer Genders* (Durham, NC: Duke University Press, 2018).
19 Paul Lovejoy, "The Children of Slavery—The Transatlantic Phase," *Slavery and Abolition* 27.2 (August 2006): 199.
20 Stephanie E. Smallwood, *Saltwater Slavery: A Middle Passage from Africa to American Diaspora* (Cambridge, MA: Harvard University Press, 2007), 71.
21 Sowande' M. Mustakeem, *Slavery at Sea: Terror, Sex, and Sickness in the Middle Passage* (Urbana: University of Illinois Press, 2016), 38.
22 Ibid., 39.
23 Walter Johnson, *Soul by Soul: Life Inside the Antebellum Slave Market* (Cambridge, MA: Harvard University Press, 1999), 58.
24 Ibid.
25 Hortense Spillers, "Mama's Baby, Papa's Maybe: An American Grammar Book," *diacritics* 17.2 (1987): 64–81.
26 Sigmund Freud, *Civilization and Its Discontents* in *The Freud Reader*, edited by Peter Gay, 727 (New York: W.W. Norton, 1989).
27 Spillers, "Mama's Baby, Papa's Maybe," 72.
28 Stephen Jay Gould, *Ontogeny and Phylogeny* (Cambridge, MA: Belknap Press of Harvard University Press, 1977), 157.
29 At least, this is one way in which Woodward reads responses to the old body. See *Aging and Its Discontents*, 177.
30 Woodward, *Aging and Its Discontents*, 170. Emphasis in original.
31 Ibid.
32 Alexander Weheliye argues in *Habeas Viscus: Racializing Assemblages, Biopolitics, and Black Feminist Theories of the Human* (Durham, NC: Duke University Press, 2014) that the flesh is a key concept for imagining alternative routes to being human and free, beyond the purview of liberal humanism. Along with *Habeas Viscus* and Alexis Pauline Gumbs's *Spill: Scenes of Black Feminist Fugitivity* (Durham, NC: Duke University Press, 2016), *Black Age* returns to and retools the analytics of Spillers and, more broadly, black literary studies of the 1970s through the 1990s, to intervene in trends in social and political thought that address the historical development of western humanism.
33 Frantz Fanon, *Black Skin, White Masks* (New York: Grove Press, 1967), 11. As Lewis Gordon summarizes, "The sociogenic pertains to what emerges from the social world, the intersubjective world of culture, history, language, economics. In that world, [Fanon] reminds us, it is the human being who brings such forces into existence." See Gordon, "Through the Zone of Nonbeing: A Reading of Black Skin, White Masks in Celebration of Fanon's Eightieth Birthday," *CLR James Journal* 11.1 (2005): 1–43.
34 Fanon, *Black Skin, White Masks*, 113.

35. For a discussion about how various nationalist regimes managed the meaning of race following the postwar "break," including an account of racial liberalism, see Jodi Melamed, *Represent and Destroy: Rationalizing Violence in the New Racial Capitalism* (Minneapolis: University of Minnesota Press, 2011).
36. Cedric Robinson describes how these two strains of black politics developed in relation to each other after World War II, in *Black Movements in America* (New York: Routledge, 1997), 123–153.
37. Ibid., 135.
38. For an account of how colorism factored into the NAACP's support of Rosa Parks over Claudette Colvin, see Monique Morris, *Pushout: The Criminalization of Black Girls in Schools* (New York: New Press, 2016), 22–23. In a 2009 National Public Radio segment, Colvin claims of Parks, "Her skin texture was the kind that people associate with the middle class. [. . .] She fit that profile." Although both Morris and Cedric Robinson state that the 15-year-old Claudette was pregnant at the time of her arrest, she did not become pregnant until after that. See Margot Alder, "Before Rosa Parks, There Was Claudette Colvin," March 15, 2009, www.npr.org.
39. "The Gary Declaration: Black Politics at the Crossroads," in *Modern Black Nationalism: from Marcus Garvey to Louis Farrakhan*, edited by William L. Van Deburg, 143 (New York: New York University Press, 1997).
40. Paul Gilroy, "Living Memory: A Meeting with Toni Morrison," in Gilroy, *Small Acts: Thoughts on the Politics of Black Culture* (New York: Serpent's Tail, 1994), 179.
41. Daylanne K. English, *Each Day Redeem: Time and Justice in African American Literature* (Minneapolis: University of Minnesota Press, 2013), 122. English refers to the strategic presentism of Black Nationalist projects of the late 1960s and early 1970s, which were foundational to the Black Arts and Black Power movements.
42. Morris, *Pushout*, 22.
43. As Keeanga-Yamahtta Taylor puts it, "Black men and women may experience racism differently in the world, but they had common interests in overcoming it—interests that could not be realized in struggles separated along the lines of gender." *How We Get Free: Black Feminism and the Combahee River Collective* (Chicago: Haymarket Books, 2017), 7.
44. For fuller accounts of this, see Keeanga-Yamahtta Taylor, *From #BlackLivesMatter to Black Liberation* (Chicago: Haymarket Books, 2016), and Kevin Alexander Gray, Jeffrey St. Clair, and JoAnn Wypijewski, eds., *Killing Trayvons: An Anthology of American Violence* (Petrolia, CA: CounterPunch Books, 2014).
45. For instance, see media articles that circulated shortly after Trayvon's death, such as John Blake, "Trayvon's Death: Echoes of Emmett Till?" March 24, 2012, http://inamerica.blogs.cnn.com, or Nicolaus Mills, "A Longer Look at the Emmett Till-Trayvon Martin Comparison," July 17, 2013, www.huffingtonpost.com.
46. Michael J. Dumas and Joseph Derrick Nelson, "(Re)Imagining Black Boyhood: Toward a Critical Framework for Educational Research," *Harvard Educational Review* 86.1 (2016): 27–47. Emphasis in original.

47 Fanon, *Black Skin, White Masks*, 111.
48 Farah Jasmine Griffin provides a cogent account of these developments in "Thirty Years of Black American Literature and Literary Studies: A Review," *Journal of Black Studies* 35.2 (2004): 165–174.
49 Ferguson, *The Reorder of Things*, 125.
50 Ibid., 122.
51 Deborah McDowell explores the epistemic and historical stakes of this distinction for the scholarly practices of black women to notable effect. See "Recycling: Race, Gender, and the Practice of Theory" in *Studies in Historical Change*, edited by Ralph Cohen, 246–263 (Charlottesville: University Press of Virginia, 1992), and *The Changing Same: Black Women's Literature, Criticism, and Theory* (Bloomington: Indiana University Press, 1995).
52 Nell Irvin Painter explains that Olaudah Equiano's 1789 slave narrative achieved canonical status because of a "diasporic turn in African-American history in the 1980s and 1990s." Painter attributes this turn to the lasting legacy of "the Black Power era, in which black Americans appeared as colonized people in the context of decolonization and independence in the Third World." I suggest here that the Black Power era leaves numerous traces in black literary studies during this era. Painter is quoted in Jennifer Howard, "Unraveling the Narrative," *Chronicle of Higher Education* 52.3, September 9, 2005, www.chronicle.com, np.
53 Stephen Best, "On Failing to Make the Past Present," *Modern Language Quarterly* 73.3 (2012): 456. Also see Stephen Best, *None Like Us: Blackness, Belonging, Aesthetic Life* (Durham, NC: Duke University Press, 2018).
54 See Joyce A. Joyce, "The Black Canon: Reconstructing Black American Literary Criticism," *New Literary History* (1987): 335–344; Henry Louis Gates, Jr., "What's Love Got to Do with It? Critical Theory, Integrity, and the Black Idiom," *New Literary History* 18.2 (1987): 345–362; Houston A. Baker, Jr., "In Dubious Battle," *New Literary History* 18.2 (1987): 363–369; and Joyce's counter-response, "'Who the Cap Fit': Unconsciousness and Unconscionableness in the Criticism of Houston A. Baker, Jr., and Henry Louis Gates, Jr.," *New Literary History* (1987): 371–384.
55 Barbara Christian, "The Race for Theory," *Cultural Critique* 6 (1987): 62.
56 Ibid., 58.
57 David Scott, *Omens of Adversity: Tragedy, Time, Memory, Justice* (Durham, NC: Duke University Press, 2014), 6. Emphasis in original.
58 Spillers et al., "'Whatcha Gonna Do?': Revisiting 'Mama's Baby, Papa's Maybe: An American Grammar Book,'" *Women's Studies Quarterly* 35.½ (2007): 306.
59 Ibid. In a conversation between Spillers, Saidiya Hartman, Farah Jasmine Griffin, Shelly Eversley, and Jennifer Morgan, neither Hartman nor Morgan believe that Spillers's argument is "contained by feminism" and instead, reaches toward, in Spillers' words, "a larger human project" (303). Spillers argues that reaching a new humanism requires intellectually working through gender's historical constitution and social reproduction.
60 Ibid., 304.

61 Sylvia Wynter's focus on the absence of Caliban's "woman" in Shakespeare's *The Tempest* reveals gendered pairs as a constitutive aspect of western humanism. See Sylvia Wynter, "Beyond Miranda's Meanings: Un/silencing the 'Demonic Ground' of Caliban's 'Woman,'" in *The Black Feminist Reader*, edited by Joy James and T. Denean Sharpley-Whiting (Malden, MA: Blackwell, 2000).

62 Of the image, Foreman writes: "The photograph places Jacobs in a semiotic system in which readers see a symbolic Aunt Martha and gentle, genteel womanhood as the opening image of *Incidents in the Life of a Slave Girl*" (40). See P. Gabrielle Foreman, *Activist Sentiments: Reading Black Women in the Nineteenth Century* (Urbana: University of Illinois Press, 2009).

63 Best, "On Failing to Make the Past Present," 457.

64 Toni Morrison, *Beloved* (New York: Vintage International, 2004), 301.

65 Ann Stoler makes this observation in *Race and the Education of Desire: Foucault's History of Sexuality and the Colonial Order of Things* (Durham, NC: Duke University Press, 1995): "Students of colonial discourses in Africa, Asia, and the Americas have often commented on a common thread: namely, that racialized Others invariably have been compared and equated with children, a representation that conveniently provided a moral justification for imperial policies of tutelage, discipline and specific paternalistic and materialistic strategies of custodial control" (150). Of course, she challenges this interpretation with an insightful reversal, which is that white children of the eighteenth and nineteenth centuries were themselves deemed as brutish.

66 On this point, I think of Cheryl I. Harris's groundbreaking 1993 essay, "Whiteness as Property" (*Harvard Law Review* 106.8 [June 1993]: 1707–1791) as evidence of how property is a constitutive aspect of white, western humanism overall and, more specifically, liberal humanism.

67 The recapitulation of black reason arises from "Conversation: Achille Mbembe and David Theo Goldberg on *Critique of Black Reason*," *Theory, Culture, & Society*, www.theoryculturesociety.org, and Mbembe's *Critique of Black Reason* (Durham, NC: Duke University Press, 2017).

68 As scholars have elucidated, white women, like black subjects, have been dispossessed of adulthood. For instance, Claudia Nelson's *Precocious Children and Childish Adults: Age Inversion in Victorian Literature* (Baltimore, MD: Johns Hopkins University Press, 2012) argues that the "child-woman" represented presumptive naturalness of female developmental stasis in relation to their male counterpart. Corinne Field's *The Struggle for Equal Adulthood: Gender, Race, Age, and the Fight for Citizenship in Antebellum America* (Chapel Hill: University of North Carolina Press, 2014) argues that white women understood the legal age of adulthood as a political matter and treated it as such during the time between the American Revolution and the Civil War.

69 Orlando Patterson, *Slavery and Social Death: A Comparative Study* (Cambridge, MA: Harvard University Press, 1982), 5.

70 Ibid.

71 David Theo Goldberg, *Racist Culture: Philosophy and the Politics of Meaning* (Malden, MA: Blackwell, 2000), 156.
72 I am influenced by the sorts of black reason Mbembe thinks of as constitutive of modernity itself. As he puts it, "The history of modernity is not so much about the progress of reason as it is about *the history of reason's unreason*" ("Conversation," np, emphasis in original).
73 Goldberg, *Racist Culture*, 157. Emphasis in original.
74 John Stuart Mill, *On Liberty* (New York: Cambridge University Press, 1989), 13.
75 Ibid.
76 This refers to the term's primary meaning, which emerged in the fifteenth century. Of equal relevance for my discussion is an extended definition, "a period of immaturity; an early stage in the growth or development of something." Together, both connotations capture various legal, social, and natural registers of age, which modern black subjectivity troubles. See "nonage, n.1 & 2," *OED Online*, www.oed.com.
77 Fred Moten, *In the Break: The Aesthetics of the Black Radical Tradition* (Minneapolis: University of Minnesota Press, 2003), 176.
78 Fanon, *Black Skin, White Masks*, 180.
79 Gordon, "Through the Zone of Nonbeing," 21. Emphasis in original.
80 Fanon, *Black Skin, White Masks*, 33.
81 See Saidiya Hartman, "Venus in Two Acts," *Small Axe* 26 (2008): 1–14.
82 Michele Wallace, *All the Women Are White, All the Blacks Are Men, but Some of Us Are Brave: Black Women's Studies*, edited by Gloria T. Hull, Patricia Bell Scott, and Barbara Smith (Old Westbury, NY: Feminist Press, 1982), 5.
83 "The Combahee River Collective Statement," published in Keeanga-Yamahtta Taylor's collection of interviews, *How We Get Free*, 17.
84 Ibid.
85 For Fanon's discussion about the black Antillean child's abnormal development, see "The Negro and Psychopathology" in *Black Skin, White Masks*. Also see Spillers's trenchant critique of Fanon's presumption that the black family's isolation from whiteness is possible in any colonial context in her 1996 essay. See Hortense Spillers, "All the Things You Could Be by Now If Sigmund Freud's Wife Was Your Mother," in *Black, White, and in Color: Essays on American Literature and Culture* (Chicago: University of Chicago Press, 2003). I take up Spillers's response to Fanon in chapter 3.
86 Alice Walker, *In Search of Our Mothers' Gardens* (San Diego: Harcourt,1983), xi.
87 Toni Morrison, *Sula* (New York: Vintage International, 2004), 52.
88 I imagine black trans historiography, notably Snorton's groundbreaking *Black on Both Sides*, in conversation with historiographical and ethnographic works on black girlhood, such as Marcia Chatelain's *South Side Girls: Growing Up in the Great Migration* (Durham, NC: Duke University Press, 2015), Cox's *Shapeshifters: Black Girls and the Choreography of Citizenship* (Durham, NC: Duke University Press, 2015), Monique Morris's *Pushout*, LaKisha Michelle Simmons's *Crescent*

City Girls: The Lives of Young Black Women in Segregated New Orleans (Chapel Hill: University of North Carolina Press, 2015), and Nazera Sadiq Wright's *Black Girlhood in the Nineteenth Century* (Urbana: University of Illinois Press, 2016).
89 Farah Jasmine Griffin, "On Black Girlhood," *Public Books*, www.publicbooks.org, np.
90 Matt Richardson, *The Queer Limit of Black Memory: Black Lesbian Literature and Irresolution* (Columbus: Ohio State Press, 2013), 8.
91 Spillers, "Mama's Baby, Papa's Maybe," 61.

1. SHAPE-SHIFTERS AND BODY SNATCHERS

1 For the backstory and impact of the photo, see Jenny Zhang, "Powerful Story Behind the Young Protestor Hugging a Police Officer at a Ferguson Demonstration," December 1, 2014, www.mymodernmet.com; Joseph Rose, "Portland Photographer Behind Viral Ferguson Rally 'Hug Photo' Knew 'This Kid Was Special,'" November 30, 2014, www.oregonlive.com; and "150,000 Facebook Posters Share Story of Young Protestor's Tearful Hug with Portland Officer," November 29, 2014, www.oregonlive.com.
2 On black boys as pets, see Yi-Fu Tuan, *Domination and Affection: The Making of Pets* (New Haven, CT: Yale University Press, 1984), 141–142.
3 Lori Merish, "Cuteness and Commodity Aesthetics: Tom Thumb and Shirley Temple," in *Freakery: Cultural Spectacles of the Extraordinary Body*, edited by Rosemary Garland Thomson (New York: New York University Press, 1996), 190.
4 See Gary Fishgall, *Gonna Do Great Things: The Life of Sammy Davis Jr.* (New York: Scribner, 2003), 14, and the television documentary, Julie Shaw, dir., *Living with Michael Jackson*, 2003.
5 Tina M. Campt, *Listening to Images: An Exercise in Counterintuition* (Durham, NC: Duke University Press, 2017).
6 In this interpretation, the image is haunted by federal and local legislative efforts to undermine the civil rights movement by denying welfare benefits to the "illegitimate" children of black single mothers. By the 1960s, single black mothers who were deemed to be unsuitable caregivers increasingly lost their children to a racially transforming child welfare system. Half a century later, Devonte would be another black child in the system who had been taken from his black mother. See Laura Briggs, *Somebody's Children: The Politics of Transracial and Transnational Adoption* (Durham, NC: Duke University Press, 2012), 41–48.
7 See Robin Bernstein, *Racial Innocence: Performing American Childhood from Slavery to Civil Rights* (New York: New York University Press, 2011). Bernstein refers to such deflection as "racial innocence."
8 I am referring to former police officer Darren Wilson's grand jury testimony on his version of the events that led him to fatally shoot Michael Brown. Remarking on a moment of transformation, Wilson had testified: "He looked up at me and had the most intense aggressive face. The only way I can describe it, it looks like a demon, that's how angry he looked" (225). *State of Missouri vs. Darren Wilson*, Grand Jury Volume V, September 16, 2014. http://apps.washingtonpost.com.

9   Robin D. G. Kelley speaks to this point with regard to George Zimmerman being found not guilty for the shooting death of unarmed teenager Trayvon Martin in 2012: "Martin died and Zimmerman walked because our entire political and legal foundations were built on an ideology of settler colonialism—an ideology in which the protection of white property rights was always sacrosanct" (299). See Robin D. G. Kelley, "How the System Worked: The US v. Trayvon Martin," In *Killing Trayvons: An Anthology of American Violence*, edited by Kevin Alexander Gray, Jeffrey St. Clair, and JoAnn Wypijewski (Petrolia, CA: CounterPunch Books, 2014).
10 For useful readings of *Wild Seed* in this regard, see Madhu Dubey, "Octavia Butler's Novels of Enslavement," *Novel* 46.3 (2013): 345–363, and Alys Weinbaum, *The Afterlife of Reproductive Slavery: Biocapitalism and Black Feminism's Philosophy of History* (Durham, NC: Duke University Press, 2019).
11 C. Riley Snorton, "Transfiguring Masculinities in Black Women's Studies," *Feminist Wire*, May 18, 2011, np. www.thefeministwire.com.
12 This insight is indebted to trans analytical frameworks advanced by Jack Halberstam and Snorton. Most notable are Jack Halberstam's *Female Masculinity* (Durham, NC: Duke University Press, 1998) and *In a Queer Time and Place: Transgender Bodies, Subcultural Lives* (New York: New York University Press, 2005).
13 I refer to Saidiya Hartman's account of the choices black women and girls made while living in northern slums during the turn of the twentieth century in *Wayward Lives, Beautiful Experiments: Intimate Histories of Social Upheaval* (New York: W.W. Norton, 2019). Hartman's work presents an occasion to trouble the categorical distinctions of gender in assessing the historical experiences of black childhood; I situate Baldwin's recollection of his boyhood in relation to the girls and women living in similar urban dwellings 40 years earlier.
14 On these relations, see Tuan, *Dominance and Affection*.
15 James Baldwin, *No Name in the Street* (New York: Laurel, 1986), 178–179.
16 See Saidiya Hartman, *Scenes of Subjection: Terror, Slavery, and Self-Making in Nineteenth-Century America* (New York: Oxford University Press, 1997), 53–54 and 79–112.
17 On black visuality and "the Fanonian moment," see Nicole Fleetwood, *Troubling Vision: Performance, Visuality, and Blackness* (Chicago: University of Chicago Press, 2011), 21–28.
18 See Phillip Atiba Goff et al., "The Essence of Innocence: Consequences of Dehumanizing Black Children," *Journal of Personality and Social Psychology* 106.4 (2014): 526–545, and Frank Edwards et al., "Risk of Being Killed by Police Use-of-Force in the U.S. by Age, Race/Ethnicity, and Sex," *PNAS* 116.34 (2019): 16793–16798.
19 Frantz Fanon, *Black Skin, White Masks* (New York: Grove Press, 1967), 112.
20 During his grand jury testimony, Wilson laid claim to childhood to signify that he was the deserving recipient of protection. Referring to Michael, Wilson stated, "[W]hen I grabbed him, the only way I can describe it is I felt like a five-year-old

holding onto Hulk Hogan. [. . .] Hulk Hogan, that's just how big he felt and how small I felt just from grasping his arm" (212). *State of Missouri vs. Darren Wilson*.
21 For a wide-ranging discussion about the arc of Wynter's work and her thinking on human genres, see Wynter and Katherine McKittrick, "Unparalleled Catastrophe for Our Species? Or, to Give Humanness a Different Future: Conversations," in *Sylvia Wynter: On Being Human as Praxis*, edited by Katherine McKittrick, 9–89 (Durham, NC: Duke University Press, 2015).
22 See C. Riley Snorton, *Black on Both Sides: A Racial History of Trans Identity* (Minneapolis: University of Minnesota Press, 2017).
23 Snorton, "Transfiguring Masculinities in Black Women's Studies," np.
24 Exemplary of such work that spans from the 1990s to the early 2000s is Michael Awkward's *Negotiating Difference: Race, Gender, and the Politics of Positionality* (Chicago: University of Chicago Press, 1995); Marcellus Blount's and George Cunningham's edited volume, *Representing Black Men* (New York: Routledge, 1996), to which I will return; Phillip Brian Harper, *Are We Not Men? Masculine Anxiety and the Problem of African-American Identity* (New York: Oxford University Press 1996); Hazel Carby, *Race Men* (Cambridge, MA: Harvard University Press, 1998); Devon Carbado's edited volume, *Black Men on Race, Gender, and Sexuality: A Critical Reader* (New York: New York University Press, 1999); Mark Anthony Neal's *New Black Man* (New York: Routledge, 2005); and Ronald L. Jackson II's *Scripting the Black Masculine Body: Identity, Discourse, and Racial Politics in Popular Media* (Albany: State University of New York Press, 2006).
25 Blount and Cunningham, *Representing Black Men*, xii. Emphasis mine.
26 Snorton, "Transfiguring Masculinities in Black Women's Studies," np.
27 "The Combahee River Collective Statement," in *How We Get Free: Black Feminism and the Combahee River Collective*, edited by Keeanga-Yamahtta Taylor, 17 (Chicago: Haymarket Books, 2017).
28 Snorton, "Transfiguring Masculinities in Black Women's Studies," np. Emphasis mine.
29 Michele Wallace, *Black Macho and the Myth of the Superwoman* (New York: Verso, 1999), 17.
30 Ibid., 19.
31 Toni Morrison interview with Alan Yentob. See Jill Nicholls, dir., *Toni Morrison Remembers*, 2015. My transcription.
32 Grace Kyungwon Hong, *The Ruptures of American Capital: Women of Color Feminism and the Culture of Immigrant Labor* (Minneapolis: University of Minnesota Press, 2006), 37.
33 Ibid., 61.
34 Morrison, *The Bluest Eye* (New York: Plume, 1994), 20.
35 Ibid.
36 Recall Spillers's assertion that, as cargo stowed in slave ships, "one is neither female, nor male, as both are taken into 'account' as *quantities*. The female in 'Middle Passage,' as the apparently smaller physical mass, occupies 'less room'

[...] But she is, nevertheless, quantifiable by the same rules of accounting as her male counterpart." Hortense Spillers, "Mama's Baby, Papa's Maybe: An American Grammar Book," *diacritics* 17.2 (1987): 72.
37 Toni Morrison, *Sula* (New York: Vintage, 2004), 52.
38 Ibid., 23.
39 Aimee Cox, *Shapeshifters: Black Girls and the Choreography of Citizenship* (Durham, NC: Duke University Press, 2015), 231.
40 Uri McMillan, *Embodied Avatars: Genealogies of Black Feminist Art and Performance* (Durham, NC: Duke University Press, 2015).
41 Ibid., 13.
42 On this point see Karen Sánchez-Eppler, *Dependent States: The Child's Part in Nineteenth-Century American Culture* (Chicago: University of Chicago Press, 2005), xxiii–xxiv.
43 Ibid., xxv. Emphasis mine.
44 Harriet Beecher Stowe, *Uncle Tom's Cabin* (New York: W.W. Norton, 2018).
45 See Hortense Spillers, "Changing the Letter: The Yokes, the Jokes of Discourse, or, Mrs. Stowe, Mr. Reed," in Spillers, *Black, White, and in Color: Essays on American Literature and Culture*, 193–194 (Chicago: University of Chicago Press, 2003).
46 Richard Yarborough, "Strategies of Black Characterization in *Uncle Tom's Cabin* and the Early Afro-American Novel," in *New Essays on Uncle Tom's Cabin*, edited by Eric Sundquist, 47 (New York: Cambridge University Press, 1986).
47 For a discussion on how the standard elderliness of Tom accompanied the sentimentality of minstrel songs, see Sarah Meer, *Uncle Tom Mania: Slavery, Minstrelsy and Transatlantic Culture in the 1850s* (Athens: University of Georgia Press, 2005), 29.
48 Yarborough, "Strategies of Black Characterization," 50.
49 Ibid.
50 On this point, see Bernstein, *Racial Innocence*.
51 "After placing 'the fair, high-bred child, with her golden head' beside 'her black, keen, subtle, cringing, yet acute neighbor' as 'representatives of their races,' Stowe emphasizes that insurmountable, essential racial differences will continue to differentiate these two, even as she uses the child to bridge persistent distinctions between slave and citizen" (232). See Caroline Field Levander, "'Let Her White Progeny Offset Her Dark One': The Child and the Politics of Nation Making," *American Literature* 76.2 (2004): 221–246.
52 See Tavia Nyong'o, "Racial Kitsch and Black Performance," *Yale Journal of Criticism* 15.2 (2002): 375–376.
53 Harry and Topsy are united by the shared obligation of enslaved children to introduce themselves to white adult strangers with a song and dance, a performance that invariably reveals the essence of their blackness, racial amalgamation notwithstanding. I describe Harry's performance later in this discussion; for Topsy's similar one, see *Uncle Tom's Cabin* (New York: W.W. Norton, 2018), 228.
54 By virtue of this function, Bell yokes Harry with the enslaved Cassy's son Henry, and Henrique St. Clare. See Bell, "'So Wicked': Revisiting *Uncle Tom's Cabin*'s

Sentimental Racism through the Lens of the Child," in *The Children's Table: Childhood Studies and the Humanities*, edited by Anna Mae Duane (Athens: University of Georgia Press, 2013).

55 Indeed, Harry's performance can be read as indicative of his total abjection, as Lauren Berlant suggests of the scene in the 1927 filmic version of the novel. See Berlant, "Poor Eliza," *American Literature* 70.3 (1998): 649.

56 On the transition of the American child's social value, from laborer in a market economy to a figure of familial affection, see Sánchez-Eppler, *Dependent States*.

57 Spillers, "Mama's Baby, Papa's Maybe," 74–75.

58 See Lori Merish, *Sentimental Materialism: Gender, Commodity Culture, and Nineteenth-Century American Literature* (Durham, NC: Duke University Press, 2000), 154–155.

59 As Daina Ramey Berry notes, "children under age ten had low monetary values, and appraisers rarely used gender to differentiate value for the first decade of children's lives" (46). See Berry, *The Price for Their Pound of Flesh: The Value of the Enslaved, from Womb to Grave, in the Building of a Nation* (Boston: Beacon Press, 2017.

60 Harriet Beecher Stowe, *Uncle Tom's Cabin* (New York: W.W. Norton, 2018), 13.

61 Ibid., 13–14.

62 According to Berry, like young children, "the elderly and superannuated had low economic values" (136). While the average sale values for children under age ten ranged from $236 for females and $258 for males, the range for the elderly was between $301 for females and $546 for males. These figures are lower than the sale values of the enslaved whose ages ranged from 23 to 39, which were an average of $494 for females and $792 for males. See Berry, *The Price for Their Pound of Flesh*.

63 On the enchantment of the fetishized commodity, see Karl Marx, *Capital: Volume I: A Critique of Political Economy* (New York: Penguin Classics, 1992), 163–164.

64 Walter Johnson, *Soul by Soul: Life Inside the Antebellum Slave Market* (Cambridge, MA: Harvard University Press, 1999), 119.

65 William Wells Brown, *Clotel; or, the President's Daughter: A Narrative of Slave Life in the United States* (Boston: Bedford/St. Martin's, 2000), 89.

66 Ibid., 90. The older men may have accurately kept their own time—their own lived experiences of their ages—by using the growing time of corn or potatoes as a proxy, but black age is revealed to be a site of such profound dispossession that it is entirely removable from the progression of time itself, as the commodity is.

67 Johnson, *Soul by Soul*, 145.

68 On this temporal structure of the commodity and its relation to sexuality, see Michael Ralph, "Commodity," *Social Text* 27.3 (2009): 83.

69 This is the point that Edward E. Baptist makes of slave traders' noted desires for "fancy maids." See Edward E. Baptist, "'Cuffy,' 'Fancy Maids,' and 'One-Eyed Men': Rape Commodification, and the Domestic Slave Trade in the United States," *American Historical Review* 106.5 (2001): 1619–1650.

70 Stowe, *Uncle Tom's Cabin*, 14.

71 Ibid., 15.

72 Ibid.
73 Johnson, *Soul by Soul*, 133.
74 Ibid., 147.
75 Jacqueline Rose, *The Case of Peter Pan or The Impossibility of Children's Fiction* (London: Macmillan Press, 1984), 93.
76 Ibid., 88–91.
77 With regard to the novel's remarkable sales in its first year of publication—over 300,000 copies—Yarborough reminds us that this is all the more astounding when these figures likely excluded large populations of the country, including much of the South, the illiterate, and those who borrowed rather than purchased books. See "Strategies of Black Characterization," 46.
78 Zaron Burnett III, "The Sad and Strange Life and Death of Devonte Hart: The Crying Black Boy Who Famously Hugged a Cop," *MEL Newsletter*, www.melmagazine.com.
79 Such an enduring economy of appearance and absence speaks to why an intersectional framework in which to analyze structural conditions of anti-black violence remains necessary. See Kimberlé Crenshaw et al., "Say Her Name: Resisting Police Brutality against Black Women," African American Policy Form, 2015. www.aapf.org/sayhernamereport/
80 *Get Out*, directed by Jordan Peele, 2017.
81 Jack Finney, *Invasion of the Body Snatchers: A Novel* (New York: Touchstone, 2015).
82 Johnson, *Soul by Soul*, 134.
83 See Cheryl I. Harris's classic essay, "Whiteness as Property," *Harvard Law Review* 106.8 (1993): 1707–1791.
84 Kobena Mercer, *Welcome to the Jungle: New Positions in Black Cultural Studies* (New York: Routledge, 1994), 45.
85 Weinbaum, *The Afterlife of Reproductive Slavery*, 11.

2. VAMPIRES AND RELICS

An earlier version of this chapter appears as "Any Other Age: Vampires and Oceanic Lifespan." Copyright © 2016 Johns Hopkins University Press and St. Louis University. This article first appeared in *African American Review* 49, 4 (Winter 2016): 313–327.

1 Benjamin Reiss, *The Showman and the Slave: Race, Death, and Memory in Barnum's America* (Cambridge, MA: Harvard University Press, 2010), 53.
2 Ibid., 52.
3 Phineas T. Barnum, *The Life of P.T. Barnum* (Urbana and Chicago: University of Illinois Press, 2000), 148.
4 Fred Moten, *In the Break: The Aesthetics of the Black Radical Tradition* (Minneapolis: University of Minnesota Press, 2003), 22.
5 Frederick Douglass, *Narrative of the Life of Frederick Douglass* (Mineola, NY: Dover Publications, 1995), 1.

6 Harriet A. Jacobs, *Incidents in the Life of a Slave Girl: Written by Herself* (Cambridge, MA: Harvard University Press, 1987), 28.
7 Uri McMillan, *Embodied Avatars: Genealogies of Black Feminist Art and Performance* (New York: New York University Press, 2015), 63. As McMillan points out, Heth was not the only "ancient negress" to be put on display. Two other similar performances were those of "Joice Heth's Grandmother" and "Mother Boston." See McMillan, *Embodied Avatars*, 30–33.
8 There are numerous examples of the "childlike negro" as pervasively figural. For one discussion regarding black immaturity as the premise of early American emancipation law, see Sharon Braslaw Sundue's "'Beyond the Time of White Children': African American Emancipation, Age, and Ascribed Neoteny in Early National Pennsylvania," in *Age in America: The Colonial Era to the Present*, edited by Corinne T. Field and Nicholas Syrett, 47–65 (New York: New York University Press, 2015).
9 Foucault, quoted in Achille Mbembe, *Critique of Black Reason* (Durham, NC: Duke University Press, 2017), 17–18.
10 Ibid., 18.
11 Reiss, *The Showman and the Slave*, 42.
12 As part of her notable work on women in American plantation slavery, Deborah Gray White discusses the two archetypes in comparative terms:
> Mammies were always older than their charges and when white children reached adulthood and recorded their remembrances they were likely to remember Mammy as elderly. However, Mammy's age might also be a metaphor for the asexuality attributed to her. Among Anglo-American Protestant middle and upper classes, the Victorian maternal ideal was understood in terms of asexuality. Very likely the Jezebel image of black females got in the way of a perception of young or middle-aged black women as maternal domestics. Old age, thus, put Mammy beyond the pale of the carnal, above the taint of Jezebel. (60)

In other words, "old age" brokers a negotiation between an ideal of (maternal) femininity and black femaleness, which could only bear an approximate relation to proper femininity. See Deborah Gray White, *Ar'n't I a Woman? Female Slaves in the Plantation South* (New York: W.W. Norton, 1999).
13 McMillan, *Embodied Avatars*, 26.
14 See Kimberly Wallace-Sanders, *Mammy: A Century of Race, Gender, and Southern Memory* (Ann Arbor: University of Michigan Press, 2008). The term "black mammy" "served as a generic name for all slave women who served as a wet nurse or baby nurse for white children" (7). She quotes an early scholar of slavery, Jesse Parkhurst, to make the point that there were various names for the women who provided childcare on the plantation. Although the matter of age is not Wallace-Sanders's focus, these names make distinctions according to age, in addition to modes of maternity. One figure "is referred to as the 'Black Mammy,' a name probably given to distinguish her from the real mother and also from the elderly slave

woman, 'Mammy,' who took care of slave children while their mothers worked in the fields or in master's home" (Parkhurst, quoted in Wallace-Sanders, 6).

15 P. Gabrielle Foreman, "The Spoken and the Silenced in *Incidents in the Life of a Slave Girl* and Our Nig," in *Callaloo* 13.2 (1990): 317. For a full discussion on strategies of representation in Jacobs's narrative, see P. Gabrielle Foreman, *Activist Sentiments: Reading Black Women in the Nineteenth Century* (Urbana: University of Illinois Press, 2009).

16 In an introduction to a special issue of *Slavery and Abolition* on children in slavery, Gwyn Campbell, Suzanne Miers, and Joseph C. Miller speculate about historical conditions the jezebel stereotype conceals: "Girls, modern psychiatry and sociology suggest, react to abusive parents by fleeing to a no less abusive male protector, often through sexual promiscuity. Would it be worth considering the stereotyped 'Jezebel' and other aspects of masters' notorious sexual abuses of their young slave girls by treating them in this, or some other, way as the children whom they were" (176). The question refers to how the master perceived adolescent behavior of enslaved children: rebelliousness (for boys) or promiscuity (for girls) were politicized and thus divorced from considerations of juvenile development (175–176). See Gwyn Campbell, Suzanne Miers, and Joseph C. Miller, "Children in European Systems of Slavery: Introduction," *Slavery and Abolition* 27.2 (2006): 163–182.

17 See Hortense Spillers, "Mama's Baby, Papa's Maybe: An American Grammar Book," *diacritics* 17.2 (1987): 67. I will return to Spillers's work later this chapter.

18 Saidiya Hartman, "Venus in Two Acts," *Small Axe* 26 (2008): 11.

19 Ibid., 12.

20 Ibid., 6.

21 See Saidiya Hartman, *Lose Your Mother* (New York: Farrar, Strauss, and Giroux, 2007).

22 Hartman, "Venus in Two Acts," 13.

23 Ernest J. Gaines, *The Autobiography of Miss Jane Pittman* (New York: Bantam Books, 1972), v.

24 I will return to this era's historiography in the following chapter.

25 See Charles H. Rowell and Octavia Butler, "An Interview with Octavia Butler," *Callaloo* 20.1 (1997): 51.

26 See Michelle V. Rowley, "Whose Time Is It? Gender and Humanism in Contemporary Caribbean Feminist Advocacy," *Small Axe* 31 (2010): 3.

27 Fanon, *Black Skin, White Masks*, 8.

28 Rowley, "Whose Time Is It?," 5.

29 Gwen Bergner remarks that "typically, contemporary readers dismiss Fanon's condemnation as so obviously sexist that it does not merit analysis" (83). See "Who Is That Masked Woman? Or, the Role of Gender in Fanon's *Black Skin, White Masks*," *PMLA* 110.1 (1995): 75–88.

30 Fanon, *Black Skin, White Masks*, 42.

31 Ibid., 47.

32 Ibid., 31.
33 Ibid., 32–33. Emphasis in original.
34 In this instance, McClintock refers to the way Homi Bhabha relegates the question of women of color in the colonial context to an afterthought in his consideration of Fanon's work in "Remembering Fanon: Self, Psyche, and the Colonial Condition." See Anne McClintock, "Fanon and Gender Agency," in *Rethinking Fanon: The Continuing Dialogue*, edited by Nigel Gibson, 283–293 (Amherst, NY: Humanity Books: 199).
35 McClintock, "Fanon and Gender Agency," 285.
36 Giselle Liza Anatol, *The Things That Fly in the Night: Female Vampires in Literature of the Circum-Caribbean and African Diaspora* (New Brunswick, NJ: Rutgers University Press, 2015), 35.
37 Ibid., 221.
38 Ibid., 17.
39 Omise'eke Natasha Tinsley, "Black Atlantic, Queer Atlantic: Queer Imaginings of the Middle Passage." *GLQ* 14.2-3 (2008): 191–215, 197.
40 Anatol, *The Things That Fly in the Night*, 7–8. Anatol argues that cultural producers of more recent generations rework terrifying earlier aspects of the soucouyant that had come out of a collective experience of enslavement in order to explore her potential power. Now, "she is horrifying because she can strip off her own skin and penetrate the skins of others; she is also the one who draws blood, not leaks it. She is a powerful actor, not acted upon" (9).
41 Tinsley, "Black Atlantic, Queer Atlantic," 212. Emphasis in original.
42 Spillers, "Mama's Baby, Papa's Maybe," 72.
43 Ibid., 67.
44 Ibid.
45 Ibid., 66.
46 Alexander G. Weheliye, *Habeas Viscus: Racializing Assemblages, Biopolitics, and Black Feminist Theories of the Human* (Durham, NC: Duke University Press, 2014), 41.
47 Spillers, "Mama's Baby, Papa's Maybe," 80.
48 Octavia Butler, *Fledgling* (New York: Seven Stories Press, 2005), and Jewelle Gomez, *The Gilda Stories* (Ithaca, NY: Firebrand Press, 1991).
49 Anatol, *The Things That Fly in the Night*, 175. Emphasis in original.
50 Ashraf Rushdy, "Neo-Slave Narrative" in *The Oxford Companion to African American Literature*, edited by William L. Andrews, Frances Smith Foster, and Trudier Harris, 533 (New York: Oxford University Press, 1997, eBook).
51 Butler, *Fledgling*, 4.
52 Melissa J. Strong, "The Limits of Newness: Hybridity in Octavia E. Butler's *Fledgling*," *FEMSPEC* 11.1 (2010): 27–43, 11.
53 Butler, *Fledgling*, 77, 76.
54 In 1951, without having given consent and without her knowledge, Lacks's cervical cancer cells were harvested. Later that same year, Lacks died of her cancer at the

young age of 31. However, her harvested cancer cells resulted in the immortal "HeLa" cell line that enabled decades of biomedical research, the profits from which her family received no compensation. For one comprehensive account of these events, see Rebecca Skloot, *The Immortal Life of Henrietta Lacks* (New York: Broadway Books, 2010).

55 James Doucet-Battle, "Bioethical Matriarchy: Race, Gender, and the Gift in Genomic Research," *Catalyst: Feminism, Theory, Technoscience* 2.2 (2016): 1–28, 4.
56 Stephanie Camp discusses the way body parts of the enslaved were conceptually isolated. She writes, "By the antebellum period, planters had so thoroughly assimilated ideas that reduced enslaved people to their bodies that they often referred to them by their parts: 'hands' was a common term, and 'heads' was not unfamiliar" (64). See Stephanie Camp, *Closer to Freedom: Enslaved Women and Everyday Resistance in the Plantation South* (Chapel Hill: University of North Carolina Press, 2004), 64.
57 Robyn Wiegman, "Intimate Publics: Race, Property, and Personhood," *American Literature* 74.4 (2002): 867–868.
58 Holloway claims that the transgression of identitarian boundaries in *Fledging* allows "us to probe what identity might mean, and more important, what it means to be human in an (arguably) postracial era." See Karla F. C. Holloway, *Legal Fictions: Constituting Race, Composing Literature* (Durham, NC: Duke University Press, 2004), 87–88.
59 Butler, *Fledgling*, 1.
60 Orlando Paterson, *Slavery and Social Death: A Comparative Study* (Cambridge, MA: Harvard University Press, 1982), 5.
61 Butler, *Fledgling*, 105.
62 Octavia Butler, *Kindred* (Boston: Beacon Press, 2003).
63 Ashraf Rushdy discusses the challenge of classifying *Kindred* within a single genre. Regarding the novel's representation of historical time, Rushdy notes that "*Kindred* is a novel of memory" (136). See Ashraf H. A. Rushdy, "Families of Orphans: Relation and Disrelation in Octavia Butler's *Kindred*," *College English* 55.2 (1993): 136.
64 Butler, *Kindred*, 135–136.
65 We learn that Shori has a younger brother, Stefan, whose "light brown" skin indicates that he, like she, is "an experiment" (76). As Stefan explains, "I should have been you, so to speak. We have the same black human mother" (76). Stefan and Shori's other male relatives are killed shortly after Shori is re-introduced to them in her amnesic state, which evokes a condition of which both the vampire and relic are figurative: Black femaleness is presumed more likely or able to survive than black maleness, for the sake of black historical survival, overall. The gendered difference of this condition is regarded as tenuous here since Stefan "should have been" Shori. Not only does this indicate that there is a fungible quality to gendered subject positions within the category of blackness. It also suggests that black female gender has been deliberately constituted as a status of survival in the black cultural imagination.

66 See Paul Lovejoy, "The Children of Slavery—the Transatlantic Phase," *Slavery and Abolition* 27.2 (August 2006): 199.
67 Gwyn Campbell, "Children and Slavery in the New World: A Review," *Slavery and Abolition*, 27.2 (August 2006): 261.
68 The politicizing of age is particularly pronounced during the adolescence years of the enslaved, according to Gwyn Campbell et al. Of adolescent slaves, "It would . . . have been an arbitrary and abusive pseudo 'parent' whose authority they defied. . . . The masters, of course, treated this distorted version of every male child's passage to adulthood through disobedience subversion in the highly politicized context they created by enslaving adult men and construing them as 'boys.' Adolescence thus became 'rebellion.'" See Campbell et al., "Children in European Systems of Slavery: Introduction," *Slavery and Abolition* 27.2 (2006): 175–176.
69 Spillers, "Mama's Baby, Papa's Maybe," 67. Emphasis in original.
70 As Rushdy notes, "[t]he debate currently rages between those who argue that slavery led to the 'infantilization' of adult Africans . . . and those who argue that slaves formed viable internal communities, family structures, and protective personae that allowed them to live rich, coherent lives within their own system of value" (45). See Ashraf H. A. Rushdy, "Daughters Signifyin(g) History: The Example of Toni Morrison's *Beloved*," in *Beloved: A Casebook*, edited by William L. Andrews and Nellie Y. McKay (New York: Oxford University Press, 1999).
71 Butler, *Fledgling*, 60.
72 Ibid., 84.
73 Phillip Atiba Goff et al., "The Essence of Innocence: Consequences of Dehumanizing Black Children," *Journal of Personality and Social Psychology* 106.4 (2014): 527.
74 Monique W. Morris, *Pushout: The Criminalization of Black Girls in Schools* (New York: New Press, 2016), 34.
75 In *The Arcades Project*, Walter Benjamin notes that, "There is a not-yet-conscious knowledge of *what has been*: its advancement has the structure of awakening," Walter Benjamin, *The Arcades Project* (Cambridge, MA: Belknap Press, 2002), 883.
76 Jewelle Gomez, *The Gilda Stories*, 9.
77 Ibid.
78 Ibid., 10.
79 Wilma King, *Stolen Childhood: Slave Youth in Nineteenth-Century America* (Bloomington: Indiana University Press, 2011), xix.
80 Gomez, *The Gilda Stories*, 11.
81 Ibid., 10. Emphasis mine.
82 Harriet Jacobs, *Incidents in the Life of a Slave Girl* (Cambridge, MA: Harvard University Press, 1987), 28.
83 Corinne T. Field, *The Struggle for Equal Adulthood: Gender, Race, Age, and the Fight for Citizenship in Antebellum America* (Chapel Hill: University of North Carolina Press, 2014), 93.

84 See Saidiya Hartman, *Scenes of Subjection: Terror, Slavery, and Self-Making in Nineteenth-Century America* (Oxford: Oxford University Press, 1997), 105.
85 Gomez, *The Gilda Stories*, 45.
86 Miriam Jones, "*The Gilda Stories*: Revealing the Monster at the Margins," in *Blood Read: The Vampire as Metaphor in Contemporary Culture*, edited by Joan Gordon and Veronica Hollinger, 164 (Philadelphia: University of Pennsylvania Press, 1997).
87 Hartman, *Scenes of Subjection*, 105.
88 Gomez, *The Gilda Stories*, 62.
89 Ibid., 126.
90 Reiss, *The Showman and the Slave*, 50.
91 Hartman, "Venus in Two Acts," 2. Emphasis in original.
92 Ibid., 1.
93 Hartman, *Lose Your Mother*, 138.
94 Hartman, "Venus in Two Acts," 8.
95 Alisa LaGamma, "Eternal Ancestors: The Art of the Central African Reliquary," *African Arts* 40.4 (Winter 2007): 34.
96 McMillan, *Embodied Avatars*, 38.
97 Ibid., 39–40.
98 In her cultural history of the zombie, Sarah Juliet Lauro writes, "the myth's history reveals that the zombie's ambivalence as living and dead is paralleled in its simultaneity as a figuration of both slavery and rebellion" (10). This latter figurative possibility evokes a fearful exertion of will that Heth's role as relic was designed to downplay. For more on the zombie's oceanic origins, see Sarah Juliet Lauro, *The Transatlantic Zombie: Slavery, Rebellion, and Living Death* (New Brunswick, NJ: Rutgers University Press, 2015).
99 Barnum, *The Life of P.T. Barnum*, 155–156. Emphasis in original.
100 Reiss, *The Showman and the Slave*, 70.
101 By offering the impossible suggestion that the Delany sisters will have a subsequent "one hundred years" after the "first" one hundred, the subtitle of this work evokes the logic of the immortal relic. Sarah Delany and A. Elizabeth Delany, *Having Our Say: The Delany Sisters' First One Hundred Years*, edited by Amy Hill Hearth (New York: Dell, 1994).
102 Ibid., xvi.
103 Mary Helen Washington, "Reading between the Lines," *Women's Review of Books* 11.4 (1994): 10.
104 Gaines, *The Autobiography of Miss Jane Pittman*. In this way, Gaines's novel may be added to other work of "black literary postmodernism," which eschews the mediation of print culture in favor of vernacular culture that is ostensibly more accessible to everyday black people. For a thoroughgoing discussion on this topic, see Madhu Dubey, *Signs and Cities: Black Literary Postmodernism* (Chicago: University of Chicago Press, 2003).
105 Gaines, *Autobiography*, v.

106 For the full interview, see Jerome Tarshis, "The Other 300 Years: A Conversation with Ernest J. Gaines, Author of *The Autobiography of Miss Jane Pittman*," in *Conversations with Ernest Gaines*, edited by John Lowe, 72–79 (Jackson: University Press of Mississippi, 1995). Emphasis in original.
107 Gaines, *Autobiography*, vi–vii.
108 Ibid., vii.
109 Ibid., viii.
110 Ibid., 4.
111 Ibid., 8.
112 Ibid., 9.
113 Ibid.
114 Douglass, *Narrative*, 39.
115 Gaines, *Autobiography*, 38.
116 Ibid., 63.
117 Ibid., 104.
118 Ibid., 97.
119 Ibid.
120 Ibid., 211.
121 For more on this argument, see Roderick Ferguson, *The Reorder of Things: The University and Its Pedagogies of Minority Difference* (Minneapolis: University of Minnesota Press, 2012).
122 Ibid., 215–216.
123 Ibid., 240.
124 Ibid., 236.
125 Ibid., 240.
126 Ibid., 242.
127 Ibid., 243.
128 Ibid., 242.
129 Hartman, "Venus in Two Acts," 3.
130 August Wilson, *Gem of the Ocean* (New York: Theatre Communications Group, 2006).
131 Ibid., 43.
132 Ibid., 52.
133 Middleton A. Harris et al., *The Black Book* (New York: Random House, 1974).
134 Ibid., np.
135 Toni Morrison, *The Bluest Eye*, "Forward," x.
136 Toni Morrison, *God Help the Child* (New York: Alfred A. Knopf, 2015), 6.

3. THE MASS AND MEN

1 As Spillers notes, "African persons [. . .] were in movement across the Atlantic, but they were also *nowhere* at all" (72, emphasis in original). Hortense Spillers, "Mama's Baby, Papa's Maybe: An American Grammar Book," *diacritics* 17.2 (1987): 64–81.

2 Olaudah Equiano, *The Interesting Narrative of the Life of Olaudah Equiano, or Gustavus Vassa, the African*, in *The Classic Slave Narratives*, edited by Henry Louis Gates, Jr., 36–37 (New York: Mentor, 1987).
   It evokes the "magic" that Octavia Butler will reimagine nearly 200 years later in her novel *Wild Seed*. A few lines before the mention of clouds that seem like land, Equiano writes, "During our passage I first saw flying fishes, which surprised me very much: they used frequently to fly across the ship, and many of them fell on the deck" (36). On her voyage across the Atlantic, Anyanwu looks out at the sea, "watching the leaping fish" (79). But as she attempts to take its shape, she realizes that "it was more like a land thing than a fish. Inside, it is much like a land animal" (80). In the spirit of Butler's speculative fiction, I imagine that Equiano, for a fleeting instant, draws a connection between the "land"—the location to which some (human) beings do or do not belong—and an embodying processing I refer to in this book as "Oceanic."
3 Gwyn Campbell et al. speculate about "the feelings of helplessness" that boys on slave ships must have had, and note that "the Equiano narrative of isolation, vulnerability and desolation" captures this experience. See Gwyn Campbell, Suzanne Miers, and Joseph C. Miller, "Children in European Systems of Slavery: Introduction," *Slavery and Abolition* 27.2 (2006): 166.
4 This is how Kincaid describes what occurred on Antigua and the other Caribbean islands after the arrival of Columbus. Upon finding indigenous communities he did not know existed, Columbus "empties the land of these people, and then he empties the people [. . .]. It is when this land is completely empty that I and the people who look like me begin to make an appearance" (623). See Jamaica Kincaid, "In History," *Callaloo* 24.2 (2001): 620–626.
5 On the point of land, historical retrieval, and remains, Wynter makes an important distinction between the production unit of the "plantation," and the "plot" on which enslaved populations grew crops to sustain themselves. See Sylvia Wynter, "Novel and History, Plot and Plantation," *Savacou* 5 (1971): 95–102.
6 Equiano, *The Interesting Narrative of the Life of Olaudah Equiano*, 37.
7 Ibid., 76.
8 See Neferti X. M. Tadiar, "Decolonization, 'Race,' and Remaindered Life under Empire," *Oui Parle: Critical Humanities and Social Sciences* 23.2 (2015): 135–160. I quote from Tadiar's discussion of racial capitalism in this current moment of late empire: currently, "[identitarian] codes now [. . .] operate within numerous calculative procedures of attribution, where they act as variables for partitioning and bundling organic and inorganic masses, matters, and potentials in new modes of value production and life extraction, which have resulted in both a proliferation of social differences [. . .] and a staggeringly profound breach in the fates of human beings" (136). Equiano's description of plantation slavery throughout the Caribbean illustrates an earlier modern version of this separation and combination of modes of life and capabilities as valuable or disposable. "Blackness" is constituted through the life and labor extraction of commodities relegated outside of the realm of humanity.

9   Equiano, *The Interesting Narrative of the Life of Olaudah Equiano*, 76.
10 Elizabeth DeLoughrey, "Yam, Roots, and Rot: Allegories of the Provision Grounds," *Small Axe* 15.1 (2011): 61. Achille Mbembe refers to this as the outcome of the Atlantic period of trade, from the fifteenth century to the nineteenth century, when he notes of the eighteenth century in particular, "it was [. . .] during this period that people and cultures were increasingly conceptualized as individualities closed in upon themselves. Each community—and even each people—was considered a unique collective body endowed with its own power. The collective also became the foundation for a history shaped, it was thought, by forces that emerged only to destroy other forces, and by struggle that could result only in liberty or servitude" (16–17). See Achille Mbembe, *Critique of Black Reason* (Durham, NC: Duke University Press, 2017).
11 As Saidiya Hartman describes, the transition from slavery to freedom was a "non-event," as it transformed the technologies of slavery-era subjection to fit the obligations of liberalism. See Saidiya Hartman, *Scenes of Subjection: Terror, Slavery, and Self-Making in Nineteenth-Century America* (New York: Oxford University Press, 1997), 116.
12 Walter Johnson, *River of Dark Dreams: Slavery and Empire in the Cotton Kingdom* (Cambridge, MA: Belknap Press, 2013). Johnson's discussion about how a particular strain of cotton reshaped both the Mississippi Valley and the enslaved people who worked the land during the rise of "the Cotton Kingdom" from the 1830s onward informs my thinking about the co-constitution of what he calls "land" and "hand." As Johnson writes, a dominance of one cotton plant "produced both a radical simplification of nature and a radical simplification of human being: the reduction of landscape to cotton plantation and of human being to 'hand'" (8).
13 For a robust account of how this single-leader paradigm has been overly identified with black political life, see Erica Edwards, *Charisma and the Fictions of Black Leadership* (Minneapolis: University of Minnesota Press, 2012).
14 Hortense Spillers, "Mama's Baby, Papa's Maybe: An American Grammar Book," *diacritics* 17.2 (1987): 66.
15 Hortense Spillers, "'All the Things You Could Be by Now, If Sigmund Freud's Wife Was Your Mother': Psychoanalysis and Race," in Spillers, *Black, White, and in Color: Essays on American Literature and Culture*, 383–384 (Chicago: University of Chicago Press, 2003).
16 See Raymond Williams, *Keywords: A Vocabulary of Culture and Society* (New York: Oxford University Press, 1983). Falling in line with the various subsequent versions that extend Williams's project, I make a modest attempt to think of the "mass" as a term that captures the dynamism of ongoing social transformation. In such a word, as Williams explains, "We find a history and complexity of meanings; conscious changes, or consciously different uses; innovation, obsolescence, specialization, extension, overlap, transfer; or changes which are masked by a nominal continuity so that words which seem to have been there for centuries, with continuous general meanings, have come in fact to express radically different

or radically variable, yet sometimes hardly noticed, meanings and implications of meaning" (17).
17 Spillers, "All the Things You Could Be by Now," 395.
18 For a discussion on the commodification of race through the mass production of folk culture in this era, see Sonnet Retman, *Real Folks: Race and Genre in the Great Depression* (Durham, NC: Duke University Press, 2011).
19 Spillers, "Mama's Baby, Papa's Maybe," 66.
20 See Walter Johnson, "Time and Revolution in African America: Temporality and the History of Atlantic Slavery," in *Rethinking American History in a Global Age*, edited by Thomas Bender (Berkeley: University of California Press, 2002). As Johnson reminds us, the "natural" time of enslaved people, which "savagery, primitivism, and biological lassitude" index, was an invention made to suit the "temporal frames of reference defined by slavery and race" (154). The dominant temporality of enslavement, which the slaveholders determined, overshadowed alternative temporalities of enslaved people, and was a constitutive part of an embodying process. As such, black bodies took on the look and meaning of temporality, a condition that I term throughout this book as "age." Thus, historical temporalities such as savagery, primitivism, and laziness find unstable translations as age.
21 Spillers, "All the Things You Could Be by Now," 394–397.
22 Ibid., 381.
23 Ibid., 394.
24 Ibid., 395.
25 Quoted in ibid., 389. Emphasis in original.
26 Stanley M. Elkins, *Slavery: A Problem in American Institutional and Intellectual Life* (Chicago: University of Chicago Press, 1976), 86.
27 Ibid., 82.
28 Ibid.
29 Ibid., 84.
30 Ibid., 130.
31 Ibid.
32 Spillers, "All the Things You Could Be by Now," 389.
33 Elkins, *Slavery*, 88, 101.
34 Ibid., 102.
35 In addition to explicitly relying on Freudian paradigms of selfhood and development, Elkins justifies his interest in the reality of a distinctly American slave "personality" by ostensibly following the lead of "a wide-spread, respectable, and productive enterprise among our psychologists and social scientists" (86).
36 Elkins specifically pulls from the Freudian-derived concept of "infantile regression" (117) to discuss the making of Sambo but bypasses the conceptual openness of the oceanic. In other words, he bypasses both the oceanic feeling and the Ocean, as a site that trafficked in the production of social meanings that would shape the modern western world, of which the American plantation is obviously a part.

37 Sigmund Freud, *Civilization and Its Discontents* in *The Freud Reader*, edited by Peter Gay, 727 (New York: W.W. Norton, 1989).
38 Ibid., 723.
39 Fred Moten, *In the Break: The Aesthetics of the Black Radical Tradition* (Minneapolis: University of Minnesota Press, 2003), 176.
40 Key examples of this work include John Blassingame, *The Slave Community: Plantation Life in the Antebellum South* (New York: Oxford University Press, 1979), Eugene D. Genovese, *Roll, Jordan, Roll: The World the Slaves Made* (New York: Vintage Books, 1976), and Herbert G. Gutman's *The Black Family in Slavery and Freedom, 1750–1925* (New York: Vintage Books, 1976).
41 Deborah Gray White, *Ar'n't I a Woman? Female Slaves in the Plantation South* (New York: W.W. Norton, 1999).
42 See Jennifer Morgan, *Laboring Women: Reproduction and Gender in New World Slavery* (Philadelphia: University of Pennsylvania Press, 2004), 48–49, 74.
43 White, *Ar'n't I a Woman*, 21.
44 Ibid., 20.
45 White, *Ar'n't I a Woman*, 60, and Kimberly Wallace-Sanders, *Mammy: A Century of Race, Gender, and Southern Memory* (Ann Arbor: University of Michigan Press, 2008), 7.
46 Hartman, *Scenes of Subjection*, 171.
47 Ibid., 178.
48 Ibid.
49 See David Theo Goldberg, *The Racial State* (Malden, MA: Blackwell, 2002), 45, 55, n6.
50 Ibid., 45.
51 Toni Morrison, *Beloved* (New York: Vintage International, 2004), 147.
52 Ibid., 12.
53 Ibid., 147.
54 Ibid., 148.
55 Frantz Fanon, *Black Skin, White Masks* (New York: Grove Press, 1967), 140.
56 Morrison, *Beloved*, 149.
57 Ibid., 152.
58 Ibid.
59 Ibid.
60 On the evolution of the syphilis study from a defunded version to the subsequent Tuskegee Study of Untreated Syphilis in the Negro Male, see James H. Jones, *Bad Blood: The Tuskegee Syphilis Experiment* (New York: Free Press, 1993), 91–100.
61 Quoted in Allan Brandt, "Racism and Research: The Case of the Tuskegee Syphilis Experiment," in *Tuskegee's Truths: Rethinking the Tuskegee Syphilis Study*, edited by Susan M. Reverby, 20 (Chapel Hill: University of North Carolina Press, 2000).
62 To the degree that their manhood is recognizable, it is through the logic that men, unlike women, have "a definite time" of contracting the disease.

63 For further discussion on the role of scientific racism as the precondition of the Tuskegee study, see Brandt, "Racism and Research." Of the turn of the century, he writes, "Physicians studying the effects of emancipation on health concluded almost universally that freedom had caused the mental, moral, and physical deterioration of the black population. They substantiated this argument by citing examples in the comparative anatomy of the black and white race" (16).
64 Toni Morrison, *Sula* (New York: Vintage International, 2004).
65 Ibid., 5–6.
66 Ibid., 68.
67 Ibid., 52.
68 Ibid.
69 Ibid., 53.
70 Ibid., 174.
71 Ibid., 58.
72 Ibid., 59.
73 For a discussion of the unthinkable intersection between "race" and female gender during early modern, European conquest, see Sylvia Wynter, "Beyond Miranda's Meanings: Un/silencing the 'Demonic Ground' of Caliban's 'Woman,'" in *The Black Feminist Reader*, edited by Joy James and T. Denean Sharpley-Whiting (Malden, MA: Blackwell, 2000).
74 Morrison, *Sula*, 157.
75 Ibid., 63.
76 Ibid., 29.
77 Ibid., 92.
78 See Gloria T. Hull, Patricia Bell Scott, and Barbara Smith, eds., *All the Women Are White, All the Blacks Are Men, But Some of Us Are Brave: Black Women's Studies* (Old Westbury, NY: Feminist Press, 1982).
79 Morrison, *Sula*, "Forward," xiii.
80 Ibid., 115.
81 Ibid., 142.
82 Ibid., 149.
83 Harriet Beecher Stowe, *Uncle Tom's Cabin* (W.W. Norton, 2018). See Tavia Nyong'o, "Racial Kitsch and Black Performance," *Yale Journal of Criticism* 15.2 (2002): 371–391.

   As Nyong'o observes regarding Topsy, which holds for the pickaninny in general, she is not only "genderless" but also "part of a disturbing and disgusting surplus. The violence done upon her is the performance of waste" (377).
84 See Robin Bernstein, *Racial Innocence: Performing American Childhood from Slavery to Civil Rights* (New York: New York University Press, 2011). Bernstein argues that "both Topsy's hardening through abuse and her conversion into sensation" are ultimately done away with through the subsequent cultural salience of the ever insensate and inhuman figure of the pickaninny (51). More broadly, Bernstein argues that "children's culture or performances" and "bodies" become the repositories for

a racial argument, such as black unfitness for citizenship, "when a racial argument is effectively countered or even delegitimized in adult culture" (51). As I suggest, if black children are such neutralizing repositories for no-longer-legitimate racist logic, then the concept of black childhood itself instantiates historical transformation. In other words, black childhood marks the embodiment of a temporality that cannot simply be described as emergent, or on the way to adulthood, but rather as out of sync with the dominant time of culture. Thus, it signifies various other temporalities. The deweys beg the question of what version of temporality—residual, ruptured, continuous—is felt during the post–civil rights era.

85   Harriet Beecher Stowe, *Uncle Tom's Cabin* (New York: W.W. Norton, 2018), 227.
86   Ibid., 228.
87   Ibid., 230.
88   Ibid., 231.
89   Ibid.
90   Ibid.
91   As Bernstein argues, the key difference between Stowe's Topsy and the pickaninny, which arise as minstrel caricature in the stage productions of *Uncle Tom's Cabin* throughout the end of the nineteenth century, and as vulgar imagery in children's books, decorative items, and other material forms, is that the character of the 1852 novel is capable of conversion, transformation—in a word, spiritual, moral, and developmental growth, whereas the pickaninny of later years is permanently insensate.
92   See Kenneth W. Goings, *Mammy and Uncle Mose: Black Collectibles and American Stereotyping* (Bloomington: Indiana University Press, 1994), for a discussion on the political and cultural developments during the period between the 1880s and 1930, in relation to the mass production of black collectibles.
93   Patricia A. Turner, *Ceramic Uncles and Celluloid Mammies: Black Images and Their Influence on Culture* (New York: Anchor Books, 1994), 16.
94   See Morgan, *Laboring Women*. Morgan writes of the mid-seventeenth century, "Terminology such as 'pickaninnies' was rare—the more common terms such as 'increase' and 'produce' suggest that slaveowners understood quite early the value of the reproductive lives of laboring women in their evolving conception of themselves as owners of human property" (82). More directly related to the futurity that black children instantiated for the slave owner—perhaps as "increase" at one historical juncture and "pickaninnies" in another—is Morgan's claim that, "When planters looked to 'increase,' they crafted real and imagined legacies. [. . .] Slaveowners whose prospects might have seemed somewhat bleak looked to black women's bodies in search of a promising future for their own progeny" (83).
95   For a discussion on the social flux in the Black Belt after the Civil War, and the evolution of late antebellum slave leasing to ongoing practices of involuntary servitude in the 1950s, see Douglas A. Blackmon, *Slavery by Another Name: The Re-Enslavement of Black Americans from the Civil War to World War II* (New York: Anchor Books, 2009).

96 Morrison, *Sula*, 69.
97 See Pamela Thurschwell, "Dead Boys and Adolescent Girls: Unjoining the Bildungsroman in Carson McCullers's *The Member of the Wedding* and Toni Morrison's *Sula*," *ESC: English Studies in Canada* 38.3 (2013): 105–128. Thurschwell refers to the deweys as a note on which to conclude, rather than as a starting point.
98 Morrison, *Sula*, 84–85.
99 Stowe, *Uncle Tom's Cabin*, 227.
100 Although the deweys seem to spend most of their time in the novel unsupervised, a particularly pointed scene depicting their lack of need for care is as follows: "two deweys came in [to Sula's bedroom] with their beautiful teeth and said, 'We sick.' Sula turned her head slowly and murmured, 'Get well'" (128). Sula caught the redheaded dewey by his shirt and held him by the heels over the banister until he wet his pants. The other dewey was joined by the third, and they delved into their pockets for stones, which they threw at her. [. . .] deprived of all weapons except their teeth, Sula had dropped the first dewey on the bed and was fishing in her purse. She gave each of them a dollar bill which they snatched and then scooted off down the stairs to Dick's to buy the catarrh remedy they loved to drink (129).
101 Michael Awkward, "A Black Man's Place in Black Feminist Criticism," in *The Black Feminist Reader*, edited by Joy James and T. Denean Sharpley-Whiting, 102 (Malden, MA: Blackwell, 2000).
102 For a discussion about the value of enslaved subjects throughout the entire life cycle, see Daina Ramey Berry, *The Price for Their Pound of Flesh: The Value of the Enslaved, from Womb to Grave, in the Building of a Nation* (Boston: Beacon Press, 2017). Of the commensurate value of children across gender, Berry writes, "children under age ten had low monetary values, and appraisers rarely used gender to differentiate value for the first decade of children's lives" (46).
103 See Phillip Atiba Goff et al., "The Essence of Innocence: Consequences of Dehumanizing Black Children," *Journal of Personality and Social Psychology* 106.4 (2014): 526–545.
104 Morrison, *Sula*, 158.
105 Ibid., 160.
106 Ibid., 5.
107 Ibid., 161.
108 Ibid.
109 Ibid., 162.
110 Ibid.
111 Ibid., 163.
112 Ibid., 170.
113 Ibid., 174.
114 Roderick Ferguson, *The Reorder of Things: The University and Its Pedagogies of Minority Difference* (Minneapolis: University of Minnesota Press, 2012), 131.
115 Ernest J. Gaines, *A Gathering of Old Men* (New York: Vintage Contemporaries, 1992).

116 Spillers, "Mama's Baby, Papa's Maybe," 67.
117 Ferguson's analysis of this story exposes the way Black Nationalist historiography of this era is produced. As he interprets Bambara's story, which depicts Miss Hazel's, a middle-aged black woman's, indignant responses to her politicized (or, in the current parlance, "woke") children as they attempt to regulate her behavior. Her biggest offense is taking an elderly black man, Bovanne, seriously, which she expresses by flirting and dancing with him at a political fundraiser, where the story takes place. She does this to counteract the younger generation's disingenuous appreciation for the elders of the neighborhood, and their flagrant disregard for his presence. As Ferguson puts it, Miss Hazel and Bovanne "are buried so that the young people's intelligence and intelligibility might be established" (121).
118 Ferguson, *The Reorder of Things*, 123.
119 Ibid., 124.
120 Ibid., 118.
121 Ibid., 122.
122 Gaines, *A Gathering of Old Men*, 32.
123 Ibid.
124 Ibid., 86–87.
125 Joel Chandler Harris, *The Complete Tales of Uncle Remus* (Boston: Houghton Mifflin, 1983), xxvii.
126 212, *State of Missouri vs. Darren Wilson*, Grand Jury Volume V, September 16, 2014. http://apps.washingtonpost.com
127 Ferguson, *The Reorder of Things*, 132.
128 Gaines, *A Gathering*, 41.
129 Ibid., 42.
130 Ibid., 48.
131 Ibid., 49.
132 Hartman, *Scenes of Subjection*, 154.
133 See Trevor Dodman, "'Belated Impress': *River George* and the African American Shell Shock Narrative," *African American Review* 44 ½ (2011): 149–166. Regarding repression of or silence about the capacious term for war-related injury, Dodman writes, "black histories from the period rarely mention the shell-shocked. African American narratives of the First World War simply do not attend to their experiences [. . .]. Numerous memoirs, histories of specific combat units, newspaper articles, magazine pieces, short stories, poems, plays, and novels from the period unfold with virtual silences about black shell shock" (157).
134 Gaines, *A Gathering*, 43.
135 Ibid., 6.
136 Ibid., 16.
137 Ibid., 44.
138 Ibid., 45.
139 Ibid., 46.
140 Ibid., 7.

141 Ibid., 11.
142 Elsa Saeta and Izora Skinner, "Interview with Ernest Gaines," in *Conversations with Ernest Gaines*, edited by John Lowe, 250 (Jackson: University Press of Mississippi, 1995).
143 Walter Benjamin, "Theses on the Philosophy of History," in *Illuminations: Essays and Reflections*, edited by Hannah Arendt, 257–258 (New York: Schocken Books, 1969).
144 S. D. Chrostowska, "Angelus Novus, Angst of History," *diacritics* 40.1 (2012): 49.
145 Gaines, *A Gathering*, 59.
146 Ibid., 88.
147 Ibid.
148 Ibid., 89.
149 Michael Sartisky, "Writing about Race in Difficult Times: An Interview with Ernest J. Gaines," in *Conversations with Ernest Gaines*, edited by John Lowe, 257 (Jackson: University Press of Mississippi, 1995).
150 See William Parrill, "An Interview with Ernest Gaines," in *Conversations with Ernest Gaines*, edited by John Lowe, 187 (Jackson: University Press of Mississippi, 1995). The southern part of Louisiana, where Gaines was raised and where *A Gathering of Old Men* is set, saw the growth of commercial industry that broke down previous organizations of ownership and labor. In 1986, Gaines remarked upon this shift, and how it is represented in his 1983 novel: "During the sixties [. . .] [l]arger companies took over and leased this place; soy beans took over and oil wells took over, and Cajuns were moved out as well. [In addition to blacks who had previously migrated North.] In *A Gathering of Old Men*, that's what it is all about. The ones who loved the land, worked the land, and then were kicked off the land" (187).
151 See Madhu Dubey, *Signs and Cities: Black Literary Postmodernism* (Chicago: University of Chicago Press, 2003). As Dubey explains, "capital relocated from its established bases in the Northeast and Midwest to less developed regions in the third world and the 'Sunbelt' South, in search of higher tax incentives, lower wages, and weaker labor unions" (25).
152 Gaines, *A Gathering*, 94.
153 Ibid.
154 Jodi Melamed, "Racial Capitalism," *Critical Ethnic Studies*, 1.1 (spring 2015): 78–79.
155 Gaines, *A Gathering*, 187.
156 Ibid., 190.
157 Ibid., 187.

4. GHOSTS

1 Wilma King, *Stolen Childhood: Slave Youth in Nineteenth-Century America*, second edition (Bloomington: Indiana University Press, 2011), 7.
2 See Vincent Carretta, "Olaudah Equiano or Gustavus Vassa? New Light on an Eighteenth-Century Question of Identity," *Slavery and Abolition* 20.3 (1999): 96–

105, and *Equiano, the African: Biography of a Self-Made Man* (Athens: University of Georgia Press, 2005).

3 For a discussion on the representational politics of naming, see Paul Lovejoy, "Olaudah Equiano or Gustavus Vassa—What's in a Name?" *Atlantic Studies* 9.2 (2012): 165–184. In this chapter, I follow the convention of using "Olaudah Equiano" to refer to the literary persona of African origin.

4 Avery Gordon, *Ghostly Matters: Haunting and the Sociological Imagination* (Minneapolis: University of Minnesota Press, 2001), 8.

5 As Gordon puts it, such a haunted reality is experienced, "not as cold knowledge, but as a transformative recognition" (8).

6 Speaking about the afterlives of Marxist thought in the wake of Soviet totalitarianism's end, the "spirit of Marxism," Jacques Derrida claims that "we intend to understand *spirits* in the plural and in the sense of specters, of untimely specters that one must not chase away but sort out, critique, keep close by, and allow to come back." See Jacques Derrida, *Specters of Marx* (New York: Routledge, 2006), 109. Emphasis in original.

7 Lisa Lowe, *The Intimacy of Four Continents* (Durham, NC: Duke University Press, 2015), 40–41.

8 Gordon, *Ghostly Matters*, 190.

9 Olaudah Equiano, *The Interesting Narrative of the Life of Olaudah Equiano, or Gustavus Vassa, the African*, in *The Classic Slave Narratives*, edited by Henry Louis Gates, Jr. (New York: Mentor, 1987), 12.

10 Ibid., 25.

11 There is no guarantee that the differently gendered Equiano siblings moved toward the horizon of adulthood in the same way. Yet, the opening of *The Interesting Narrative* suggests a degree of parity that might have extended to the status of adulthood. For instance, "The dress of both sexes is nearly the same. [. . .] When our women are not employed with the men in tillage, their usual occupation is spinning and weaving cotton" (14).

12 Walter Johnson, "Time and Revolution in African America: Temporality and the History of Atlantic Slavery," in *Rethinking American History in a Global Age*, edited by Thomas Bender, 149 (Berkeley: University of California Press, 2002).

13 King, *Stolen Childhood*, 8.

14 Michelle M. Wright, *Physics of Blackness: Beyond the Middle Passage Epistemology* (Minneapolis: University of Minnesota Press, 2015), 83.

15 See Saidiya Hartman, "Venus in Two Acts," *Small Axe* 12.2 (2008): 1–14.

16 In addition to Carretta's biographical work, see S. E. Ogude, "Facts into Fiction: Equiano's Narrative Reconsidered," *Research in African Literatures* 13.1 (1982): 31–43.

17 Jenny Sharpe, *Ghosts of Slavery: A Literary Archaeology of Black Women's Lives* (Minneapolis: University of Minnesota Press, 2003).

18 Christina Sharpe, *In the Wake: On Blackness and Being* (Durham, NC: Duke University Press, 2016), 53.

19 William Boelhower, "'I'll Teach You How to Flow': On Figuring Out Atlantic Studies," *Atlantic Studies* 1.1 (2004): 28–48, 32.
20 Hartman, "Venus in Two Acts," 13.
21 Two notable works on the racial implications of Sigmund Freud's 1917 essay, "Mourning and Melancholia," are Anne Anlin Cheng, *The Melancholy of Race: Psychoanalysis, Assimilation, and Hidden Grief* (New York: Oxford University Press, 2001) and Jermaine Singleton's *Cultural Melancholy: Readings of Race, Impossible Mourning, and African American Ritual* (Urbana: University of Illinois Press, 2015).
22 See Rebecca Epstein, Jamilia J. Blake, and Thalia González, "Girlhood Interrupted: The Erasure of Black Girls' Childhood," Georgetown Law's Center on Poverty and Inequality, 2017, www.endadultificationbias.org.
23 For the former slave, "autobiography, a genre of liberal political narrative that affirms individual right, may precisely contribute to the 'forgetting' of the collective subject of colonial slavery" (50). See Lowe, *The Intimacy of Four Continents*, 50–70.
24 Ibid., 70.
25 See Frank Wilderson and Saidiya Hartman, "The Position of the Unthought," *Qui Parle* 13.2 (2003): 183–201, 184–185.
26 Equiano, *The Interesting Narrative*, 29.
27 Nazera Sadiq Wright, *Black Girlhood in the Nineteenth Century* (Urbana: University of Illinois Press, 2016), 27.
28 See Farah Jasmine Griffin, "On Black Girlhood," *Public Books*, www.publicbooks.org. Griffin puts it this way: "When ordinary black girls are located in the archive it is often in writings that record violence against them, list them as chattel, or portray them as one-dimensional stereotypes" (np).
29 On this point, see Sylvia Wynter, "Beyond Miranda's Meanings: Un/silencing the 'Demonic Ground' of Caliban's 'Woman'" in *The Black Feminist Reader*, edited by Joy James and T. Denean Sharpley-Whiting (Malden, MA: Blackwell, 2000).
30 Douglass, *Narrative of the Life of Frederick Douglass* in *The Classic Slave Narratives*, edited by Henry Louis Gates, Jr. (New York: Mentor, 1987), 273.
31 As Gates notes, Equiano's narrative deploys "the trope of chiasmus," which is "a favorite device in Douglass's *Narrative*" (xiv). Gates exemplifies this rhetorical favoritism by citing Douglass's most famous chiasmus, "how a man was made a slave [. . .] how a slave was made a man," which has the implicit effect of binding Equiano and Douglass together with a rhetorical strategy that shores "gender" as a constitutive aspect of western humanism. See Gates, "Introduction," *The Classic Slave Narratives*, xiii–xiv.
32 Derrida, *Specters of Marx*, 58–59.
33 Equiano, *The Interesting Narrative*, 37.
34 Ibid., 44.
35 Fred Moten, *In the Break: The Aesthetics of the Black Radical Tradition* (Minneapolis: University of Minnesota Press, 2003), 22.

36 Ramesh Mallipeddi refers to these two moments, in which Equiano recounts his sense of belonging during his youthful servitude, as an examples of the text's politically expansive framework of kinship. See Ramesh Mallipeddi, *Spectacular Suffering: Witnessing Slavery in the Eighteenth-Century British Atlantic* (Charlottesville: University of Virginia Press, 2016), 188.

37 For an extended account of how a burgeoning middle class in eighteenth-century Britain informed the ideological dimensions of childhood, see Andrew O'Malley, *The Making of the Modern Child: Children's Literature and Childhood in the Late Eighteenth Century* (New York: Routledge, 2003).

38 Douglass, Narrative of the Life of Frederick Douglass in The Classic Slave Narratives, 258.

39 Ibid., 259.

40 Ibid., 55.

41 Ibid., 53.

42 See Houston Baker, *Blues, Ideology, and Afro-American Literature: A Vernacular Theory* (Chicago: University of Chicago Press, 1987). Baker turns away from the narrative significance of Equiano's sister when he pushes past Equiano's losses along the First Passage in order to get to the overrepresented origin of black diasporic subjectivity, the Middle Passage. As he claims, "the full import of loss is felt less in sentiment than in terror. Having arrived at the coast, Equiano encounters *the full, objective reality of his commercially deportable status*" (32, emphasis mine). Mallipeddi illustrates how the narrative creates a framework of kinship that does not privilege blood relations or families but, rather, redefines kin beyond blood and ancestry. One outcome of this generally astute observation is that the textual significance of Equiano's sister loses its specificity. Thus, Mallipeddi observes that, "for Equiano, water is as thick as blood: his strength of attachment to [shipmate Richard] Baker seems equaled only by that of his female sibling" (191).

43 Carretta, *Equiano the African*, 73.

44 Hartman, "Venus in Two Acts," 12.

45 See Singleton, *Cultural Melancholy*, 8–9.

46 As Derrida puts it, "Repetition *and* first time: this is perhaps the question of the event as question of the ghost." *Specters of Marx*, 8.

47 See Charles Chesnutt, "Superstitions and Folk-Lore of the South," in *Charles W. Chesnutt: Stories, Novels, and Essays* (New York: Library of America, 2002).

48 Charles Chesnutt, "The Wife of His Youth," in *Charles W. Chesnutt: Stories, Novels, and Essays*, 101–112.

49 Ibid., 101.

50 Ibid.

51 Ibid., 104.

52 Ibid.

53 Ibid., 101.

54 Catherine Keyser, "'The Wave of a Magician's Wand': Romance, Storytelling, and the Myth of History in 'The Wife of His Youth,'" *American Literary Realism* 44.3 (2012): 215.
55 See Saidiya Hartman, *Scenes of Subjection: Terror, Slavery, and Self-Making in Nineteenth-Century America* (New York: Oxford University Press, 1997) for an influential response to this historiographic project of retrieving the person from the veil of the slave. There, Hartman examines quotidian practices of the enslaved that cannot be reduced to the meaning of resistance in a liberal humanist sense, which has been frequently applied to the lives of the enslaved. She writes, "too often the interventions and challenges of the dominated have been obscured when measured against traditional notions of the political and its central features: the unencumbered self, the citizen, the self-possessed individual, and the volitional and autonomous subject" (61).
56 Chesnutt, "The Wife of His Youth," 104.
57 Ibid., 104–105.
58 See Werner Sollors, *Neither Black nor White Yet Both: Thematic Explorations of Interracial Literature* (New York: Oxford University Press, 1997), 10–16. Sollors observes that Chesnutt likely signifies on the allusions to racial ambiguity in the poems.
59 Chesnutt, "The Wife of His Youth," 105. Emphasis mine.
60 Ibid.
61 Ibid.
62 Ibid.
63 Keyser, "'The Wave of a Magician's Wand,'" 217.
64 Chesnutt, "The Wife of His Youth," 107.
65 Ibid.
66 Ibid., 101–102.
67 Ibid., 102.
68 Ibid., 111.
69 Ibid., 108.
70 Chesnutt describes the relic-like origins of his own conjure stories in "Superstitions and Folk-Lore of the South," along with his attempts to capture a vanishing storytelling tradition by interviewing "half a dozen old women" in the South. See Chesnutt, "Superstitions and Folk-Lore of the South," in *Charles Chesnutt: Stories, Novels, and Essays* (New York: The Library of America, 2002), 865.
71 Chesnutt, "The Wife of His Youth," 110.
72 See Toni Morrison, "The Future of Time: Literature and Diminished Expectations" in *The Source of Self-Regard* (New York: Vintage International, 2020), 117. Morrison makes this point about collective, rather than individually possessive, claims to the future that "*the* child," as opposed to "*our* child," connotes.
73 Chesnutt, "The Wife of His Youth," 107.

74 For a detailed account of the health crisis that accompanied emancipation, see Jim Downs, *Sick from Freedom: African-American Illness and Suffering during the Civil War and Reconstruction* (New York: Oxford University Press, 2012). For a careful historiography of post-emancipation sexual violence and its relation to gender and racial terror in the midst of black struggles for full citizenship, see Hannah Rosen, *Terror in the Heart of Freedom: Citizenship, Sexual Violence, and the Meaning of Race in the Postemancipation South* (Chapel Hill: University of North Carolina Press, 2009).
75 Chesnutt, "The Wife of His Youth," 107.
76 Toni Morrison, *God Help the Child* (New York: Alfred A. Knopf, 2015), 3.
77 See Grace Kyungwon Hong's discussion about *The Bluest Eye* in *The Ruptures of Capitalism: Women of Color Feminism and the Culture of Immigrant Labor* (Minneapolis: University of Minnesota Press, 2006).
78 Toni Morrison, *The Bluest Eye* (New York: Vintage International, 2007), 4.
79 Morrison, *God Help the Child*, 10.
80 Ibid., 17.
81 Ibid., 16.
82 Ibid., 14.
83 See Erica Burman, "Deconstructing Neoliberal Childhood: Towards a Feminist Antipsychological Approach," *Childhood* 19.4 (2011): 423–438.
84 For an extended discussion on neoliberal feminism, see Catherine Rottenberg, *The Rise of Neoliberal Feminism* (New York: Oxford University Press, 2018). The concept of American innocence is shot throughout Baldwin's work, but for a well-known account, see James Baldwin *The Fire Next Time* (New York: Vintage International, 1993).
85 Morrison, *God Help the Child*, 133.
86 Ibid., 8.
87 Ibid., 8–9.
88 Ibid., 57.
89 As Walker mentions, "Like Sweetness, Morrison doesn't seem to want to touch Bride either—at least not tenderly." Kara Walker, "Toni Morrison's *God Help the Child*," *New York Times*, April 13, 2015, np. www.nytimes.com.
90 See "The Combahee River Collective Statement," in *How We Get Free: Black Feminism and the Combahee River Collective*, edited by Keeanga-Yamahtta Taylor, 17 (Chicago: Haymarket Books, 2017).
91 Morrison, *God Help the Child*, 56.
92 Walker, "Toni Morrison's *God Help the Child*," np.
93 Morrison, *God Help the Child*, 134.
94 Ibid., 4.
95 Ibid., 42.
96 Ibid.
97 Michele Elam, "Baldwin's Boys," *CR: The New Centennial Review* 16.2 (2016): 27–28.

98 Morrison, *God Help the Child*, 177.
99 Ibid., 178.
100 Ibid., 177.
101 Ibid., 178.
102 Ibid.
103 Morrison, "The Future of Time," 117.

EPILOGUE

1 Obama's "respectability politics" had been a topic of frequent commentary. One variation on this theme, which explains a frequently observed dynamic between Obama and black people, is William A. Darity, Jr., "How Barack Obama Failed Black Americans," *The Atlantic*, December 22, 2016. www.theatlantic.com.
2 Ralph Ellison, *Invisible Man* (New York: Vintage International, 1995), 94.
3 See Keeanga-Yamahtta Taylor, *From #BlackLivesMatter to Black Liberation* (Chicago: Haymarket Books, 2016), 148.
4 Elizabeth Day, "#BlackLivesMatter: The Birth of a New Civil Rights Movement," *The Guardian*, July 19, 2015, www.theguardian.com.
5 Kimberlé Williams Crenshaw and Andrea J. Richie, "Say Her Name: Resisting Police Brutality against Black Women," African American Policy Form, 2015. www.aapf.org/sayhernamereport/
6 Kevin Quashie, *Black Women, Identity, and Cultural Theory: (Un)Becoming the Subject* (Piscataway, NJ: Rutgers University Press, 2004), 11. Emphasis in original.
7 Kiese Laymon, *Heavy: An American Memoir* (New York: Scribner, 2018), 238.
8 Ibid., 239.
9 *The Untold Story of Emmett Louis Till*, directed by Keith Beauchamp, 2005.

INDEX

Page numbers in *italics* indicate photos.

absence, 88
abuse, 3, 5
activism, 17–18, 21–22, 207–8
adulthood: adultification, 174; for Africans, 228n70; age in, 149; for black men, 54, 122; blackness in, 53; for black women, 41; childhood compared to, 66–67; for children, 36–37; exclusion from, 19; freedom in, 126, 154; gender in, 71–72; after girlhood, 104; in hegemony, 7; language of, 114–15; manhood compared to, 68; men as, 33–38; perceptions of, 52–53; performance in, 78; in slavery, 178–79; as status, 99–100; in western humanism, 158–59; white, 146; for whiteness, 56; for white women, 216n68
Africa, 10, 171–72, 177
African American studies, 23–24
Africans: adulthood for, 228n70; blackness of, 126; boyhood for, 124; as commodity, 91; as diasporic, 89–90, 215n52; Middle Passage for, 132, 134; New World for, 155; Oceanic lifespans for, 91–92, 109; slavery of, 124–25; slave trade for, 11–12, 41; for Spillers, 37
Afro-futurism, 92–93
Agamben, Giorgio, 25
age: in adulthood, 149; age-shifting, 38–39, 45–47, 66; as arbitrary, 10; in black literature, 203–8; blackness and, 28, 37, 51, 188; for black people, 5–6, 54–55; for black women, 27, 111, 120; categories, 57; as commodity, 62; dispossession of, 14, 35–36, 222n66; for Fanon, 21; functions of, 7–8; in *A Gathering of Old Men*, 126–30; gender related to, 22, 41, 136–37, 146; in *Get Out*, 48–49; for Hartman, 173; hegemony of, 52, 126–27; of Heth, 102; history and, 8, 29–33, 98, 118; for humanity, 37–38; in human time, 185–86; in immortality, 105; in liberalism, 20; maturation related to, 98–99; meanings of, 3–4; for Morrison, 6; in narratives, 6–7; in New World, 121; no-age, 31, 33; in the Oceanic, 125; old, 12–14; perceptions of, 82–83, 141–42, 154–55; politics of, 228n68; racialization of, 69–70; as racial value, 76; of relics, 119–22, 183; in segregation, 19; during slave trade, 67; for Snorton, 54; temporality of, 9, 81–82; temporal logic of, 155–64; time related to, 40–41; as transitional, 60; trauma of, 76–77; untimeliness of, 28, 37; untimely, 45–46, 61, 171; for vampires, 103
aggregation, 125
Aging and Its Discontents (Woodward), 12–13
All the Women are White, All the Black Are Men, But Some of Us Are Brave (Wallace), 34–35
alternative historiography, 111–19
alternative humanity, 10–11, 14

amnesia, 188–89
Anatol, Giselle Liza, 89–90, 226n40
"Angelus Novus" (Klee), 161
antebellum South, 97
anthropological knowledge, 31–32
anti-black violence, 73
anti-slavery fiction, 67
Arn't I a Woman (White), 139
artificial childhood, 13–14, 92–100
artificial girlhood, 109
artificial immortality, 110
artificial maturity, 139
Atlantic Ocean: for black writers, 14–15; modernity related to, 10; ocean lifespans, 11; as relic, 84–85; temporality related to, 12; transatlantic cultural exchange, 10, 67–68
autobiography: of Barnum, P. T., 109; conventions of, 112; of Heth, 81; history related to, 6; oral history and, 110; from slave trade, 169; temporality in, 166. *See also* Equiano, Olaudah
The Autobiography of Miss Jane Pittman (Gaines), 39–40, 86–87, 111–19

Baker, Houston, Jr., 24, 242n42
Baldwin, James, 43, 49–50, 196, 200
Bambara, Toni Cade, 157
Baptist, Edward E., 68
Baraka, Amiri, 18–19
Barnum, Bret, 42, 43, 45, 50
Barnum, P. T., 39, 81–82, 92, 107, 109, 119
Bell, Camille, 73
Bell, Sophia, 63
Beloved (Morrison), 26–28, 121–22, 139–42
Benjamin, Walter, 25
Bernstein, Robin, 62, 140–41, 235n84, 236n91
Best, Stephen, 23–24
Beyoncé, 192
Bhabha, Homi, 226n34
biology, 93–95, 226n54
black activism, 7
black age. *See specific topics*

black Antillean children, 15–16, 35, 136–37, 217n85
The Black Book (Morrison), 27, 121–22
black boys, 43–50; gender for, 38; in liberal humanism, 60; plantations for, 55; in *Uncle Tom's Cabin*, 61–71; for western humanism, 51–52
black children: abuse against, 5; crime against, 21; dehumanization of, 100; for Fanon, 132–33; freedom for, 151–52; in *Heavy*, 207–8; hegemony for, 4–5; images of, 42, 43–44; Morrison for, 57–58; performance by, 62–63, 65–66; pickaninnies for, 151; in white culture, 204–5
black culture: for black people, 199; as commodity, 129–30; ghosts in, 177; imagination in, 4; in *Sula*, 144–45; vampires for, 120–21; white culture compared to, 137–38, 184
black dehumanization, 15–17, 91
black diaspora, 52
black embodiment: "avatars" as, 59; for Barnum, P. T., 107; of blackness, 143; of black women, 102; in culture, 38–39; for Fanon, 141; in *Get Out*, 73–74; of Heth, 81–82, 92, 106, 109; infantilization from, 129; in the Oceanic, 144; from slavery, 45, 118–19, 203; for Spillers, 90–91; stereotypes of, 63; temporality and, 3–4, 144; for untimeliness, 3, 39; vampires for, 105–6
blackface minstrelsy, 69–71
black femaleness, 137
black feminism, 192–202; black women for, 52; counter-nationalism in, 54; exclusion for, 88; for Ferguson, 158–59; in fiction, 65; gender for, 204; historiography for, 54–55, 142; liberal humanism for, 71–72, 213n32; politics of, 23; radical, 19–20; scholarship, 8, 22–23, 34–35; second-wave, 199; shape-shifting for, 46–47; Spillers on, 25–26; *Sula* for, 126–30, 206; untimeliness for, 20

"A Black Feminist's Search for Sisterhood" (Wallace), 1
black gender, 50–60
black girlhood: in *The Gilda Stories*, 100–106; human time in, 148; in literature, 46, 55–58; patriarchy for, 54; studies, 37; violence against, 241n28
black history, 118, 238n133
black humanity, 119
black immortality, 95
black infantilism, 69–70
black liberalism, 15, 17–19, 18–19, 26
black literature, 24–25, 26, 203–8, 229n104
Black Lives Matter, 45, 206
Black Macho and the Myth of the Superwoman (Wallace), 55
black male adulthood, 122
black male feminism, 52–53, 72
black manhood, 17; hypervisibility of, 44, 52–53; in literature, 47; patriarchy of, 53–54; shape-shifting in, 47–48; in US, 142–43; for Wallace, 55
black masculine leadership, 116
black masculinity, 122
black men, 54, 122, 136
black nationalism, 238n117; childhood for, 23; liberation movements, 157; presentation of, 18–19; in *Sula*, 159–60
blackness: in adulthood, 53; of Africans, 126; age and, 28, 37, 51, 188; Baldwin on, 49–50; biology of, 94–95; of black Antillean children, 136–37; black embodiment of, 143; for black people, 127; childhood and, 94; for children, 151; in colorism, 196–97; in culture, 61; as ethnicity, 91–92; exclusion for, 96–97; in fiction, 108–9; gender and, 20, 37; hypervisibility of, 46; imagination of, 131; immaturity related to, 74–75; infantilization of, 149; for liberal humanism, 29, 82–83; after Middle Passage, 153; modern, 8, 46; as naive, 70; New World, 11–12, 132; as no-age, 31, 33; the Oceanic for, 137; for Spillers, 60; in untimeliness, 29, 35; untimely, 16, 28, 122
Black Panther Party, 19, 156
black people: age for, 5–6, 54–55; age-shifting for, 47; black culture for, 199; blackness for, 127; citizenship for, 235n84; dispossession for, 110–11; exclusion of, 2–3; gender for, 22–23, 25; hegemony for, 3–4; history of, 203–8; hypervisibility of, 39; leadership for, 116–17; manhood for, 126, 137–38; maturation for, 199–200; patriarchy for, 76; racism for, 214n43; social inclusion for, 78–79; socialization of, 55–56; suffering for, 190–91; terminology for, 55; violence against, 192, 203–8; for white culture, 110–11; in World War I, 159–60
Black Power, 143
black racial formation, 5–6
black racialization, 9
Black Skin, White Masks (Fanon), 13, 15–17, 34, 87–88
black storytelling, 110–12
black teenagers, 50–51
black untimeliness, 15–17, 54–55, 62, 168
black women, 6, 226n34; adulthood for, 41; age for, 27, 111, 120; black embodiment of, 102; for black feminism, 52; for Butler, 115; as children, 89; colorism for, 191–92; for Combahee River Collective, 76; coming of age for, 169; dehumanization for, 58–59; exclusion of, 88–89; Ferguson on, 22–23; gender for, 136; as ghosts, 181–82; for Hartman, 119; history for, 33–38; literary culture for, 6; as mammies, 83–84, 224n12, 224n14; relationships between, 148–49; reproductive rights for, 201–2; slavery for, 81; during slave trade, 68–69; as spectacle, 92; untimeliness for, 20; as vampires, 86. *See also* black feminism

black writers, 14–15, 87–92
Blount, Marcellus, 53–54
The Bluest Eye (Morrison), 6, 47, 56, 79, 193
boyhood, 124
Brand, Dionne, 10, 87
Brent, Linda, 84
Brown, Michael, 38, 43, 50–51, 218n8, 219n20; dehumanization of, 52; Martin compared to, 73
Brown, William Wells, 67
Burman, Erica, 195–96
Butler, Octavia, 39–40; black women for, 115; Gaines compared to, 111; Gomez compared to, 85–86, 104; slavery for, 46, 87; time for, 97; vampires for, 93

Camp, Stephanie, 227n56
Campbell, Gwyn, 98–100, 231n3
Campt, Tina, 44
Capécia, Mayotte, 88
Caribbean, 124–25, 135
Carretta, Vincent, 165, 180
Celestine, Priscilla, 72–73
Cheng, Anne, 180
Chesnutt, Charles, 168, 243n70. *See also* "The Wife of His Youth"
Child, Lydia Maria, 27
childhood: adulthood compared to, 66–67; artificial, 13–14, 92–100; for black nationalism, 23; blackness and, 94; for Combahee River Collective, 197; discipline in, 63–64; dispossession of, 3, 19, 56–58, 84–85, 148; femininity in, 34–35; ghosts, 197; for Hart, D., 72–73; infantilization during, 152; neoliberal, 195–96; racialization of, 139; seniority compared to, 129; after slavery, 70; stolen, 102
childlike Negro, 99, 224n8
children: adults for, 36–37; artificial childhood, 13–14; black, 100, 132–33; black Antillean, 15–16, 35, 136–37, 217n85; blackness for, 151; black women as, 89; in *The Bluest Eye*, 79; during colonialism, 32–33; Committee to Stop Children's Murders, 73; as commodity, 222n59, 222n62; constancy for, 147–48; definitions of, 44; emotional vulnerability of, 51; freedom for, 114; gender for, 8, 83–84; in *Get Out*, 77–78; literature for, 56; perceptions of, 44; prepubescent, 122; primitive society related to, 32; racialization of, 216n65; slavery for, 221n53; in slave trade, 65; social protection of, 3, 21; stolen girlhood, 103; violence against, 1–2. *See also* black children
choice, 96
Christian, Barbara, 24–25
Chrostowska, S. D., 161
citizenship, 159, 194, 221n51, 235n84
Civilization and Its Discontents (Freud), 11
civil rights, 16–18, 116–17, 129, 155, 218n6
civil status, 104
Clark, Taliaferro, 143
class issues, 18
Cleaver, Eldridge, 156
Clotel (Brown, W.), 67, 76–77
Coleman, Gary, 44
colonialism: black racial formation through, 5–6; children during, 32–33; for Fanon, 87–88; history of, 23–24; human time in, 33; the mass in, 132–33; New World, 90
colorism, 214n38; blackness in, 196–97; for black women, 191–92; in *The Bluest Eye*, 193; in citizenship, 194; dispossession and, 197–98; perceptions in, 194–95
Colvin, Claudette, 18–19, 22
Combahee River Collective, 8, 23, 47, 76, 197
Committee to Stop Children's Murders, 73
commodity: Africans as, 91; age as, 62; black culture as, 129–30; children as,

222n59, 222n62; history as, 67–68; in shape-shifting, 65; spectacle as, 70, 82
conformity, 18
consent, 96, 104–5
constancy, 128, 131, 147–50
Cosby, Bill, 120–22
counter-history, 9
counter-nationalism, 54
counter-temporality, 85–86
Cox, Aimee, 58–59
Crenshaw, Kimberlé, 206–7
crime, 21, 27–28, 45, 63–64
criticism, 23–24
Cullors, Patrisse, 206
culture: anti-black violence in, 73; black embodiment in, 38–39; black infantilism in, 69–70; blackness in, 61; cultural ethics, 103; cultural politics, 74–75; ghosts in, 40–41, 173–74; Hart, D., in, 38–39, 42, 43–45, 49–52; Jacobs for, 37; literary, 6, 89; Morrison for, 23; shape-shifting in, 46, 49; Spillers for, 24; time and, 151–52; transatlantic cultural exchange, 10, 67–68; vampires for, 106. *See also* black culture; white culture
Cunningham, George, 53–54

Davis, Angela, 22–23
Davis, Sammy, Jr., 44
Davis, Sherry, 72–73, 80
dehumanization: of black children, 100; for black women, 58–59; of Brown, M., 52; history of, 197; in racialization, 32
Delany, Elizabeth, 110–11
Delany, Sarah, 110–11
DeLoughrey, Elizabeth, 125
Derrida, Jacques, 25, 165, 177, 183, 240n6
discipline, 63–64
dispossession: of age, 14, 35–36, 222n66; for black people, 110–11; of childhood, 3, 19, 56–58, 84–85, 148; colorism and, 197–98; of gender, 91; history of, 104–5;

193; of humanity, 29, 100; of human time, 54; maturation related to, 72–73; of memory, 76; for men, 49, 52–53; in New World, 155; the Oceanic as, 109; of time, 33, 143
DNA. *See* biology
Doucet-Battle, James, 95
Douglass, Frederick, 82–83, 114, 176–79
"A Dream of Fair Women" (Tennyson), 186
dreams, 104
Dumas, Michael J., 21

Elam, Michele, 199–200
Elkins, Stanley, 40, 55, 233nn35–36; Fanon compared to, 134–37; historiography by, 152–53; infantilization for, 133–34; maleness for, 149; plantations for, 133
emancipation. *See* freedom
Emancipation Proclamation, 86
English, Daylanne, 18–19
enslaved children, 70–71
enslaved men, 40
Equiano, Olaudah, 41, 215n52, 231n2, 240n11; for Gates, 241n31; for Lowe, 164; Middle Passage for, 123–25, 242n42. *See also* specific topics
Equiano Girl: in Africa, 171–72; ghosts related to, 167–68, 172–81; untimeliness for, 178
"The Essence of Innocence" (study), 100
ethnicity, 91–92
Europe: Africa for, 172; historical time for, 140; modernity in, 125–26; New World for, 124–25
exclusion: as abuse, 5; from adulthood, 19; for black feminism, 88; for blackness, 96–97; of black people, 2–3; of black women, 88–89; humanist, 72; social, 46
exploration, 123–24

family, 171–72, 174–75, 179–80
fancy market, 68–69, 222n69

Fanon, Frantz, 1, 13, 213n33; age for, 21; black Antillean children for, 217n85; black children for, 132–33; black dehumanization for, 15–17; black embodiment for, 141; black women for, 33–34; colonialism for, 87–88; Elkins compared to, 134–37; gender for, 88–89; history for, 31; the mass for, 133–34; philosophy of, 8; sociogeny for, 51
femaleness, 135–36, 137
femininity, 34–35, 71, 135–36
feminism, 194, 196, 199, 227n56. *See also* black feminism
Ferguson, Roderick, 7, 238n117; black feminism for, 158–59; on black women, 22–23; civil rights era for, 116; hegemony for, 155; "My Man Bovanne" for, 157
fiction: anti-slavery, 67; black feminism in, 65; blackness in, 108–9; Heth in, 97; within historiography, 40; infantilization in, 195–96; motherhood in, 64; plantations in, 112, 115–16; race relations in, 62–63; rape in, 104–5; relics in, 117–18; slavery in, 76–77, 113–14; time in, 198–99; transatlantic cultural exchange in, 67–68; women in, 85; World War I in, 144–45
Finney, Jack, 74–75
The Fire Next Time (Baldwin), 43
Fledgling (Butler), 39, 85, 92–100, 119
Foreman, P. Gabrielle, 27, 84
Foucault, Michel, 83
Fraser, Nancy, 159
freedom: activism for, 207–8; in adulthood, 126, 154; for black children, 151–52; for children, 114; consent as, 105; in mixed-racial organizations, 189; for the Oceanic, 154; after slavery, 190, 232n11; in *Sula*, 145–55; universal, 5; violence after, 244n74
Freeman, Elizabeth, 5
Freud, Sigmund, 8, 11, 132, 134–35, 233nn35–36

Gaines, Ernest, 39–40, 86–97; as alternative historiography, 111–19; for black literature, 229n104; labor for, 239n150; manhood for, 126–30; philosophy of, 161; plantations for, 156. *See also specific works*
Garner, Margaret, 27–28
Garza, Alicia, 205–6
Gates, Henry Louis, Jr., 24, 176–77, 241n31
A Gathering of Old Men (Gaines), 40, 126–30, 156–64
Gem of the Ocean (Wilson, A.), 119–20
gender: in adulthood, 71–72; age related to, 22, 41, 136–37, 146; black, 50–60; for black boys, 38; for black feminism, 204; blackness and, 20, 37; for black people, 22–23, 25; for black women, 136; for children, 8, 83–84; dispossession of, 91; for Fanon, 88–89; for Hartman, 219n13; for humanity, 26; interventions, 28; in labor, 135; of manhood, 137–38; politics, 52–53; race and, 35–36; racialization of, 148; sexuality and, 91–92; as social category, 59, 142; for Stowe, 48; in time, 103–4; for Tinsley, 90; untimely gender pairing, 188; whiteness and, 33–38
Get Out (Peele), 39, 48–49, 73–80
ghosts: in black culture, 177; black women as, 181–82; childhood, 197; in culture, 40–41, 173–74; Equiano Girl related to, 167–68, 172–81; for feminism, 196; history of, 166–67; in *The Interesting Narrative of the Life of Olaudah Equiano*, 165–68; melancholia of, 180, 182–83; modernity for, 168–69; for Morrison, 41, 202; Oceanic lifespans of, 164; of slavery, 172–73; temporality of, 165–66; untimeliness of, 40, 166; untimely, 41, 166, 240n6; in "The Wife of His Youth," 182–92
The Gilda Stories (Gomez), 39, 85–86, 92–93, 100–106
Gilmore, Ruth Wilson, 3, 211n6

Gilroy, Paul, 1, 10, 171
girlhood: adulthood after, 104; artificial, 109; in Fledgling, 119; maturation from, 154–55, 193–94; in Middle Passage, 167–68; protection during, 113–14; as relic, 114–15; during slavery, 107; in Sula, 146–48; violence in, 206–7. See also specific topics
God Help the Child (Morrison), 41, 122, 168–69, 192–202
Goldberg, David Theo, 31–32, 139
Gomez, Jewelle, 39–40, 85–86, 93, 104. See also specific works
Gordon, Avery, 166, 170
Gordon, Lewis, 33–34, 213n33
Great Britain, 10, 125
Green, Kai M., 9
Grenada Revolution, 25
Griffin, Farah Jasmine, 37
Guess Who's Coming to Dinner (film), 74

Halberstam, Jack, 5
Haley, Alex, 87
Hart, Devonte: childhood for, 72–73; civil rights related to, 218n6; in culture, 38–39, 42, 43–45, 49–52; Davis, Sherry, for, 80
Hart, Jennifer, 49
Hart, Sarah, 49
Hartman, Saidiya, 85, 106–7, 159, 212n17, 232n11; age for, 173; black women for, 119; gender for, 219n13; maturation for, 138–39; Middle Passage for, 165; politics for, 137–38, 243n55; sentimentality for, 175–76
Having Our Say (Hearth), 110–11
Hearth, Amy Hill, 110–11
Heavy (Laymon), 207–8
hegemony: adulthood in, 7; of age, 52, 126–27; for black children, 4–5; for black people, 3–4; categories of, 41; for Ferguson, 155; hegemonic time, 144, 166–67; in modernity, 31; of white culture, 134

Heth, Joice, 39–40; age of, 102; autobiography of, 81; for Barnum, P. T., 109, 119; black embodiment of, 81–82, 92, 106, 109; in fiction, 97; in The Gilda Stories, 85–86; as history, 86; for McMillan, 83–84, 108–9, 224n7; objecthood for, 59; as relic, 83, 108, 116; for Spillers, 92
historical consciousness, 128–29
historical constitution, 135
historical temporalities, 37
historical time, 28, 140
historical violence, 158
historicism, 37
historiography: alternative, 111–19; for black feminism, 54–55, 142; by Elkins, 152–53; fiction within, 40; of slavery, 55, 243n55; temporality with, 22–28; writing, 106
history: age and, 8, 29–33, 98, 118; autobiography related to, 6; black, 118, 238n133; of black activism, 7; of black people, 203–8; for black women, 33–38; of Caribbean, 124–25; as collective, 113; of colonialism, 23–24; as commodity, 67–68; of consent, 104; counter-history, 9; criticism of, 23–24; of dehumanization, 197; of dispossession, 104–5, 193; for Fanon, 31; of feminism, 227n56; of ghosts, 166–67; of Grenada Revolution, 25; Heth as, 86; of humanity, 4–5, 154; of human time, 161; imagination of, 39–40; of Jacobs, 26–27; literary, 24–25; of lost information, 109–10; for Lowe, 167, 175; of the mass, 161–62; mediation of, 108; of modernity, 217n72; for Morrison, 27–28; of New Orleans, 67; obscurity in, 160–61; oral, 110; of racial violence, 196; scholarship of, 111–12; of slavery, 4, 23–24, 173; sociogeny in, 15–16; of suffering, 190–91; time and, 25; truth in, 119–22; of untimeliness, 19, 188; Washington, G., in, 116; of World War I, 162–63

Holloway, Karla, 96
Hong, Grace, 6, 47, 56–57, 72
humanist exclusion, 72
humanistic scholarship, 59
humanity: age for, 37–38; alternative, 10–11, 14; dispossession of, 29, 100; fairness in, 105; gender for, 26; history of, 4–5, 154; human development, 12; imagination for, 7, 38; non-humanity, 29; racial abuse for, 4
human time: age in, 185–86; in black girlhood, 148; in colonialism, 33; conflations of, 8; dispossession of, 54; history of, 161; infantilization without, 152; inhuman time, 14; in New World, 124; untimeliness and, 185; in US, 142–43, 150; for western humanism, 29–31

I Am a Martinique Woman (Capécia), 88
imagination: in black culture, 4; of blackness, 131; of history, 39–40; for humanity, 7, 38; of liberal humanism, 167; of Morrison, 121–22; national, 19; slavery in, 28; of white culture, 84; of whiteness, 48–49
immaturity, 72, 74–75
immortality, 105, 110
Incidents in the Life of a Slave Girl (Yellin), 26–27, 82
infantilization, 129; of blackness, 149; during childhood, 152; for Elkins, 133–34; in fiction, 195–96; without human time, 152; infantile helplessness, 135; in manhood, 138–39; for Moten, 135; racial, 153
inhuman time, 14
innocence, 196
In Search of Our Mothers' Gardens (Walker, A.), 35–36
The Interesting Narrative of the Life of Olaudah Equiano (Equiano), 41, 123–25, 164, 165–68, 170–71, 176. *See also* Equiano Girl

Invasion of the Body Snatchers (Finney), 74–75
"It's Nation Time" (Baraka), 18–19

Jacobs, Harriet, 26–28, 37, 82, 103
Jazz (Morrison), 112
Je Suis Martiniquaise (Capécia), 88
Jezebels, 84, 225n16
Jim Crow segregation, 186
Johnson, Walter, 4, 11, 232n12, 233n20
Jones, Miriam, 104
Joyce, Joyce A., 24–25

Kaluuya, Daniel, 73–74
Keyser, Catherine, 185, 188
Kincaid, Jamaica, 124, 231n4
Kindred (Butler), 87, 97–98, 227n65
King, Wilma, 165, 171
Klee, Paul, 161

labor, 135, 139, 239n150
Lacks, Henrietta, 95, 227n54
LaGamma, Alisa, 108
language, 114–15
lateral maturity, 206
Latin America, 133
Laymon, Kiese, 207–8
leadership, 113, 116–17, 156
legal activism, 17–18
Levander, Caroline, 62
Lewis, Emmanuel, 44
liberal humanism, 15; agency for, 186; black boys in, 60; for black feminism, 71–72, 213n32; blackness for, 29, 82–83; imagination of, 167; politics of, 30; slavery for, 153–54; whiteness in, 47
liberalism: age in, 20; black, 15, 17–19; manhood in, 48; politics of, 41; progressive, 128; in scholarship, 6; teleology for, 30; Western, 7
liberal nationalism, 17
liberation, 126–27. *See also* freedom
liminality, 185–86

literary culture, 6, 89
literary history, 24–25
literature, 46–48, 55–58. *See also specific literature*
"Living Memory" (Gilroy), 1
Lloyd, David, 212n13
Lorde, Audre, 7–8
lost information, 109–10
Louis, Joe, 116
Lovejay, Paul, 10
Lowe, Lisa, 6, 164, 167, 175

maleness, 146, 149
Mallipeddi, Ramesh, 242n36
"Mama's Baby, Papa's Maybe" (Spillers), 11, 24, 81, 90–91, 132
Mammies, 83–84, 224n12, 224n14
manhood: adulthood compared to, 68; in *Beloved*, 139–42; for black people, 126, 137–38; for Gaines, 126–30; in *A Gathering of Old Men*, 156–64; gender of, 137–38; infantilization in, 138–39; in liberalism, 48; for Spillers, 129; in *Uncle Tom's Cabin*, 133. *See also* black manhood
"Margaret" (Tennyson), 186
Martin, Trayvon, 153, 219n9; Brown, M., compared to, 73; for Obama, B., 203–5; perceptions of, 51; Till compared to, 8, 15–22
Marxism, 240n6
the mass: in Africa, 177; in colonialism, 132–33; for Fanon, 133–34; history of, 161–62; in "Mama's Baby, Papa's Maybe," 132; in modernity, 130–31; for Morrison, 40; Oceanic lifespans of, 129, 131; old men as, 163–64; for Spillers, 129–30; temporality for, 137–44
maturation, 217n76; age related to, 98–99; artificial maturity, 139; for black people, 199–200; dispossession related to, 72–73; from girlhood, 154–55, 193–94; for Hartman, 138–39; lateral maturity,

206; on plantations, 116–17; regret in, 200–201; in *Uncle Tom's Cabin*, 128; of vampires, 101–2; for Walker, A., 146
Mbembe, Achille, 29, 83, 217n72, 232n10
McClintock, Anne, 88–89, 226n34
McMillan, Uri, 59, 82–84, 108–9, 224n7
mediation, 108, 112
Melamed, Jodi, 163
melancholia, 180, 182–83
memory, 76
men: as adults, 33–38; dispossession for, 49, 52–53; enslaved, 40. *See also specific topics*
Merish, Lori, 44
Middle Passage: for Africans, 132, 134; blackness after, 153; for Equiano, 123–25, 242n42; girlhood in, 167–68; for Hartman, 165; for Spillers, 170–71
Mill, John Stuart, 32–33
Million Man March, 52–53
minstrel performance, 64, 69–71
mixed-racial organizations, 184–86, 189
modern blackness, 8, 46
modernity: Atlantic Ocean related to, 10; in Europe, 125–26; for ghosts, 168–69; hegemony in, 31; history of, 217n72; the mass in, 130–31; the Oceanic related to, 10–15; racialization in, 102–3; slavery related to, 82
modern slavery, 52
Morgan, Jennifer, 135
Morris, Monique, 19
Morrison, Toni, 1; age for, 6; for black children, 57–58; for culture, 23; ghosts for, 41, 202; historical concerns for, 18; history for, 27–28; for Hong, 56–57; imagination of, 121–22; the mass for, 40; for readers, 112; slavery for, 26; Wallace related to, 47. *See also specific works*
Moten, Fred, 33, 135
motherhood, 57, 64–65, 79–80
"Moynihan Report," 76

Mustakeem, Sowande' M., 10–11
"My Man Bovanne" (Bambara), 157

NAACP. *See* National Association for the Advancement of Colored People
Narrative (Douglass), 82, 176–77
natal alienation, 30
National Association for the Advancement of Colored People (NAACP), 17–18
National Black Political Convention, 18
nationalism, 53
national liberation, 126–27
Nelson, Joseph Derrick, 21
neoliberal childhood, 195–96
neoliberal feminism, 194
neoliberal ideology, 96
neo-slave narratives, 97, 100
New Orleans, Louisiana, 67
Newton, Huey, 156
Newton, Isaac, 130
New World: for Africans, 155; age in, 121; blackness, 11–12, 132; colonialism, 90; dispossession in, 155; for Europe, 124–25; exploration of, 123–24; human time in, 124; slavery, 85, 131; social order, 91
no-age, 31, 33
non-humanity, 29
non-normative temporality, 107
Nyong'o, Tavia, 62–63, 235n83

Obama, Barack, 203–5, 245n1
Obama, Michelle, 192
objecthood, 59
the Oceanic: age in, 125; black embodiment in, 144; for blackness, 137; as dispossession, 109; freedom for, 154; in *Get Out*, 78–79; modernity related to, 10–15; "oceanic feeling," 8; as redemptive, 135; slave trade related to, 170–71; vampires related to, 83–87; women as, 37

Oceanic lifespans: for Africans, 91–92, 109; for alternative humanity, 10–11, 14; of ghosts, 164; of the mass, 129, 131; during slave trade, 120–21; for vampires, 85, 87
old age, 12–14
On Liberty (Mill), 32–33
oral history, 110

Parks, Rosa, 18, 214n38
Pascal, Michael Henry, 179
patriarchy: of black manhood, 53–54; for black people, 76; in slavery, 64–65
Patterson, Orlando, 30, 96–97
Peele, Jordan, 39, 48–49
perceptions: of adulthood, 52–53; of age, 82–83, 141–42, 154–55; of children, 44; in colorism, 194–95; of crime, 45; of Martin, 51; of teenagers, 20–22, 46; with untimeliness, 198–99
performance: in adulthood, 78; age-shifting as, 66; by black children, 62–63, 65–66; for McMillan, 82; minstrel, 64, 69–71; race in, 69–70; untimeliness of, 60
philosophy, 8, 29, 32–33
photography, 1–2
pickaninnies, 149–50, 150–51, 236n94
plantations, 232n12; for black boys, 55; for Elkins, 133; enslaved children on, 70–71; in fiction, 112, 115–16; for Gaines, 156; maturation on, 116–17; for slavery, 40, 67, 135; system of, 134
Poitier, Sidney, 74
politics: of age, 228n68; of black feminism, 23; black liberalism in, 18–19; of conformity, 18; cultural, 74–75; gender, 52–53; for Hartman, 137–38, 243n55; of leadership, 113; of liberal humanism, 30; of liberalism, 41; political-economic transformations, 5; of slavery, 99; of universal freedom, 5

post-civil rights era, 155
prepubescent children, 122
primitive society, 32
progressive liberalism, 128
protection, 35, 113–14
protest, 21–22
psychoanalysis, 134–35
psychology, 8, 11, 132, 233nn35–36

Quashie, Kevin, 207

race: biology with, 93–94; categories of, 61; class issues compared to, 18; gender and, 35–36; in performance, 69–70; racial formation, 36; relations, 1–2, 21, 62–63; for white culture, 88
"The Race for Theory" (Christian), 24–25
racial abuse, 4
racial capitalism, 2–3, 143, 231n8
racial hierarchies, 56
racialization, 9, 14; of age, 69–70; of childhood, 139; of children, 216n65; dehumanization in, 32; of gender, 148; for Jacobs, 82; in modernity, 102–3; racial infantilization, 153; of violence, 90–91
racial untimeliness, 45
racial violence, 196
racism, 87–88, 143–44, 214n43, 235n63
radical black feminism, 19–20
Rancière, Jacques, 157
rape, 104–5
reclamation, 3
regret, 200–201
Reiss, Benjamin, 81, 105, 109–10
relationships, 98, 148–49
relics: age of, 119–22, 183; Atlantic Ocean as, 84–85; in fiction, 117–18; girlhood as, 114–15; Heth as, 83, 108, 116; untimeliness of, 82–83; vampires related to, 87, 106–11

Representing Men (Blount/Cunningham), 53
reproductive rights, 201–2
resilience, 145–46
revisionism, of slavery, 87
Rice, Tamir, 153
Richardson, Matt, 37
Robinson, Cedric, 17
Robinson, Jackie, 116
Roediger, David, 70
Roots (Haley), 87
Rose, Jacqueline, 70
Rosen, Hannah, 192
Rowley, Michelle, 88
Rushdy, Ashraf, 93

Sánchez-Eppler, Karen, 2, 5, 59–60
"Say Her Name" (Crenshaw), 206–7
scholarship: black feminism, 8, 22–23, 34–35; black literature in, 24–25; of history, 111–12; humanistic, 59; liberalism in, 6; on *Sula*, 146
scientific racism, 143–44, 235n63
scientific time, 109
Scott, David, 25
Seale, Bobby, 156
second-wave black feminism, 199
segregation, 19, 117, 186
seniority, 129
sentimentalism, 175–80
sexuality, 91–92
sexual purity, 104
sexual violence, 27
shape-shifting: in black manhood, 47–48; commodity in, 65; for Cox, 58–59; in culture, 46, 49
sharecropping, 162–63
Sharpe, Christina, 10, 172
Sharpe, Jenny, 172
Singleton, Jermaine, 181
"Sir Launcelot and Queen Guinevere" (Tennyson), 187
sites of transition, 50–60

slavery: adulthood in, 178–79; of Africans, 124–25; black embodiment from, 45, 118–19, 203; for black women, 81; for Butler, 46, 87; childhood after, 70; for children, 221n53; citizenship after, 221n51; after civil rights, 129; civil status in, 104; crime during, 27–28, 63–64; disavowal of, 75; family during, 171–72; in fiction, 76–77, 113–14; freedom after, 190, 232n11; ghosts of, 172–73; girlhood during, 107; historiography of, 55, 243n55; history of, 4, 23–24, 173; in imagination, 28; in Latin America, 133; for liberal humanism, 153–54; modern, 52; modernity related to, 82; for Morrison, 26; New World, 85, 131; patriarchy in, 64–65; plantations for, 40, 67, 135; politics of, 99; remembering, 188–89; reproductive afterlife of, 79; resilience after, 145–46; revisionism of, 87; slave girls, 84; slave-owners during, 98; for Spillers, 52; time during, 233n20; violence of, 60, 118–19
Slavery (Elkins), 40, 55
slave trade: for Africans, 11–12, 41; age during, 67; autobiography from, 169; blackface minstrelsy related to, 71; black women during, 68–69; Britain in, 10; for Campbell, 231n3; children in, 65; documents, 10–11; family during, 179–80; Great Britain in, 10, 125; in *The Interesting Narrative of the Life of Olaudah Equiano*, 170–71; in literature, 48; Oceanic lifespans during, 120–21; the Oceanic related to, 170–71; Portugal in, 10; for Spillers, 84, 220n36; violence of, 67, 106–7; whiteness during, 68
Snorton, C. Riley, 46, 52, 54
social exclusion, 46
social inclusion, 78–79
socialization, 55–56

social order, 30
social protection, 3, 21
sociogeny, 15–16, 51
sociology, 37
soucouyants, 89–90
Soul by Soul (Johnson), 11
spectacle, 70, 82
Specters of Marx (Derrida), 165
Spillers, Hortense, 8, 11–12, 81, 123, 215n59; absence for, 88; Africans for, 37; black dehumanization for, 91; black embodiment for, 90–91; on black feminism, 25–26; blackness for, 60; for culture, 24; Freud for, 132; Heth for, 92; historical constitution for, 135; historical time for, 28; manhood for, 129; the mass for, 129–30; Middle Passage for, 170–71; post–civil rights era for, 155; slavery for, 52; slave trade for, 84, 220n36
stereotypes: of black embodiment, 63; of childlike Negro, 99, 224n8; of Jezebels, 225n16; of Mammies, 224n14; of pickaninnies, 150–51, 236n94
stolen childhood, 102
stolen girlhood, 103
Stoler, Ann, 216n65
Stowe, Harriet Beecher, 38–39, 48, 128. See also *Uncle Tom's Cabin*
Strong, Melissa J., 94
Sula (Morrison), 40, 47; black culture in, 144–45; for black feminism, 126–30, 206; black girls in, 58; black nationalism in, 159–60; freedom in, 145–55; *A Gathering of Old Men* compared to, 163; girlhood in, 146–48

teenagers, 20–22, 46, 50–51
teleology, 30
temporality: of age, 9, 81–82; of age-shifting, 45–46; Atlantic Ocean related to, 12; in autobiography, 166; black embodiment and, 3–4, 144;

counter-temporality, 85–86; of ghosts, 165–66; historical temporalities, 37; with historiography, 22–28; for the mass, 137–44; non-normative, 107; temporal logic, 155–64; temporal progression, 141–42; of time, 126; of vampires, 100

Tennyson, Alfred, 186–88
"Theses on the Philosophy of History" (Benjamin), 25
Till, Emmett, 1–3, 8, 14–22, 153, 208
Till-Mobley, Mamie, 1–3, 14, 21, 205, 208
time: age related to, 40–41; for Butler, 97; culture and, 151–52; dispossession of, 33, 143; in fiction, 198–99; gender in, 103–4; hegemonic, 144, 166–67; historical, 28, 140; history and, 25; linear schema of, 153; scientific, 109; during slavery, 233n20; temporality of, 126; untimely, 29; western humanism for, 29–30; for women, 88–89. *See also* human time
Tinsley, Omise'eke, 10, 90
Tometi, Opal, 206
transatlantic cultural exchange, 10, 67–68
"Transfiguring Masculinities in Black Women's Studies" (Snorton), 52
trauma, 76–79
truth, in history, 119–22
Turner, Patricia A., 151
"Tuskegee Study of Untreated Syphilis in the Negro Male," 142–43, 234n60

Uncle Tom's Cabin (Stowe), 38–39, 48, 236n91; black boys in, 61–71; humanist exclusion in, 72; manhood in, 133; maturation in, 128
United States (US): Africa and, 10; black manhood in, 142–43; civil rights in, 16–18; human time in, 142–43, 150; innocence in, 196; nationalism in, 53; political-economic transformations in, 5; post-civil rights era in, 155; sharecropping in, 162–63; "Tuskegee Study of Untreated Syphilis in the Negro Male" in, 142–43, 234n60
universal freedom, 5
untimeliness: of age, 28, 37; black, 15–17, 54–55, 62, 168; black embodiment for, 3, 39; for black feminism, 20; with black liberalism, 26; blackness in, 29, 35; for black women, 20; for Equiano Girl, 178; of ghosts, 40, 166; history of, 19, 188; human time and, 185; perceptions with, 198–99; of performance, 60; philosophy of, 29; racial, 45; of relics, 82–83; for Scott, 25; of un-aging, 13–14; for women, 194; in zone of nonbeing, 15–16
untimely age, 45–46, 61, 171
untimely blackness, 16, 28, 122
untimely flesh, 20–22
untimely gender pairing, 188
untimely ghosts, 41, 166, 240n6
untimely juvenility, 192
untimely perspectives, 200–201
untimely time, 29
untimely youth, 3
US. *See* United States

vampires: age for, 103; for black culture, 120–21; for black embodiment, 105–6; black women as, 86; for black writers, 87–92; as counter-temporality, 85–86; for culture, 106; in *Fledgling*, 85; in *The Gilda Stories*, 92–93; in literary culture, 89; maturation of, 101–2; in neo-slave narratives, 97; Oceanic lifespans for, 85, 87; the Oceanic related to, 83–87; relationships related to, 98; relics related to, 87, 106–11; temporality of, 100; for western humanism, 83
Vassa, Gustavas. *See* Equiano
"Venus in Two Acts" (Hartman), 85, 165

violence: anti-black, 73; against black girls, 241n28; against black people, 192, 203–8; against children, 1–2; after freedom, 244n74; in girlhood, 206–7; historical, 158; racial, 196; racialization of, 90–91; sexual, 27; of slavery, 60, 118–19; of slave trade, 67, 106–7; against women, 121

Walker, Alice, 8, 35–37, 146
Walker, Kara, 198
Wallace, Michele, 1, 23, 34–35, 47, 55
Washington, George, 81, 97–98, 109, 116
Washington, Mary Helen, 110, 112
Weinbaum, Alys, 79
Wenger, O. C., 143
western humanism: adulthood in, 158–59; black boys for, 51–52; human time for, 29–31; vampires for, 83
Western liberalism, 7
White, Deborah Gray, 135, 139, 224n12
white adulthood, 146
white culture: black children in, 204–5; black culture compared to, 137–38, 184; black people for, 110–11; exploration for, 123–24; hegemony of, 134; imagination of, 84; race for, 88; segregation from, 117
white femininity, 71
white maleness, 146
whiteness: adulthood for, 56; for black Antillean children, 35; gender and, 33–38; in *Get Out*, 75–76; imagination of, 48–49; in liberal humanism, 47; during slave trade, 68
white patriarchal gaze, 64
White Skin, Black Masks (Fanon), 1
white supremacy, 192
white women, 48, 216n68
Wiegman, Robyn, 95–96
"The Wife of His Youth" (Chesnutt), 168–69, 182–92
Wild Seed (Butler), 46
Williams, Allison, 74
Williams, Raymond, 232n16
Wilson, August, 119–20
Wilson, Darren, 43, 50–51, 218n8, 219n20
Winfrey, Oprah, 192
"Womanist" theory, 35–37
women: in fiction, 85; protection of, 35; slave girls, 84; as *soucouyants*, 89–90; time for, 88–89; untimeliness for, 194; violence against, 121; white, 48, 216n68. *See also* black women
Woodward, Kathleen, 5, 12–14
World War I, 144–45, 159–60, 162–63
Wright, Michelle, 171
Wright, Nazera, 176
Wynter, Sylvia, 52, 88, 124, 231n5

xenophobia, 94

Yarborough, Richard, 61–62, 223n77
Yellin, Jean Fagan, 26–27
youth. *See* childhood

Zimmerman, George, 21, 205, 219n9
zombies, 229n98
zone of nonbeing, 15–16

ABOUT THE AUTHOR

HABIBA IBRAHIM is Associate Professor in the Department of English at the University of Washington in Seattle. She is author of *Troubling the Family: The Promise of Personhood and the Rise of Multiracialism*.

www.ingramcontent.com/pod-product-compliance
Lightning Source LLC
Chambersburg PA
CBHW020401080526
44584CB00014B/1125